SEX TRAFFICKING, SCANDAL, AND THE TRANSFORMATION OF JOURNALISM, 1885–1917

SEX TRAFFICKING, SCANDAL, AND THE TRANSFORMATION OF JOURNALISM, 1885–1917

GRETCHEN SODERLUND

THE UNIVERSITY OF CHICAGO PRESS
CHICAGO AND LONDON

GRETCHEN SODERLUND is assistant professor of media history in the University of Oregon's School of Journalism and Communication.

The University of Chicago Press, Chicago 60637
The University of Chicago Press, Ltd., London

Printed in the United States of America

22 21 20 19 18 17 16 15 14 13   1 2 3 4 5

ISBN-13: 978-0-226-02136-2 (cloth)
ISBN-13: 978-0-226-02153-9 (paper)
ISBN-13: 978-0-226-02167-6 (e-book)

Library of Congress Cataloging-in-Publication Data
Soderlund, Gretchen, 1970–
Sex trafficking, scandal, and the transformation of journalism, 1885–1917 / Gretchen Soderlund.
pages; cm
Includes bibliographical references and index.
ISBN 978-0-226-02136-2 (alk. paper) — ISBN 978-0-226-02153-9 (pbk.: alk. paper) — ISBN 978-0-226-02167-6 (e-book) 1. Human trafficking—Press coverage—New York (State)—New York—History. 2. Human trafficking—Press coverage—Illinois—Chicago—History. 3. Sensationalism in journalism—United States—History. 4. Journalism—United States—History. I. Title.
HQ144.S69 2013
306.3'62—dc23   2012043194

♾ This paper meets the requirements of ANSI/NISO Z39.48-1992 (Permanence of Paper).

FOR DAN

CONTENTS

PREFACE

In the seventy-two years between 1835 and 1907, the tone and style of news coverage of prostitution changed dramatically. Some of these changes can be glimpsed in the following three stories drawn from the daily papers of New York and Chicago. In 1835, the *New York Sun* printed this lewd and jocular account of two brothel marauders in its "Crime Beat" section: "On Saturday night a gentleman named Thomas H. Niven, a carpenter by trade, and another named William Westervelt, a merchant, went to the nunnery of Mrs. Phebe Doty, No. 35 Leonard street, on some special embassy, and while there, as charged, became riotous and disorderly, violated the peace and dignity of the *sanctum sanctorium* of Mrs. Doty's domicil, and then to clap the climax of their sin, actually abused in a shameless manner the venerable lady herself."[1] This satirical example from the premier Jacksonian-era penny press paper figured madams and clients as little more than public nuisances and fodder for jokes about religion and social class. The brothel's existence was a mundane, if annoying, aspect of city life in the 1830s. The story lampooned commercial sex and its potential consequences—a "climax" followed by the "clap." Notably, the paper publicly announced the names of the male brothel visitors and their respective trades. Yet Niven and Westervelt's public outing was not intended to shame or humiliate; their transgressions were meant to entertain readers, who were cast as knowing participants in the story's puns and wordplay. Mrs. Doty, the object of the men's crime, took the brunt of the *Sun*'s jest. She was mockingly referred to as a "venerable lady," while her "nunnery" was represented as a sacred altar and vagina. The story only alluded to the extent of Niven and Westervelt's abuses. The madam's victimization drew little sympathy from the *Sun*'s police reporter. In the end, these working-class men's drunken evening was a fleeting amusement worth only a short anecdote in the police blotter section.

Thirty-two years later, the *Chicago Tribune* published a letter from a pious writer imploring "good Christian people" to contribute to a fallen women's rescue home:

> I call upon all City Missionaries and all good Christian people, and especially on all women reposing by the mercy of heaven in virtuous homes to direct their charitable aid to the enlargement, support, and needful encouragement of the Magdalen Asylum, truly the house of the kindest of shepherds, truly the asylum of the most penitent and heart broken Magdalens and for the most shame-stricken outcast of society. It is an institution that will succeed in accomplishing an amount of good which few dream of, only needing aid to make it efficient for every class of unfortunate women and girls, from those who have taken one downward step, to those who have drained to the dregs of infamy and prostitution.[2]

The floridly sentimental language of Christian piety replaced the *Sun*'s mockingly sacrilegious puns. Newspaper readers were called upon to recognize themselves as "good Christian people." Specific appeals were made to middle- and upper-class women "reposing by the mercy of heaven in virtuous homes." The protections and comforts afforded by social class were depicted as God-given. Class and domesticity served as protection against sin, but they also challenged middle-class women to help the less fortunate. Prostitutes were simultaneously agents of their own destruction and objects of pity, unfortunate sinners with the capacity for redemption. If Mrs. Doty was a known member of the community, the prostitutes referred to in this letter existed on the depraved margins of society.

By 1907, the tone and substance of coverage had shifted once again. The *Chicago Tribune* printed the following article entitled "Rally to Crush White Slave Sin: Many Organizations Represented at Meeting Launching New Crusade":

> Charges that Chicago is rapidly becoming the greatest "white slave" center of the world and that a powerful syndicate for traffic in young girls exists in the city has stirred reform organizations to form a large organization for the express purpose of combating the evil. . . . At the rally, Miss Rose Johnson stirred her hearers to action by asserting there are paid agents in Egypt and Panama receiving many young and innocent girls from Chicago, and that they are sold into bondage. . . . Assis-

> tant State's Attorney C. G. Roe furnished additional information as to the traffic. "There is a great Chicago syndicate for the traffic in young girls," said Mr. Roe. "I believe the state should give us a force of detectives to ferret out the agents in this business."[3]

This story's fact-based, informative style represented prostitutes as victims of a well-organized conspiracy. Commercial sex was no longer seen as a local issue but as one of international import. An image of a vast and coordinated system forcing unsuspecting white girls into sexual servitude replaced the earlier image of the dissolute, fallen woman. Trafficked girls were wholly innocent, and neither piety nor social class insulated them from harm. An organized foe mandated a similarly coordinated response, prompting demands for state intervention. Despite an alleged abundance of white slaves and traffickers, names were never mentioned in this account, while activities of anti-vice activists and public officials figured prominently. If the Civil War account appealed to economically privileged women ensconced in the domestic sphere, this story featured a female activist with a public presence on the front line of reform.

These newspaper stories were all products of their social and historical contexts, and each represented a radical break in the regulation and representation of commercial sex. It is notable that the level of specificity of the stories waned as the scale of the perceived problem grew: the *Sun*'s crime story highlighted the concrete event of Niven and Westervelt's escapades, and the *Tribune*'s white slavery story used the occasion of the reform rally to represent an elusive yet apparently widespread conspiracy. The rally, itself occasioned by *charges* of trafficking in women in Chicago by muckraking magazines, was the event that provided access to this conspiracy. Thus the *Tribune* story on sex trafficking constituted one link in a mass-mediated public conversation: initial charges of white slavery in mass-circulation magazines provided the impetus for the public meeting, which became the event mandating the *Tribune*'s report. Finally, the *Tribune* itself became a forum publicizing the voices calling for state intervention into the white slavery issue.

This book considers the conditions within news industries and anti-vice movements that made this final representation possible. It considers how forced prostitution (also referred to as sex trafficking, sexual slavery, and, during the period in question, white slavery) become the dominant framework for understanding and regulating prostitution in the early twentieth century. In doing so, it chronicles how relations between anti-vice reformers and the print media were built up and then undone between 1885 and

1917. During the nineteenth century, the print media featured stories of prostitution that varied from the satiric to the serious-minded. Like the *Sun*'s crime story, some reportage described events surrounding prostitution, while others, like the *Tribune*'s two stories, connected the activities of anti-vice activists to prostitution on the streets and in the community.

Between 1885 and 1917 in England and the United States, monthly mass-distribution magazines and daily newspapers began to generate their own popular meanings, images, and associations around prostitution, which frequently conflated all sexual commerce with sexual slavery. In 1907, stories began to proliferate in the American news media of white women kidnapped and sold into prostitution by organized bands of immigrants, often alleged to be conspiring with elected officials. While some serialized exposés and episodic reportage portrayed an underground network of traffickers as an object of social concern, a public menace to be stopped by any means possible, others cast doubt on the phenomenon. This book explores the role played by the print media in the spread and containment of the social and moral scandal over white slavery. It asks, To what degree was knowledge of sex trafficking dependent upon emerging journalistic practices for its very construction? What do the investigative methods for obtaining information about forced prostitution, including the sources consulted, tell us about the developing role of journalism in this historical period? How did stories of forced prostitution and the scandals they generated transform media practices—institutional, professional, and cultural—during this thirty-year time period? And why did sex trafficking become the impetus for such transformations?

The theoretical questions that organize this inquiry fall outside the "myth or reality" paradigm that sometimes dominates discussions of sex trafficking, exploring instead the historical production of truth and falsity and their relationship to modes of journalistic knowledge. Reformulating white slavery as a media scandal allows us to examine the historically situated ensembles of practices, or ways of speaking, seeing, and stating propositions, that governed claims to truth and made phenomena like white slavery intelligible and plausible.[4] Yet it is insufficient to consider only those mechanisms that produced white slavery as a "real" phenomenon, particularly when trafficking claims were hotly contested in their day. Thus this book examines how claims of falsity as well as truth operate within particular historical orders and forms of cultural production, including mass media such as print journalism.

My initial foray into this topic began with a simple question: If the mass media shape how topics of national concern are discussed, defined, and developed as public debates—in short, if they frame issues for the public—do such controversies in turn shape the mass media? In other words, do public debates alter the way mass media are received by audiences, the institutional relationships they forge, and even how they promote and conceive of themselves? To examine this question, I initially went back to the Progressive Era, arguably the first period in US history saturated by a national mass media. This period provided a unique lens on this problem, since the nascent Progressive Era news media lacked today's highly developed professional protocols, institutional alliances, and conventions for framing different types of events. The Progressive period, which roughly spanned the years 1900 to 1917, in fact laid the groundwork for many developments in the media industry that exist today. These include conventions of news objectivity, the emergence of public relations as a political force, the development of national commodity audiences, the increased dependence of news on advertisers, and the forging of now-entrenched alliances between news institutions and elites.

As I delved further into newspaper and magazine reportage, it became clear that between 1885 and 1917 an epistemic change occurred in the press that was linked to different modes of information-gathering and sourcing, and to a more general shift from sensationalism to standardized procedures now referred to as journalistic objectivity. This book argues that media scandals around sex trafficking played a significant role in both of the major phases of this massive transformation, becoming one of the premier battlegrounds on which late nineteenth- and early twentieth-century struggles over journalistic knowledge took place. The book is framed by the work of William T. Stead and George Kibbe Turner, investigative journalists who instigated sex trafficking scandals on two continents. An examination of their claims, news-gathering practices, and reception by different segments of the audience reveals that in both cases the scandals that each author sought to incite became uncontainable "surplus scandals." That is, they turned on media forms themselves, resulting in skepticism, allegations of sensationalism, and, ultimately, transformations in allowable discourses and media practices. Chapter 1 elucidates the concepts of surplus scandal and sensationalism and their relationship to journalism's crusades against white slavery.

Chapter 2 focuses on Stead's 1885 exposé, "The Maiden Tribute of Modern Babylon," which argued that virgins were being sold as commodities on the streets of London to wealthy aristocrats who were seducing and ruining them. While the text itself was a mélange of knowledge-producing practices—including eyewitnessing, interviews, personal observations, visceral experiences, and fetishized accounts of girls screaming—it made major contributions to journalistic practices. The exposé constituted an early example of stunt reporting as well as the use of interviews, which were uncommon in England at the time. Although "The Maiden Tribute" entangled Stead in ethical and legal controversies, it opened up new discursive possibilities via the sex trafficking narrative for the social movements and the press not only in England but in the United States as well.

Chapter 3 examines the relationships between the American press and the Women's Christian Temperance Union (WCTU), paying particular attention to the organization's attempt to focus national attention on forced prostitution in the wake of Stead's exposé. It demonstrates that the WCTU made a number of contributions that reshaped mainstream American journalism. The organization, under the leadership of Frances Willard, launched a highly sophisticated media campaign, hired professionals to engage and critique media, created their own media, and formed a large-scale, proto–mass audience, which they proceeded to self-consciously market as a commodity audience to the press. In doing so, they redefined and redrew the boundaries of "sensationalism" while deploying sensationalism strategically themselves, merging activism with a strikingly modern media campaign.

In the 1840s the penny presses had pioneered the newspaper crusade as a strategy that allowed them to engage in prurient reporting without drawing the ire of their middle-class readerships. These early, newspaper-driven crusades had been localized, with journalistic commentary and focus stemming from a single shocking event (the murder of a beautiful young prostitute or shopgirl, about whose corpse editors would wax eloquent).[5] Chapter 4 considers Turner's muckraking exposés of white slavery in Chicago and New York. Although Turner's reports focused on particular cities, the phenomena they described were abstract, enabling readers across the United States to envision themselves as members of a larger national public similarly imperiled by widespread trafficking rings. As such, they served as a rallying point, particularly in Chicago, for social reformers who coalesced around the issue of sex trafficking and propagated a broad range of legal and institutional changes and congressional laws.

Chapters 5 and 6 argue that Turner's articles became the object of a rear guard attack on investigative journalism more generally. In this response, the object to be contained and curtailed was not white slavery per se, but the muckraking press that highlighted corporate and municipal corruption. Chapter 5 considers the surplus scandal that ensued after the publication of Turner's 1909 "The Daughters of the Poor: A Plain Story of the Development of New York City as the Leading Center of the White Slave Trade of the World, Under Tammany Hall," in *McClure's Magazine*. Turner's allegations threw a wrench into the upcoming municipal elections and incited an undercover investigation into trafficking in New York City. The *New York Times* initially drew from a stock of sentimental narratives to describe the investigation and the ensuing criminal trial. However, as the investigation into trafficking in the city grew increasingly problematic, the *Times* developed a detached orientation toward its object, similar to that demanded of "objective" journalism.

Chapter 6 traces the transformation of the white slavery controversy after the much-publicized release of a grand jury inquiry into white slavery in New York. The grand jury, headed by none other than Standard Oil heir John D. Rockefeller Jr., issued a presentment that paradoxically became the yardstick against which the truth about white slavery was measured. The grand jury took issue with Turner's characterization of trafficking rings as vice trusts and sought to inject a less conspiratorial idiom into anti-vice crusades. Rockefeller's intervention into white slavery and prostitution helped to precipitate a rift between anti-vice movements and the press, while public debates over sensationalism (now coded as hysteria) and pornography once again resurfaced. Rockefeller's work and the closure in the 1910s of many red-light districts led to the eventual dissolution of grassroots anti-vice reform movements. In their stead, Rockefeller personally presided over the creation of the American Social Hygiene Association and its institution-based and eugenics-motivated efforts to abolish prostitution.

Scholars are only beginning to explore the historical and cultural conventions through which controversies over gender, race, and sex have historically played themselves out in the mass media.[6] This book contributes to that emerging literature by tracing the history of popular print–media depictions of sex trafficking. Doing so reveals much about the evolution of mass media practices and conventions that serve to render complex, sex-related issues intelligible to the public. By considering relationships among identity, sexuality, and the evolution of journalistic conventions, this project complicates traditional accounts of media history, which locate such developments as journalistic objectivity in the "masculine" arenas of foreign affairs, world wars, and technology—outside struggles over race, class, gender, and sexuality.[7] Likewise, while the majority of historical studies on sex slavery and vice focus on the social movements that coalesced around them, I examine the controversy over the existence and extent of white slavery, as well as the new forms of knowledge and representational practices that emerged from the controversy. Attempts to contain sex trafficking were not limited to the policing of city streets and state borders: the controversy also established and legitimated new strategies for shaping and channeling information within news industries. It is therefore worth investigating how scandals over sex trafficking helped to precipitate and reinforce developing journalistic strategies for attaining knowledge and the evolution of professional ideologies in the late nineteenth and early twentieth centuries.

An earlier version of chapter 5 was published as "Covering Urban Vice: 'White Slavery,' the *New York Times*, and the Construction of Journalistic Knowledge," *Critical Studies in Media Communication* 19, no. 4 (December 2002): 438–40.

ACKNOWLEDGMENTS

This book could never have been completed without generous support from the Illinois Program for Research in the Humanities at the University of Illinois at Urbana–Champaign and a Mellon Postdoctoral Fellowship at the University of Chicago. Several people influenced my intellectual development and provided scholarly advice and assistance during the research and writing process. My first thanks goes to the incomparable Paula Treichler, whose enthusiasm for this project has sustained me through the long process of completing it. Sonya Michel, Cary Nelson, John Nerone, and Angharad Valdivia provided valuable insights when this project was still in its infancy. Appreciation goes to Michael Silverstein, Andy Abbott, Susan Gal, Andreas Glaeser, and Lisa Wedeen for providing me with a postdoctoral experience that irrevocably changed the way I think about media institutions and altered the shape of this book. Although Carol Stabile and I have never been institutionally bonded, her work has been central to the development of my thinking from the beginning.

I owe a great debt to my friends in the academy and elsewhere who have enriched my life (and this book): Boatema Boateng, Ted Bailey, Elizabeth Bernstein, Jack Bratich, Heidi Brush, Amina Cain, Kevin Carollo, Sealing Cheng, Melissa Ditmore, Liz Emens, Alice Filmer, Kelly Gates, Grace Giorgio, David Golumbia, Jeff Harshbarger, James Hay, Timika Hoffman-Zoller, Anna Hulseberg, Janet Hutchinson, Marie Leger, Craig Matarrese, Margaret Ozierski, Liz Perea, Joy Pierce, Tracy Quan, Carrie Rentschler, Craig Robertson, Penelope Saunders, Oliver Speck, Jonathan Sterne, Lana Swartz, Mrak Unger, Daniel Vukovich, David Zoller, and Mingus Zoller. A special thanks to Gil Rodman for the MFK, a game I look forward to playing with him for years to come. Dave Hudson also deserves special acknowledgment. I am less lonely knowing that he shared a part of my childhood. In Richmond, Laura Browder, Abigail Cheever, and Carol Summers carefully read and commented on early drafts of this manuscript. Amira Pierce provided much-needed assistance with my endnotes. The teachers at the VCU Child Development Center took wonderful care of my children, providing the time and space needed to finish this project.

I am lucky to have so many family members that I can also count as close friends: Joanna York, Marianne Best, Wilhelmina Bourne, Gene Murphy, Ken McGee, Rosemary Bourne, Karl Soderlund, Billy White, and Vanessa Piccorossi. Their love has sustained me through good and bad times. My parents, Chuck and Paula Soderlund, have provided unwavering love and support. My children, Lina and Julian, make sure I exist in a state of perpetual exhaustion. But they have also taught me the meaning of unconditional love, and I am so very happy to share my life with them.

Three people I love deeply are no longer here to see the publication of this book. My grandparents, Charles and Bernice Soderlund, were always there for me and are deeply missed. My mother, Anne McCredie, passed away at the end of 2011 while this manuscript was still under review. Life is less interesting without her. She is the main reason I see the world differently than everyone else. Growing up with her taught me more about life than any formal course of education ever could.

This book is dedicated to my best friend and life partner, Dan McGee, who has read and commented on every word in this book many times over. Meeting Dan changed my life in every way. Without his strength, vision, love, and perspicacity, I shudder to think of where I would be today. Dan has always had my endless devotion, deep admiration, and undying gratitude. Now he has this book.

CHAPTER ONE

White Slavery and Journalism's Shifting Axis of Truth

In early 1909, George Kibbe Turner, an investigative reporter working for *McClure's Magazine*, toured New York City's dance halls seeking first-hand evidence of a vast trade in white women's bodies. He sought to produce an exposé that would be as successful as the one about Chicago vice he had written for *McClure's* two years earlier. It would be an added bonus if the story also happened to take down Tammany Hall in the city's upcoming election. What Turner did not count on was the level of controversy and negative publicity about his methods, conclusions, and, indeed, the very investigative enterprise of which his piece was only a small part that his article would incite.

Sexual scandals and tales of prostitution were by no means new to the press when Turner scoured the streets of New York looking for evidence of the white slave trade. Beginning in the 1830s with the murder of upscale prostitute Helen Jewett, the penny presses had discovered somewhat by accident that the combination of sex and death dramatically increased circulation rates. A competition ensued among various East Coast editors for the newest and most shocking details, transforming the event of the murder into a protracted and titillating "whodunit" mystery.[1] In the late 1890s, the trial of alleged prostitute Dora Clark, in which author Stephen Crane intervened, captivated newspaper readers nationwide and led to the reprinting of Crane's fictional *Maggie: A Girl of the Streets*. Such New York papers as Pulitzer's *New York World* and Hearst's *New York Journal*, known by contemporaries as examples of the "new journalism," also feasted on a steady diet of vice coverage.

If the press was no stranger to covering sex commerce and vice, and often did so with a deep level of amusement and fascination, between 1885 and 1909 an important subset of coverage on prostitution emerged, of which Turner's was the endnote: the high-profile sex trafficking exposé that attempted to elicit pity, shock, and horror in audiences and, in so doing, to change legislation and alter the course of elections. This coverage took the form of newspaper crusades carried out on two continents. As I use the term, a *newspaper crusade* is a structured series of interventions over time guided by activist, reformist, and moral/political agendas, but always with underlying commercial interests in mind. Newspaper crusades exist in relationship to other reform movements as responses to direct pressure from these groups or as attempts to capture or maintain a movement as a commodity audience. From William T. Stead's 1885 report on sexual slavery and child prostitution in London, "The Maiden Tribute of Modern Babylon," to George Kibbe Turner's 1907 and 1909 investigative pieces on urban vice trusts, "The City of Chicago: A Study of the Great Immoralities" and "The Daughters of the Poor: A Plain Story of the Development of New York City as a Leading Center of the White Slave Trade of the World, Under Tammany Hall," these crusading exposés constituted a specialized and unique genre of reporting in themselves, one that generated such an excess of publicity, controversy, and scandal that at each juncture it served to alter legislative agendas and transform existing journalistic practices.

WHITE SLAVERY, A MOBILE SIGNIFIER

As David Roediger has argued, slavery became a master metaphor in antebellum discussions of the white working class because of its powerful resonance with black chattel slavery, a form that "stood as the ultimate expression of denial of liberty."[2] However, northern wage laborers in the 1830s and 1840s stopped short of fully identifying with chattel slavery because of its association with pure victimization and powerlessness. Later in the nineteenth century, slavery came to signify other forms of systemic exploitation because it was an immediately recognizable system of exploitation that had been conducted in the open and had produced a stock of visual referents. As a metaphor, slavery became a rhetorically potent way of imagining inequalities of power relationships between social groups and within institutions. The phrase *white slavery* was used rhetorically during the Civil War by abolitionist newspapers in reference to working-class white Southerners and Northerners who supported the Confederacy.[3] *White slavery* was also used in reference to prostitution in non-Western countries, the oppression faced by non-Muslims in Mesopotamia, and "Mormon plural wives."[4] The term was used throughout the century in the context of discussions about the lack of legal protections for working women in the United States and abroad. One 1888 newspaper called the oppressive management and low salaries faced by telephone girls "a system of white slavery [whose] principle slave-owners live in Boston or Lowell."[5] Another periodical decried the stores that hired "frail young girls" as cash carriers, suggesting that this was "a subject upon which the energies of women reformers might concentrate themselves without any risk of provoking unfavorable comment. . . . The sympathy of all classes will be with the victims of a system which it is hardly hyperbolical to stigmatize as white slavery."[6]

As late as March 1906, newspapers and unions were referring to male laborers as white slaves. A story in the *San Francisco Call*, "Four Thousand White Slaves," featured testimony from John B. Harris corroborating recent claims by unions that white slavery was occurring in the Florida Keys. Harris was out of work for several months in Philadelphia when he replied to an employment agency's ad for work on the Florida East Coast Railroad for four and five dollars a day. When he arrived and saw the slavelike conditions of the laborers, he and fellow workers hatched an escape plan, but armed guards deterred the others. Harris, the first man to "escape and tell his story," suggested there was a conspiracy between the mayor of Miami, the police, and the railroad to keep these men laboring in bondage in the Keys.[7]

While *white slavery* was a polysemic term that encompassed a number of meanings in the late nineteenth and early twentieth century, after Stead's series in London's *Pall Mall Gazette*, the meaning of the phrase began to congeal around the notion of forced domestic and international prostitution. The appropriation and vast diffusion of this sense of the term in the United States resulted from transatlantic media flows that carried stories of virgins auctioned, seduced, and ruined from British papers to American social purity reformers. Much in the same way that the socially constructed crime "mugging" found its way from the pages of American newspapers to British ones in the 1960s, the media in this late nineteenth-century context served as "the key apparatus which formed the link and framed the passage of the terms from one context to another," in this earlier instance transmitting stories of a particularly heinous form of sexual exploitation across the Atlantic and labeling it white slavery.[8] International media flows like those that developed in the nineteenth century enabled newspapers and their readers to borrow narratives, terms, definitions, and broader topical issues from each other, enlarging the visibility of certain issues and diminishing that of others. By 1910, the diverse practices that had been variously referred to as white slavery—polygamy, indentured servitude, wage slavery, the working conditions of shop and factory girls, the southern pro-slavery mind-set, and others—were overshadowed by the image of the enchained white female prostitute.

However, *white slavery* as applied to sexual commerce was always a slippery, ambiguous, and imprecise term that was rhetorically loaded, fraught with contradictions, and prone to controversy. There was no consensus among the late nineteenth- and early twentieth-century reformers who took up the anti–white slavery mantle about the character and scope of the phenomenon. Some alleged that white slavery was a type of prostitution that existed alongside unforced prostitution; others used the term in reference to women who moved across state lines or national boundaries to engage in prostitution; some invoked it only in reference to child and teenage prostitution; while still others used it to describe all sexual commerce. White slave crusades were also harnessed to any number of overlapping and separate social and political agendas. Between 1885 and 1917, anti–white slavery campaigns were linked to crusades around temperance, women's suffrage, red-light district closures, higher wages for women, curfews for youth, increased urban surveillance, a stronger federal government, anti-immigration laws, anti-obscenity efforts, and higher age-of-consent laws, to name just a few.

The anti-vice efforts of groups like the Woman's Christian Temperance Union, the National Vigilance Committee, the American Purity Federation, the White Cross League, Jane Addams's settlement house movement, and others have been chronicled and analyzed by historians, sociologists, and legal scholars who themselves have advanced a number of cultural and social explanations to account for the emergence of white slavery as a label and as a popular explanation for why women enter prostitution. For some, white slavery was a fiction created by sentimental moral reformers. It was the crowning achievement of an irrational era during which social hysteria reigned supreme.[9] Some scholars contend that white slavery signaled a real, albeit misnamed and exaggerated, phenomenon.[10] The phenomenon has been discussed as a means of introducing pornographic, titillating fare into mass cultural texts.[11] Prostitution and white slavery have been analyzed as issues that allowed the middle class to discuss sexuality, while at the same time distancing themselves from the topic by projecting it onto prostitutes.[12]

White slavery has also been widely understood as an ideological expression of a set of interlocking cultural anxieties related to rapid industrialization, increased eastern European immigration, mass urbanization, and altered family and gender relations. Other scholars have considered particular aspects of the Progressive Era white slavery episode, including the legislative response to white slavery at local, state, and federal levels as well as the intersection of discourses about race, gender, economics, and citizenship in white slave crusades.[13] Scholarship on white slavery provides important perspectives for understanding prostitution as a social phenomenon that is inseparably linked to the production of identity through power and knowledge, strategies of urban management and surveillance, and symbolic processes that operate together to produce deviance across class, race, and gender lines.[14]

Few of these studies have considered white slavery as a media phenomenon or mass-mediated controversy. Those that do focus primarily on the popularity of white slavery narratives in films in the 1910s and the public controversies surrounding them, not on journalism or the effects of debates over white slavery on journalistic practices.[15] Yet in England and America, the campaigns against the organized sex trade and vice were also engagements with the very media that brought such activities to light through journalistic exposés. White slavery was a social construct, a model for understanding commercial sex exchanges that entered the late Victorian and Progressive public spheres by way of mass-distributed cultural productions. The trafficking networks depicted in such productions were by character abstract and often invisible, and therefore needed to be textually *represented* or *made visible* through a newspaper report, a pamphlet, a policy document, and so forth. The publication of Stead's 1885 exposé and Turner's 1907 and 1909 muckraking articles were pivotal moments in the career of the white slavery label and represent high points within anti-prostitution campaigns more generally. This movement to combat sex slavery was protracted over thirty years, but the key media moments in 1885, 1907, and 1909, respectively, took on similar contours that were specifically linked to the print media, their central locus of publicity. Despite the difference in time and place of publication, the exposés by Turner and Stead generated similar responses in terms of creating legislation, fostering a proliferation of reform activity and discourse around prostitution and sex trafficking, and, finally, being subject to a backlash (creating what I call "surplus scandal") against their methods and conclusions, a reaction that played itself out in newspapers, criminal courts, and grand juries. The publication of these exposés and the structure of the responses to them had transformative effects on media conventions, institutions, and practices in both cases. These effects, however, were not confined to the late nineteenth- and early twentieth-century print media; they were also linked to specific social movements and political agendas that were seeking not only to spur (or stifle) social change but to shape media content.

Considering sex trafficking through the lens of media interactions—existing *and* emerging media practices—allows us to trace a new trajectory for journalism that is attentive to gender, race, and sexuality, and to grasp more fully the complex relationships among late nineteenth- and early twentieth-century social movements and a growing journalistic culture. Indeed, I would argue that in order to understand the logic governing journalism, one must understand its relationship to anti-vice movements and other social and moral crusades. The reverse is also true. After 1885, social movements emerged in dialogue with and at times in opposition to journalism. As the following chapters demonstrate, the period's reform movements were inseparable from a mass-distribution print media field that simultaneously highlighted social problems, offended moral sensibilities (rendering newspapers objects of reform in their own right), and galvanized readers around issues like sex trafficking. A complex interplay of and ultimately interdependent relation among reform movements, mass news audiences, journalistic methods, and editorial decision-making evolved throughout the period in question.

WHITE SLAVERY, RACE, AND IMMIGRATION

Controversies over white slavery exposed many of the fault lines in the United States over class and gender difference, racial inequality, prevailing definitions of citizenship, immigration, industrialization, and shifting understandings of the notions of public and private. Whereas Stead's "The Maiden Tribute" raised concerns about the sexual liberties that aristocrats took with the poor in London, Turner's exposés stoked anti-Semitism by blaming eastern European Jews for trafficking in the United States. His depiction of new immigrants in "The City of Chicago" provided a powerful rationale for the enactment of measures that used sex as a justification to restrict the national and international mobility of women and minorities.

Anti-vice activists from across the United States participated in the fight to end white slavery, but the campaign's most ardent proponents (and its main detractors) were clustered in the Northeast and Midwest, particularly in the urban centers of New York City and Chicago. The meanings they attributed to white slavery drew on earlier discourses about black chattel slavery and Chinese prostitution. Many of the moral entrepreneurs whose work turned toward issues of sex trafficking after 1907 considered their work as an extension of the antebellum abolitionist movement. These activists drew more heavily on the rhetoric of blackness and whiteness and made more explicit comparisons between organized sexual slavery and chattel slavery than did Turner. According to one reform tract:

> It is slavery, real slavery that we are fighting. The term white slave isn't a misnomer or a sensational term conjured up by sensational newspapers. The words describe what they stand for. The white slave is a slave as much as the negro was before the Civil War, as the African is in the Belgian district of the Congo, as much as any people are slaves who are owned, flesh and bone, body and soul, by another person, and who can be sold at any time and place, and for any price, at that person's will; that is what slavery is, and that is the condition of hundreds—yes, of thousands—of girls at present.[16]

A popular anti-trafficking image featured a white Christian woman behind bars, her hands clasped together as if in prayer, her eyes looking mournfully up to heaven. Anti-trafficking polemics like Clifford G. Roe's *Panders and Their White Slaves* utilized this iconic image to pose the questions, "What if this Girl were your Sister? What constitutes a devil man?"[17] During the Progressive Era, this illustration served as the crusade's version of Elizabeth Margaret Chandler's famous abolitionist image of the shackled black woman with her hands clasped, similarly looking up, that asked, "Am I Not a Woman and a Sister?" The emblem was used by William Lloyd Garrison in his antislavery publication, the *Liberator*.

Despite their reliance on abolitionist language and imagery, a number of crusaders dismissed the severity of chattel slavery in order to underscore the gravity of white slavery. The title to Jean Turner Zimmermann's *Chicago's Black Traffic in White Girls* embodies this logic, as does the insert to Ernest A. Bell's *Fighting the Traffic in Young Girls*, which promised "thirty-two pages of striking figures showing the workings of the blackest slavery that has ever stained the human race."[18] In this formulation, black slavery merely primed the public for the horrors of white slavery.

While some reformers self-identified as heroic abolitionists, few aligned themselves with the contemporary struggles of blacks. Roe and Turner, for instance, were overt xenophobes whose white slavery narratives were also tirades about the loss of Anglo-Saxon dominance in the context of unprecedented eastern and southern European immigration. Even Jane Addams, whose work on white slavery and prostitution argued forcefully for pluralism and women's suffrage, said comparatively little about black prostitution. The more general absence of concern for the black prostitute was curi-

Figure 1.1. Iconic abolitionist image. From the *Liberator* (17 March 1832).

ous, given that the creation of segregated red-light districts in the 1890s had pushed these thriving yet undesirable zones into the poorest urban areas. By the early twentieth century, vice districts and black neighborhoods increasingly occupied the same geographic locale. As Cynthia Blair reminds us, "Black prostitutes actively participated in the transformations that shaped the racial and sexual landscape in cities like Chicago."[19] Kevin Mumford suggests that the white slavery panic congealed a number of northern fears about racial mixing. Although scant attention was paid to black prostitution in the extensive Progressive Era literature on the social evil, "social scientific studies of white slavery . . . revealed, through their elision of blackness, that the worthy fallen woman was coded as white."[20]

Reformers also derived their understanding of white slavery from nineteenth-century concerns about Chinese prostitution. During the Gold Rush, more than a hundred thousand Chinese laborers, many of them from Canton, flocked to the West Coast, hoping to enrich themselves and their families. Like prospectors in general, many of these men were young and single or had left wives and children behind. In 1850s California there were twelve men to every woman, a condition that ensured a flourishing sex

Figure 1.2. Iconic white slavery image. From Clifford G. Roe, *Panders and Their White Slaves* (New York: Fleming H. Revell, 1909).

trade. Chinese prostitutes, too, arrived in California between 1850 and 1880. While the first wave of Chinese sex workers was entrepreneurial, establishing their own brothels and attaining a certain degree of economic independence, by the late 1850s organizations of "fighting tongs" had established control over most of the Chinese vice trade. The tongs ran gambling, prostitution, and opium establishments that catered to a mixed clientele. They also imported thousands of Chinese women for the trade.[21]

On the West Coast the Chinese were subject to extreme racism. Euro-Americans decried the customs of the "Mongolian race" and characterized them as incapable of assimilation and, in fact, less than human. The Chinese were frequently compared to rodents and cockroaches. One newspaper reported that San Francisco's Chinatown was "the rankest outgrowth of human degradation that could be found on the continent," adding that the Chinese lived under conditions that were "scarcely one degree above those [in] which the rats of our waterfront and other vermin live and breathe and have their being."[22] While Chinese women constituted just a small percentage of the region's prostitutes, they emerged as prominent targets of community violence, anti-vice intervention, and immigration legislation. Newspapers alternated between depicting Chinese prostitutes as victims kidnapped by tongs and held in San Francisco's miniature "cribs" and as unruly and opium-addled foreign threats. Vigilance activism and increased antipathy toward Chinese laborers led to the first federal immigration law. The 1875 Page Act barred Asian women who intended to work as prostitutes and Asian male contract workers from entering the United States. This act set the precedent for restrictive Progressive Era measures that denied entry to women suspected of immigrating for "immoral purposes."[23]

Despite the decades-long ban on Chinese immigration after the 1882 Chinese Exclusion Acts, Progressive Era white slavery crusaders would make combating "yellow slavery" a priority on the West Coast. It became common for missionaries to write about yellow slavery, and for white slavery books to feature chapters on yellow slavery, tracing its origins to uncivilized practices in the homeland and alleging that the Chinaman, like the Jew, had imported immoral practices to the United States.[24] Other texts imagined a vast trade in American prostitutes throughout Asia.[25]

SURPLUS SCANDAL: WHY SEX TRAFFICKING?

The editors, journalists, and reformers who advanced the notion of white slavery in the late nineteenth and early twentieth century were pushing hard against prevailing understandings of sexuality and gender and preestablished practices of truth-gathering, as were the groups and institutions that fought to counter claims of white slavery. All were social agents who were simultaneously engaged in struggles over meaning and dominance in strategies of truth-production as well as the attainment of cultural, economic, and political power. To understand more fully the white slavery episode, it is necessary to consider the relationship between trafficking narratives, the quest for distinction among newspapers and magazines, the institutionalization of the newspaper crusade, the generation of audience identifications, and battles over legitimacy within the late nineteenth- and early twentieth-century media fields. At times these struggles over meaning and power were highly organized and sophisticated, even by today's standards of orchestrated news blitzes and media campaigns. The mediated white slavery scandals that played themselves out between 1885 and 1917 created opportunities for actors in a variety of moral reform movements, media institutions, and positions of economic and political power to transform media in ways that promoted their own agendas. At the same time, the reform movements rising up in the midst of these scandals provided ready-made, marketable audiences to news media, which in turn not only tailored their content to attract these audiences but transformed these audiences into mass readerships.

While the etymological roots of the term *scandal* predate many forms of modern media, scandals took on a new character and dimension with the arrival of the mass-distribution print media that circulated stories of transgressions beyond small communities. As John B. Thompson puts it, "The media were endowed with the capacity to make actions and events visible to others in a way that was qualitatively different from anything that had existed previously: the act of making visible was severed from the constraints of physical co-presence and reconstituted in extended stretches of time and space."[26] For James Lull and Stephen Hinerman, a media scandal ensues "when private acts that disgrace or offend the idealized, dominant morality of a social community are made public and narrativized by the media, producing a range of effects from ideological retrenchment to disruption and change."[27] While many transgressions generate scandal, the combination of sex and power has been an enduring one in British and American society. Sex scandals, often involving powerful public men and less-powerful private women (or the exposure of sex acts marked as deviant), have the power to destroy careers, rattle governing institutions, and initiate broader crises of authority.[28]

Media exposés of sex trafficking, in particular, have created scandals that expand into every domain connected to the controversy and inevitably turn back on the media as the ultimate target to be attacked. They are in many respects the ideal foci around which to wage battles over media conventions, practices, and institutions themselves. The sex trafficking scandal is thus a subset of media scandal that generates what I am calling surplus scandal, one that effectively spills into other areas (law enforcement, media, politics). The "surplus" is created in part because the scandal is about sex and in part because its object is not individual improprieties but allegations of extensive wrongdoing, abuse, and atrocities on such a level that the claims inspire sympathy coupled with moral outrage. Moreover, the abuses in a sex trafficking scandal are alleged to occur on a scale that both suggests widespread conspiracy and simultaneously incites skepticism. The skeptical moment in this process is critical because it invariably turns against the media themselves. This recursive embedding of a debate over the media itself within every major late nineteenth- and early twentieth-century debate over sex trafficking takes two forms: (1) attacks on "sensationalism" and claims that the media representations are obscene and pornographic, and (2) attacks on the methods of fact-finding that result in large-scale and ultimately transformative debates about journalism itself.

When it comes to sex, scandals do not just draw people in as readers; they draw the media into the scandals themselves, broaden the scope of the scandals, and open the media up as no longer transparent conveyers of stories but as objects of debate and attack. As the following chapters demonstrate, scandals over sex and prostitution in particular served as a social and cultural conduit for the transformation not only of discourses concerning sexuality and vice but of the practices and conventions of the media, and also of the relationships among media, social movements, and institutions of power. Such scandals turn back on the media because of their transgression of allowable (and at times credible) discourses within media and because journalists themselves also frequently violate ethical boundaries in investigating these exposés.[29]

BELIEF AND SKEPTICISM IN WHITE SLAVERY SCANDALS

Efforts by the Woman's Christian Temperance Union, the National Vigilance Committee, and other late nineteenth- and early twentieth-century religious and social reform groups to end white slavery were grounded in a moral schema that unquestioningly accepted the sexual enslavement of white women as an imminent social threat. However, not all commentators were equally convinced of the scale or severity of the country's trafficking problem. Emma Goldman wrote disparagingly of the middle-class audience that devoured sentimental white slavery exposés and the self-serving lawmakers who catered to this constituency's every whim. "The people are a fickle baby that must have new toys every day. The 'righteous' cry against the white slave traffic is just such a toy. It serves to amuse the people for a little while, and it will help to create a few more fat political jobs," wrote Goldman.[30] Walter Lippmann echoed this critique in his analysis of the Chicago Vice Commission's recommendations on white slavery: "Sensational disclosures will often make the public flare up spasmodically; but the mass of men is soon bored by intricate rules and tangles of red tape; the 'crusade' is looked upon as a melodrama of real life—interesting, but easily forgotten."[31]

These critics' predictions about the crusade's short half-life were accurate: by the onset of World War I, public opinion had shifted away from white slavery as the primary explanation for women's entry into prostitution.[32] Yet the disappearance of white slavery from the national agenda cannot completely be chalked up to the public's limited attention span, although that probably played a role. Rather, a rapid succession of events in New York City cast widespread doubt on the original allegations made in *McClure's*. The first was a scandalously botched criminal investigation into the city's sexual slave trade. The second was the release of a grand jury's findings on white slavery, which took issue with many central assumptions about white slavery. Daily newspapers in New York and elsewhere followed these events closely, weighing each detail against the vivid and elaborate depiction of underground trafficking networks laid out in *McClure's*. By June 1910, the same month in which the Mann Act was signed into law, the *New York Times* explicitly distanced itself from the white slavery controversy.

Because skepticism over the truth value of stories and debates over truth-gathering methods played such a prominent role in the media controversies surrounding white slavery, it is necessary to examine how truth is discursively produced and how this relates to journalistic institutions and practices and their relations to political authority and economic power, on the one hand, and to audiences and social movements, on the other. Of value for this discussion is Michel Foucault's emphasis on the methods underlying and enabling truth-bearing practices. For Foucault,

> truth is a thing of this world: it is produced only by virtue of multiple forms of constraint. And it induces regular effects of power. Each society has its régime of truth, its 'general politics' of truth: that is, the types of discourse which it accepts and makes function as true; the mechanisms and instances which enable one to distinguish true and false statements, the means by which each is sanctioned; the techniques and procedures accorded value in the acquisition of truth; the status of those who are charged with saying what counts as true.[33]

Foucault goes on to suggest that there is an ongoing battle over "the ensemble of rules according to which the true and the false are separated and specific effects of power are attached to the true."[34] For Foucault, truth is historically, institutionally, and disciplinarily situated. Statements that count as truth, or that produce truth effects, always exist at the center of a knowledge/power nexus, which accords only certain subjects the legitimacy and power to state "truths." Foucault suggests that disciplines and disciplinary institutions are governed at any particular moment by a regime of truth, but that these regimes, which seem so solid and truth-bearing, actually fall quite suddenly, leading to broad epochal shifts in knowledge.[35]

Foucault's understanding of changes in discourse and regimes of truth is based on the metaphor of "war and battles" rather than on language in the form of structural linguistics. While *langue* is a fixed set of rules and relationships, Foucault underscores the importance of the event, in the sense of a pivotal battle, to discursive change: "The problem is at once to distinguish among events, to differentiate the networks and levels to which they belong, and to reconstitute the lines along which they are connected and engender one another."[36] However, in his actual account of regimes of truth, Foucault tends to focus on moments of outright epistemological rupture instead of incremental changes in discourse or the smaller and recurring struggles through which knowledge and knowledge-bearing practices change. He pays less attention to the ongoing struggle over meaning and the stakes—political, economic, and institutional—involved or to the strategies deployed by institutionally situated agents and social movements in promoting and pushing back against truth effects.

Much of Foucault's writing is concerned with the applied sciences and their affiliated institutions: psychiatry, medicine, penal institutions. Prisons, psychiatric wards, and hospitals are more or less closed institutions that are dominated by professional bodies, slow to change, and thus subject to radical and abrupt paradigm shifts similar to those described by Thomas Kuhn.[37] Journalism, while not a science, has in the twentieth century nonetheless aspired to an objectivity built around skepticism as a professional norm that in some respects resembles scientific objectivity. Yet as Michael Schudson points out, the irony is that print news as it has developed in America is not a closed institution but one situated squarely in the commercial sphere that deals directly with the general public. Though journalists invoke objectivity, and many hold advanced degrees, they do not possess a specialized language that requires advanced training to speak, interpret, and apply.[38] Rather than being specialists, reporters are producers of stories who trade in accessibility and timeliness. Members of the mainstream press produce stories that bring in a stable readership for advertisers. Journalism is thus in the business of making events visible to readers and selling this product (accounts of events and other ephemera) to advertisers. Further, the modern news media interact with an unparalleled number of public and private institutions and individuals. As Kevin G. Barnhurst and John Nerone suggest, the "world that makes the news is actually a disparate collection of institutional and non-institutional sources: governments and their agencies, the police, stock markets, sports associations, entertainment industries, polling organizations, the wire services, and so forth."[39] The news media field is the only one that intersects with all of these differing institutions and sources and transmits these encounters to readerships in narrative form. The effect of these multiple overlaps is that institutions can be transformed as they come in contact with the press, and the press in turn can be transformed by its contact with other institutions.

THE BIPOLARITY OF SENSATIONALISM

The most important manner of producing truth and generating claims of falsity examined in the following chapters is sensationalism, and it needs to be clarified that sensationalism produces truth effects, despite the fact that attacks on reporting for being "sensational" tend to imply that certain news reports or newspapers are either fabricated, irrelevant, or carry false baggage in the form of excess meaning or emotion.[40] Thus in its uncritical or colloquial sense, *sensationalism* is invoked primarily as a negative accusation, an accusatory dismissal that is negatively leveled against whatever narrative or medium is being critiqued. The problem with this usage is that it neither helps us understand what sensationalism is—what practices are involved in producing allegedly "sensationalist" discourse, including what strategies are being deployed in its usage—nor helps us assess the actual truth-values of "sensational" productions. The negative category of sensationalism is, in this sense, similar to the negative category of pornography or obscenity. Supreme Court Justice Potter Stewart's famous 1964 statement about pornography comes to mind: "I shall not today attempt further to define the kinds of material I understand to be embraced. . . . But I know it when I see it." When educated viewers find a sexually laden text arousing, it is "erotica," but when they find it upsetting or tasteless, it is "pornography." Similarly parsing out what is and is not sensational is equally subjective: sensationalism in the uncritical sense becomes everything shocking that a critic finds disagreeable, while everything potentially shocking yet agreeable falls under a different category—perhaps "newsworthy."

Some historians have similarly invoked a limited analytical understanding of sensationalism. In his work on press coverage of murder trials in Richmond, Virginia, Michael Ayers Trotti takes sensationalism to mean "that subset of violent crimes that struck a chord in the community, resonating strongly enough to maintain a passionate public interest for months."[41] Similarly many studies of yellow journalism, often characterized as the media form that epitomizes press sensationalism, use the term descriptively but do not question what it means.[42] In their seven-hundred-page history of newspapers in the United States, Michael Emery, Edwin Emery, and Nancy L. Roberts define sensationalism as simply "the emphasis on emotion for its own sake."[43] A more analytical approach to sensationalism understands that sensationalism has been an important mode for producing truth effects in mass media. Sensationalism is also productive in the sense that it can lead to social and economic changes, discursive changes, and so forth. Insofar as it produces skepticism and negativity, yet also produces truths, meanings, discourses, debate, and even social change, sensationalism can be said to have a bipolar character. Insofar as it can produce meanings and social change, and alter institutional practices on such a grand scale, sensationalism as a process is thus overwhelmingly positive, even though it is colloquially and rhetorically understood primarily in a negative sense. Even as it is most often conceived of as a negative speech act, as a critique or easy dismissal of certain narratives and forms, sensationalism as critique nonetheless acts to define the allowable discourses in media and produce positive effects.[44] Sensationalism in the press, therefore, is more usefully understood as a particular form of cultural and institutional logic and practice than as simply an exaggeration or fabrication of the "facts" or the production of a rousing, titillating story.

Lisa Duggan comes closest to what I am calling positive sensationalism when she writes, "More than merely diversionary, pandering, or profiteering and prurient, the strategies of scandal and sensationalism addressed the interests of publishers and readers through politically productive narratives that intervened in prevailing definitions of equality and freedom—through the rhetorical and material organization of public and private life."[45] Thus, as a process, sensationalism is more expansive and more positive in its effects than generally recognized, and it fails to have entirely negative inhibitory effects even when such effects are explicitly intended. Both sensationalism as critique and sensationalism as strategy entail marking something as worthy or unworthy of public attention and so redefining semantic domains, cultural salience, and socially allowable discourse. Thus we can understand sensationalism in this sense as a tactic in the contests over cultural relevance and salience that occur on the battlefield of mass media.

In newspapers and in press criticism of the 1880s, 1890s, and 1900s, both negative and positive senses of the term *sensationalism* were deployed with varying degrees of self-consciousness. Each decade also witnessed shifts in the meanings, content, and forms that came under critique as "sensationalism." Hazel Dicken-Garcia demonstrates that sensationalism, in the sense of "too much attention to violence, crime, sex, and gossip about the socially prominent," was a recurring theme throughout the nineteenth century, and it appeared both as a concrete accusation leveled at a particular editor, newspaper, or story, and as an abstract criticism about the pernicious effects of imposing these topics on society.[46] This sense of violent media as the domain of sensationalism in much of the nineteenth century is underscored by Warren Francke's study showing that sensory detail formed the "core of sensationalist news" during that period and that graphic depictions of crimes and violence in nineteenth-century newspapers rendered themselves particularly vulnerable to critiques of excess and sensationalism.[47] However, while the content of the press—detailed minutia about crimes—came under attack in the nineteenth century, Michael Schudson proposes that with the advent of new journalism, "Sensationalism in the 1880s was less substance than style: how extravagantly should the news be displayed? Sensationalism meant self-advertisement."[48] Sensationalism in this sense equals blatant self-promotion, with the press calling attention to its contents with stylistic flourishes like screaming headlines and large illustrations, rather than (or in addition to) using detailed descriptions of violence to lure in readers. But as chapters 5 and 6 demonstrate, sensationalism as critique also came to be understood as the production of false or fabricated knowledge after the turn of the century. Sensationalism thus became a dismissal that could be leveled against a reporter's methods or conclusions irrespective of the stylistic or formal characteristics of the work in question.[49]

SENSATIONALISM, PUBLICITY, AND REFORM

Within the white slavery controversy, some of the most vocal white slavery publicists found themselves defending the existence of white slavery against charges of sensationalism. However, some activists were quite conscious and strategic in their use of sensationalism, while others utilized sensationalism as a strategy without recognizing it as such, often simultaneously decrying media productions other than their own (or other than those they found agreeable) as being "sensationalist."

Some white slavery crusaders viewed shock as a necessary component of publicity. For this group, exaggeration was a justified and necessary attention-grabbing strategy. Sensationalism in the form of deliberate exaggeration to shock audiences was explicitly advocated as a strategy by Harriet Laidlaw, a suffragist and white slavery campaigner, who advised an audience of women activists, "Remember ladies, it is more important to be aroused than it is to be accurate. Apathy is more of a crime than exaggeration in dealing with this subject."[50] For Laidlaw, sensationalism was strategic, justifiable, and warranted when utilized by social movements to achieve tangible political goals. Carried out in the name of the public good, exaggeration was a key strategy for alerting the public to important social issues.

While Laidlaw advocated strategic sensationalism, other white slavery activists had to defend their reform media against charges of negative sensationalism. One defense was to assert that the extreme nature of white slavery claims in fact constituted verification of the existence of the phenomenon. Unlikely, extreme, and horrifying tales of sexual slavery were therefore not exaggerations at all but, by their very nature, blunt expressions of the truth. Reformers articulating this view stressed that what appeared to be sensational distortions were actually sordid truths that society, for whatever reason, chose to deny. United States District Attorney Edwin W. Sims's chapter in Bell's *Fighting the Traffic in Young Girls* follows this logic. Sims sought to defend his representation of white slavery from the charge of "sensationalism" by describing the conditions in which white slaves were held as "horrifying and scarcely capable of exaggeration." While Sims found the sensationalism of the white slavery topic "personally repellant," he felt compelled to write about white slavery on the basis of "official knowledge of the facts." He went on, "So far as the matter of sensationalism is concerned, that may be disposed of in the simple statement that the naked recital, in the most formal and colorless phraseology, of the facts already brought to light by the 'white slave' prosecutions are in themselves so sensational that the art of the most brilliant orator, or the cunning of the cleverest writer, could not add an iota to their sensationalism."[51] Interestingly, Sims appears to be drawing a distinction between sensationalist writing, which he views as a gratuitous artifice, and sensationalism of fact, which he views as justifiable shock in reaction to uncolored facts. A subtle claim of authority lies within this distinction. Sims, an attorney and apparent connoisseur of sensationalism done right, appeals to his own access to the true facts, facts whose truth is evidenced in the sensation of shock experienced by the reader, independent of any manipulation contrived by the writer.

Sims and other moral entrepreneurs writing after 1910 had to defend graphic images and narratives of white slavery against those who sought to tone them down. Some, like *McClure's* editor Samuel S. McClure, argued that orthographic representations of sex trafficking paled in comparison to the actual experience of witnessing the phenomena. McClure called the magazine's white slavery exposés "as compared with the real truth of the subject, merely as the light of the moon to the light of the sun."[52] White slavery, he claimed, was beyond "sensationalism"; far from exaggerating the truth, he alleged that the magazine had withheld critical information deemed too shocking for the public arena.

OBJECTIVITY AND THE RISE OF INSTITUTION-BASED KNOWLEDGE

Like the term *white slavery*, news itself is a historically situated and dynamic cultural construct possessing its own logic, procedures, conventions, and narratives.[53] Far from being transparent transmitters of "the facts," news magazines and newspapers are sites of cultural production that operate according to institutional and professional rules and paradigms and within dominant political ideologies.[54] Early twentieth-century investigative journalism in muckraking magazines and objective reporting in newspapers not only had different social goals, but were guided by distinct models of communication. Investigative reporters often privileged what I call "street-based" information, while emerging objective journalists increasingly consulted "institution-based" sources. As muckraking magazines came under assault in the later Progressive Era, this journalistic mode became increasingly associated with irresponsible talk and was measured against emerging standards of rationality.

The dominant professional norm for journalists after the 1920s was objectivity. Objectivity demanded that reporters distinguish between facts and values, maintain an emotional distance from the subject matter, provide a chain of evidence and sources proving where they got their information, and dutifully cover both sides of a story.[55] Under this professional model, the journalist became a detached observer, capable of sifting through information and arriving at the facts of a case. Yet, as Elizabeth Bird points out, such "information takes the form of quotes from sources, which the journalist assembles in recognizable generic form, offering information aimed at proving the source's credibility."[56]

By the 1930s, objectivity became codified as the dominant news-production practice. Along with objectivity came a new set of relations between professional reporters and their sources. In the aftermath of World War I, reporters increasingly gravitated toward "official" sources whose credibility was derived from their affiliation with powerful institutions.[57] According to Kevin Stoker, journalistic objectivity mandated that "the accuracy of . . . information [be] measured by the credibility or official status of the source and not [by] the individual investigation of the journalist.[58] If the muckrakers were often antagonistic toward their sources, objective journalists saw it as their duty to withhold judgment and ethical posturing. While a technical and professional articulation of journalistic objectivity did not appear until the 1920s in the United States, Dan Schiller dates the emergence of objectivity in reporting to the 1830s, when the press became a commercial institution.[59] In this historical narrative, the first sign of objectivity was the press's move toward nonpartisan reporting, which created a distance between "news" and things political. The intimate connection that the press previously shared with political parties was severed, while news became a commodity potentially read by all literate citizens, regardless of party affiliation. Newspapers began to cast their nets widely in search of larger audiences, thereby changing the definition of news to that which had general appeal. In the view of other media historians, however, "this was less a development toward objectivity than it was a shift away from political partisanship."[60]

Changes in style, content, and what counts as truth (what many media historians call "journalistic innovations") occur differently in journalism than in comparatively closed disciplinary institutions. These transformations can be attributed to changing print technologies and the political economy of mass distribution, but they also have to do with news-gathering practices, the status of public discourse, regimes of intelligibility at a given historical moment, and struggles over meaning both within and outside the print media.

Some media historians argue that press transformation occurs in a piecemeal way; bits and pieces of practices that we consider essential to modern journalism could also be found at earlier moments, complicating the division of press history into distinct moments. For example, David Mindich finds ideals associated with journalistic objectivity, such as detachment and nonpartisanship, in some eighteenth-century newspapers, even during the phase that is widely considered the golden age of the partisan press, a phase of press history that has been routinely contrasted to the era of objectivity.[61] Change in this formulation is neither uniform nor linear in journalism, and the ruptures so often pointed to by historians are frequently exercises in creating boundaries around a much more amorphous field. The problem with this analysis is that it assumes that outsiders, such as scholars of media and journalism, are the only ones creating these boundaries and that the boundaries are entirely semantic and have no concrete institutional, practical, and discursive expression. I argue that epochal transformations do occur in media and journalism along the lines that Foucault suggests but that they draw upon the existing practices that Mindich points to as their raw material. Unlike in the physical and natural sciences, in journalism there is not a complete displacement of paradigms or regimes of truth, but a rise to dominance of certain practices, institutions, and players within a competitive field. Further, the impetus for these changes may arise in unusual or unexpected ways, such as from controversies over white slavery, which I believe formed an ideal catalyst for journalistic transformation because of sex trafficking's potential to create surplus scandals.

Battles over meaning, institutional power, strategies, and techniques for producing truth are thus necessary for us to understand the rise and fall of dominant regimes of truth in broader fields of knowledge. While we can see aspects of various news practices and journalistic standards in different eras, I am most interested in how practices, attitudes, and appeals to truth and falsity were utilized at particular moments in the context of struggles over mass media and how these battles transformed journalism. One of the more important battles in journalism is the struggle over whose voice counts as truth in terms of journalistic sourcing, which groups get to determine the cultural relevance and salience of particular topics, and which groups and individuals get consulted by the mass media. In other words, I am concerned with questions of who had access to mass media, who—moral reform movements, advertisers, elites—could shape media agendas, and what mechanisms and rhetorical strategies they employed to secure positions alongside journalistic institutions.

To some degree, the topics journalists chose to focus on had much to do with the worlds they were able to access given their own class status. William T. Stead, Jacob Riis, Ray Stannard Baker, and other nineteenth-century reformer-reporters observed, interviewed, and intervened in the lives of the lowest classes, partly because people who lived on the streets were not as able to shield themselves from observation or protect themselves from the potential pitfalls of representation as the elite were. As Warren Francke suggests, "For a time, it seemed, low-status reporters must interview low-status sources."[62] As journalism increasingly became professionalized, journalists were able to access sources with higher status (something many nineteenth-century reporters only dreamed of), but such access rarely occurred on reporters' own terms. These transformations in sourcing, access, and institutional connections, it seems to me, are the most pertinent for parsing out various "moments" of the press. The connections that were formed between the press and other institutions and individuals found expression in the statements that "counted as truth" in the context of reportage on particular pivotal events, the meaning of which became contested on the battleground of mass media.

The effects of skepticism and claims of falsity at the historical moments in which the majority of white slavery controversies occurred are important for understanding the specific impact of sex trafficking exposés on journalism and on reform movements. The white slavery controversy engendered enormous amounts of both belief and skepticism, leading to new truth effects and methods for arriving at them within journalism. Because skepticism came to dominate the debates over white slavery, these controversies helped to propel a journalism based on purported objectivity founded in skepticism to a position of authority and dominance over other truth-bearing practices performed by journalists. Objectivity did not obliterate other styles of news, but the ideal of objectivity became dominant within the profession and became the standard against which other forms were defined.

In the past, media historians have been content to link changes in the press, including the rise of journalistic objectivity, to the "masculine" areas of foreign affairs, wars, and technology—outside struggles over race, class, gender, and sexuality. However, we will see that this skepticism became an important weapon in the reaction to claims about white slavery and that the transformation of journalism and the dominance of objectivity as a regime of truth within journalism were already in full swing after these debates. It is true that specific practices by editor-publishers and claims of truth-telling and fairness by newspapers date back to the early nineteenth century and perhaps even earlier, as Mindich has shown. However, these practices were not fully developed and institutionalized, recognized as best practices, and accorded legitimacy; nor were they dominant within the journalistic field prior to the twentieth century.

Before relegating sensationalism to objectivity's "other," the next chapter considers the apex of sensationalism in England, the ascendancy of "new journalism" under William T. Stead, who was sensationalism's master practitioner and grand theoretician. Stead conducted the first major journalistic investigation into forced prostitution, an inquiry that played a central role in the development of his methods and in the conceptualization of sensationalism. Lest there be any doubt that sensationalism is a positive strategy for producing truth effects, let me turn not to Foucault but to Stead himself, who, writing in 1886, stated that the term *sensationalism* "covers a wonderful lack of thinking. For, after all, is it not a simple fact that it is solely by sensations experienced by the optic nerve that we see, and that without a continual stream of ever-renewed sensations we should neither hear, nor see, nor feel, nor think. Our life, our thought, our existence, are built up by a never-ending series of sensations, and when people object to sensations they object to the very material of life."[63] Stead contrasted his view to that of the "anti-sensationalist": "'You must not pump spring water unawares upon a gracious public full of nerves,' is the canon of the anti-sensationalist; if you do, it is held by some to be so grave an offence as to justify them in saying anything, even if they deny that the water was cold which aroused them into a state of indignant clamour." He noted that exaggeration was a form of sensationalism but "not the sensationalism which I am prepared to defend. The sensationalism which is indispensable is sensationalism which is justifiable. Sensationalism in journalism is justifiable up to the point that it is necessary to arrest the eye of the public and compel them to admit the necessity of action."[64] Here Stead argues that sensationalism is an essential method for revealing and communicating the truth of human experience of reality, which for him is grounded in sensory experience. He thus offers an organic model of sensationalism that flows naturally between the body and the press. In his second passage he goes so far as to make a distinction between positive sensationalism and lying or exaggeration. Positive sensationalism is that which arouses the public and is couched in terms of social reform. Herein lies a critical point. The use of sensationalism as positive strategy was championed by and inseparable from writers involved directly in social movements as well as those movements themselves, a point upon which I elaborate in the next two chapters and in the later discussion of the rise of muckraking.

CHAPTER TWO

William T. Stead and the "Soul" of Sensationalism

> I am but a comparatively young journalist, but I have seen Cabinets upset, Ministers driven into retirement, laws repealed, great social reforms initiated, Bills transformed, estimates remodeled, programmes modified, Acts passed, generals nominated, governors appointed, armies sent hither and thither, war proclaimed and war averted, by the agency of newspapers.
>
> —William T. Stead, "Government by Journalism" (1886)

The earliest journalistic effort to equate prostitution and slavery can be traced to London's daily *Pall Mall Gazette*. In July 1885, the paper's dynamic, evangelical editor, William T. Stead, created an overnight sensation with his exposé entitled "The Maiden Tribute of Modern Babylon," which appeared in four consecutive issues of the *Gazette*. Stead's account of the pervasive abduction and seduction of virgins scandalized British culture and led to the passage of social purity legislation that raised the age of consent from thirteen to sixteen. Shortly after the publication of Stead's revelations, angry demonstrators gathered in a highly publicized mass protest in Hyde Park to demand that Parliament pass stalled legislation to protect young girls. The resulting Criminal Law Amendment Act of 1885 was an omnibus piece of legislation that not only enacted new age-of-consent laws, but also greatly expanded police power to arrest prostitutes and brothel owners, leading to a national crackdown on all forms of commercial sex. The law also contained a provision making "indecent acts" between men illegal, ushering in a period of law enforcement intervention into male homosexuality in Britain. Stead's exposé altered the immediate cultural landscape, leading to a surge of anti-vice activism as various social purity vigilance groups organized to insure enforcement of the act in their localities. Working in tandem with law enforcement, groups like the National Vigilance Committee attempted to enforce a single code of sexual conduct on men and women by encouraging men to "level up" to standards of chastity expected of women in late Victorian society.

As the Criminal Law Amendment Act was being passed in Parliament, fallout from Stead's journalistic methods in "The Maiden Tribute" led to his three-month incarceration in Holloway Prison. He was tried and convicted on abduction charges for purchasing the thirteen-year-old Eliza Armstrong for five pounds. Stead argued that the girl's purchase, while not as tightly organized as it could have been, was committed in the service of a larger goal. This journalistic stunt, the centerpiece of "The Maiden Tribute," was offered as proof of London's trade in virgins. Testifying in court, Armstrong's mother, who sought the criminal charges, claimed that her understanding was that her daughter had been offered a respectable position; she had been deceived in accepting the deal. The court finally found Stead and two conspirators guilty of abduction. However, the legal and social changes instituted by Stead's piece were already in motion before his methods and morality were called into question. While other newspapers reveled in the details of Stead's arrest and proclaimed the end of his career, Stead emerged from prison with an enhanced reputation. His sentence to prison for exposing sex trafficking made the state look complicit in vice; stories of Stead's martyrdom mobilized the multinational social purity movement and helped spark similar campaigns in the United States and elsewhere.

If, as chapter 1 argues, sex trafficking is not so much discovered as created as an object of public political discourse, social movements and the press have historically been two sites where representations of sexual trafficking are produced and institutionalized. This chapter considers how alliances between reform movements and journalism around the issue of white slavery and child prostitution were forged in England. It examines the process by which a crusading journalist, temperance activists, rescue workers, and social purity reformers borrowed conventions from each other, drawing on theories, narratives, and methods for arriving at and publicizing beliefs about widespread sex slavery. Stead's exposé redefined prostitution in English popular culture and reform movements, creating a productive synergy between journalistic and reformist domains. "The Maiden Tribute" solidified a conceptual link between prostitution and coercion while establishing enduring symbolic connections between commercial sex and slavery. By focusing on the most extreme cases of "unwilling virgins," Stead's writing

Figure 2.1. William T. Stead as editor of the *Pall Mall Gazette*, 1881. From Estelle Stead, *My Father: Personal and Spiritual Reminiscences* (London: William Heinemann, 1912), 105.

revived a languishing purity movement in England and redirected this movement's reform focus toward coerced prostitution and away from other abuses.

"The Maiden Tribute" controversy had a formative impact on journalism in England and would later come to encourage certain tendencies within journalism in the United States as well. Despite complaints and protests by the press and others, Stead was an early practitioner of the interview, which came to be implemented and standardized in short order. Stead also opened up the range of allowable topics within reform movements and journalism by delivering a quick blow to the purported "conspiracy of silence" surrounding the issue of prostitution. Readers and newspapers were divided over whether Stead's report was pornographic, but—scandalous or not—such stories became permanent in England and opened up new discursive possibilities both there and in the United States. Despite any negative repercussions directed at Stead himself—the dwindling circulation at the *Gazette,* his firing, and his time in jail—the incitement to discourse about forced prostitution became a permanent fixture in journalism, one that appears even in today's papers. The censures failed to stop the inevitable redrawing of boundaries that resulted from Stead's exposé, and they failed to decrease the influence of Stead, who continued to inspire British journalists and went on to influence American reformers and early muckrakers.

"The Maiden Tribute" and its resulting surplus scandal led Stead to rethink journalistic ethics and practices. Despite his use of dubious methods, he did feel that if journalism had more power and more access to institutions and individuals, it would not have to resort to such stunts in order to produce socially valuable knowledge. His foray onto the streets of London as well as his questionable claims about the ubiquity of sexual slavery led directly to his rethinking of the relationship between journalism and other public institutions. Stead's work was marred by serious conceptual and ethical problems. On the heels of writing his sex trafficking exposé, Stead formulated one of the earliest journalistic approaches to public opinion. Significantly, these major revelations did not follow his earlier exposés, though some were famous in their own right. They followed an exposé that also happened to be a sex scandal—indeed, a surplus scandal in which concerns over the media came to predominate.

REDEFINING PASSIONATE MASCULINITY

Stead rose to prominence in the 1870s and 1880s, first writing for the *Northern Echo* and then serving as editor of London's *Pall Mall Gazette,* which sold for a penny, billed itself as "An Evening Newspaper and Review," and self-identified as a hybrid political journal and daily paper. The *Gazette* considered itself a cultured intellectual evening paper that sought a select elite readership. The *Gazette* under Stead did not trade in descriptive journalism or reprint documentary sources. Instead the paper was interested in exposés, particularly in the service of moral or political goals. Stead and his staff combined social investigation, sensationalist detail, and a keen sense of spectacle to produce a number of popular and efficacious journalistic crusades. Stead was already the most powerful and feared reporter-editor in England by the time he turned his attention to "The Maiden Tribute." Advocating what he would later call "governance by journalism," Stead employed the *Gazette* as a vehicle to force through popular legislative reforms. Appeals to readers' sense of morality, sentiment, and public dignity were mainstays of his reportorial approach. In 1884 the *Gazette* launched the "Bitter Cry" campaign against urban poverty, which persisted until a Royal Commission was formed to look into housing issues in the city. Upon the announcement of the commission, the paper's headline read: "Amid a perfect chorus of approval in Parliament and the press, the Royal Commission on the Dwellings of the poor has at length become a certainty."[1] Stead pioneered the "new journalism" during his tenure at the *Gazette*; his journalistic tone and investigative methods were so successful that they were quickly adopted by more conservative "gentleman's journal" publications like London's *Evening News*, *Daily Mail*, and *Lloyd's*. However, these papers were never as innovative as the *Pall Mall Gazette* under the editorship of Stead, whose own sense of self-importance, dogged exposure of corruption at all levels of society, and well-timed sensationalist disclosures earned him multinational fame.

Like all his exposés, Stead's work on vice fused evangelical activism with social investigation and publicity. Stead drew no distinction between religiously motivated social reform and journalism, viewing the two as collaborators in the same democratic movements. The origins of "The Maiden Tribute of Modern Babylon" were deeply embedded in the culture of Protestant social reform that he inhabited.[2] Since the 1860s, purity activists had been organizing against what they perceived as the intrusion of a Parisian-style system of state regulation of vice into England and its colonies. Many British reformers felt that the French system codified the sexual double standard into state law, implementing an "evil" system in which the state assured men easy access to prostitutes and protected men from venereal diseases by staging medical interventions on prostitutes. Their fears were seemingly realized when Parliament passed the Contagious Diseases Acts of 1864, 1866, and 1869, which mandated the registration and routine physical examination of prostitutes for venereal disease in barrack and seaport towns. Between 1865 and 1880, a powerful opposition movement, comprised of a growing Christian women's movement, Baptists, and other Nonconformists, as well as rescue workers, emerged to force Parliament to repeal the acts and to call for an end to the double standard.[3] This broad-based campaign of "new abolitionists," spearheaded in large part by Josephine Butler and Ellice Hopkins, laid the reform infrastructure that was mobilized and reconfigured in the aftermath of Stead's exposé on child prostitution.

"The Maiden Tribute" was published against this backdrop of Nonconformist and Anglican revival in which thousands of men, including Stead, participated. In 1888 Stead addressed the Edinburgh Vigilance Association. Of his crusade and the double standard of morality, he stated:

> Hitherto they had had two distinct standards of morality in relation to all questions governing the sexes. . . . In [the] face of the progressive elevation and emancipation of women, they had to face this fact, that in their ideas of sexual morality, they had either to level up or to level down. They had either to raise the standard of the male to the standard of the female, or they had to make up their minds as best they could to see the female standard leveled down to the male standard.[4]

The 1880s witnessed a proliferation of male chastity groups, the most prominent being Hopkins' White Cross Society. Members of this organization wore white crosses, symbolic of their commitment to virtuous masculinity. When the White Cross Society and representatives of other reform groups held purity lectures in vice areas and all-male institutions like medical schools, men in the audience were often moved to tears; they pledged to lead morally pure lives free of vice and frequently joined purity crusades themselves.[5]

"THOSE DREAD REGIONS OF SUBTERRANEAN VICE"

In May 1885 Stead was approached by the city chamberlain, Benjamin Scott, who was also chairman of the London Committee for Suppressing the Traffic in English Girls. Earlier that year, Scott's group had investigated a longstanding brothel ring in Chelsea that catered to wealthy patrons, including European royalty. Servants told members of the group that the wares sold in Mrs. Jeffries's brothel occasionally included girls as young as thirteen. The London Committee successfully searched for a prosecutorial angle, aiming to incite a high-profile court case to highlight the need for strong age-of-consent laws. Before the trial got under way, however, Mrs. Jeffries saved her patrons from considerable embarrassment by pleading guilty and paying a fine of two hundred pounds. As if to taunt those concerned about a conspiracy between officialdom and vice, a "wealthy friend" paid the two hundred pounds, and the well-connected madam "drove off in a brougham supplied by an earl."[6] With this flourish, Mrs. Jeffries and her friends dealt a considerable blow to social purity forces in England who hoped the trial would be the significant public event to which they could tie their age-of-consent crusade.

When this attempt at publicity failed, Scott implored Stead to use his journalistic position to intervene publicly in Parliament's handling of the Criminal Law Amendment Act, a key piece of social purity legislation that was in peril of being dropped because of a change in government. The law had many components, but the most important provision for reformers was raising the age of consent from thirteen to sixteen. Scott argued that unless the press did something to mobilize public opinion around this act, it would quietly disappear from Parliament's agenda, and a twenty-year battle for legislation protecting girls and women would be lost.

By his own account, Stead was loath to take on such a politically sensitive topic, but he ultimately determined that the cause outweighed any concerns he might have about the "risk, physical and moral," that he would face as a result of this undertaking.[7] Stead and three staff writers for the *Gazette*, whom he described as possessing "devotion and self-sacrifice, combined with a rare instinct for investigation and a singular personal fearlessness," formed a special commission to investigate vice on London's streets (61). This self-appointed commission spent months interviewing people in London's East and West Sides. The social investigators conducted extensive interviews with people involved in various ways with prostitution, including both those who directly abetted the trade and those who attempted to control or reform it. The team collected, analyzed, and checked statements from former and current brothel owners and prostitutes, professional procurers, male clients, abortionists, rescue workers, jail wardens, ex-detectives, and members of Parliament. The stories these informants told and the leads they provided formed the backbone of "The Maiden Tribute."[8]

In each of his four installments, Stead built his case for the existence of a veritable slave trade in virgins on London's streets. He claimed to have had firsthand exposure to the individuals involved and therefore spoke "not from hearsay or rumor," but from his own "investigation into the facts," drawing a distinction between hearsay and information gleaned from a formal interview (61). In addition to relying on others' testimony for insider knowledge about vice, Stead also personally oversaw the purchase of a thirteen-year-old virgin for five pounds from her mother. The stunt added credibility to Stead's claims about the existence of a "London slave market" by providing "firsthand" evidence embodied by Lily, the girl's pseudonym. The particulars of Lily's purchase and treatment in captivity by Stead ultimately led to the journalist's three-month imprisonment on abduction charges, as discussed above.

In the nineteenth century, reporting on prostitution in England and the United States had been vulnerable to charges of commerce-driven sensationalism and prurience. The visibility of heterosexual prostitution, especially in industrializing cities and port towns, was met in the Victorian era with frequent admonitions to avoid discussing the "social evil" in polite company. To stave off charges of prurient sensationalism, a journalistic report on child prostitution required strategic introduction and justification to late Victorian readers. Key social institutions had decided to maintain a conspiracy of silence around the issue. Stead felt it was incumbent on journalism, in particular the *Gazette*, to render vice orthographically visible and audible to the Victorian public in order to produce political effects. The exposé's July 4, 1885, prelude and the report's first several paragraphs were devoted to this issue of institutional silence; they proposed a "sunshine and shadow" model in which the dark spaces where vice occurred were illuminated by a new regime of institutional and public visibility. The crusading newspaper and journalist would be the catalyst for this thoroughgoing transformation in sexual expression and regulation.

The prelude, inconspicuously entitled "Notice to Our Readers," indicated that the Criminal Law Amendment Act was going to be dropped by Parliament and announced: "We have, therefore, determined, with a full sense of the responsibility attaching to such a decision, to publish the report of a Special and Secret Commission of inquiry which we appointed to examine the whole subject." The following week's report would focus on "those phases of sexual criminality which the Criminal Law Amendment Bill was framed to repress." Under the heading "Frank Warning," the prelude continued:

> All those that are squeamish, and all those that are prudish, and all those who prefer to live in a fool's paradise of imaginary innocence and purity, selfishly oblivious of the horrible realities which torment those whose lives are passed in the London Inferno, will do well not to read the *Pall Mall Gazette* of Monday and the three following days. The story

> of an actual pilgrimage into a real hell is not pleasant reading, and is not meant to be. It is, however, an authentic record of unimpeachable facts, "abominable, unutterable, and worse than fables yet have feigned or feared conceived." But it is true, and its publication is necessary. (51–52)

The "Frank Warning" gave advance notice of the sensation to come. This advertisement at once engaged sensationalism while deflecting criticism since "nothing but the most imperious sense of public duty would justify its publication."[9] It appealed to "unimpeachable facts" and the dire legal context to argue that the report's publication was necessary and to deny the journalist's own agency in its construction. Stuart Hall has argued that stock fictional narratives exert a determining force over news reports such that, in essence, "the story writes the journalist." To take Hall's insight slightly out of context, the "Frank Warning" simultaneously glorified the journalist for taking on a courageous assignment and also portrayed him as a mere conduit for any details determined abhorrent or sensationalist; he could not resist writing them if he tried.[10] Because the topic at hand is "real" and not the product of a wild imagination, the journalist's task is merely to present written narrative facts that he has collected during his investigation or pilgrimage.

The warning ostensibly served to ward off the genuinely squeamish reader, but in fact it performed a great deal of cultural work, attempting to justify and legitimate marginalized forms of representational and reading practices. It first castigated a generic, hypersensitive, and disconnected middle-class Victorian reader, and then invoked a new reader firmly grounded in urban realities through texts, neither internally occupied nor "selfishly oblivious" to the world outsider her parlor. Dressed as a warning, the prelude in fact constituted a challenge to readers to confront directly the *Gazette*'s forthcoming chronicle of "horrible realities." This representation of readership was something of a canard: as Sally Mitchell argues, popular Victorian sentimental novels, while associated with "daydreaming," had long been "strongly clustered around a complex of pain, suffering, and alienation."[11] Also, the urban scene with its host of social maladies had long been a topic in Victorian fiction and reportage.[12] The warning nonetheless legitimized the practice of reading "The Maiden Tribute" by suggesting that the exposé would transcend charges of sensationalism; and, by extension, it offered readers themselves immunity from charges of prurience. At the same time, it advertised itself as an "authentic" report that transcended imaginative capacities, thereby delivering the reader to a previously unthinkable state. Thus the real promise embedded in the "Notice to Our Readers" was deliverance of the ultimate sanctioned reading experience.

By appealing to "facts," the "Frank Warning" offered reality as the gold standard against which legal censorship or quick dismissal was unjustified. Yet Stead's lavishly peppered references to the "real" are tempered by melodramatic religious imagery figuring vice in London as an actual place, an "Inferno," a veritable hell on Earth that one enters and few exit. Billing his study as an "authentic record of unimpeachable facts," Stead constructed himself as a mythic, sacrificial figure engaging in self-endangerment to undertake a pilgrimage into hell and bring stories from the underworld to readers. In asserting that the topic "is one upon which even the coolest and most scientific observer may well find it difficult to speak dispassionately in a spirit of calm, philosophic investigation," Stead established a rhetoric of withering masculine objectivity that would be invoked in subsequent, primarily male-authored journalistic and reform tracts asserting the horrors of sex slavery (64).

The interweaving of scientific investigation and myth did not end there. Stead's central analogy was to the maidens sent from ancient Athens to die in the Labyrinth of Daedalus, from which they could "never retrace their steps." However, he pointed out that the Athenian tribute was paid only once every nine years, while "this very night in London, and every night, year in and year out, not seven maidens only, but many times seven . . . will be offered up as the Maiden Tribute of Modern Babylon." While they may have been maidens at dawn, by "tomorrow they will find themselves within the portals of the maze of London brotheldom" (58).

Like these maidens, the male social investigator also ventured into the urban labyrinth, not to fulfill the logic of the prostitutes' descent into hell, but like a detective, to discover its secrets. None of the seductions Stead described occurred outdoors. They took place in many-roomed brothels, rented hotel rooms, and the estates of wealthy gentlemen. Following popular convention, Stead referred to these spaces as streets. He also spent a great deal of time talking to street prostitutes, even though these women (and no doubt men) do not figure in his investigation. The more time Stead spent on London's literal streets, the more he asserted that a psychic identification occurred between the journalist who investigates the streets and the streetwalkers who advertise their bodies on them:

> *I have been a night prowler for weeks.* I have gone in different guises to most of the favorite rendezvous of the harlots. I have strolled along

> Ratcliff-highway, and sauntered round and round the Quadrant at midnight. I have haunted St. James Park, and twice enjoyed the strange sweetness of summer night by the sides of the Serpentine. I have been at all hours in Leicester-square and the Strand, and have spent midnight in Mile-end-road and the vicinity of the Tower. Sometimes I was alone; sometimes accompanied by a friend; and the deep and strong impression which I have brought back is one of respect and admiration for the extraordinarily good behavior of the English girls who pursue this dreadful calling. (177; my emphasis)

Despite this empathic identification, the middle-class male journalist was in fact free to wander and was subjectively granted a form of universal access to survey and represent the city streets. Nineteenth-century middle- and working-class women were not as easily granted the same privileges of mobility in movement or identification as men.[13]

Despite the attempted "scientific" investigation and assemblage of information by the special commission, as well as the fact-checking methods that Stead built into the investigation, "The Maiden Tribute" was a lurid and strikingly unreliable account of teenage prostitution in London that borrowed upon a number of popular genres to represent sexual exchange in the city as a "veritable slave trade." Stead represented a world in which rapacious aristocrats took sexual advantage of young, working-class girls throughout London. While some youths might overtly agree to their "seduction" by these wealthy men, Stead sought to prove that, despite their verbal statements of acquiescence, girls are "absolutely and totally ignorant of the nature of the act to which [they] assented" (69). This imagery of sinning rogues and clueless victims proved effective among middle-class reformers. As Deborah Gorham argues, the "imagery of individual sin, with its corresponding possibility of individual redemption, may have been comforting to these late Victorian middle-class reformers because it did not threaten the images of womanhood, childhood, and family life that formed an essential part of their worldview."[14] At a moment when notions of childhood were undergoing a radical renegotiation, Stead had to prove that the teenage victims possessed no agency in their actions in order to present them as worthy of reformist attention.

Judith Walkowitz suggests that the narrative structure of "The Maiden Tribute" fused "older cultural forms" like melodrama with contemporary ones like "pornography and fantasy, [as well as] the Gothic fairy tale." As a result, Stead "produced an unstable text and a contradictory, obsessive discourse around sexuality that remain a legacy for the modern era."[15] When

Stead condemned the "princes and dukes, the ministers and judges, and the rich of all classes" for their abuses against "the daughters of the poor," he borrowed from the rich popular tradition of melodrama, which had been successfully deployed in a variety of radical, nineteenth-century working-class and feminist campaigns. Melodrama's status as a politicized storytelling mode stemmed partly from its clear distinction of the purely innocent victim from the wholly guilty villain.[16] The victims in older melodramas tended to be working class and often female. While Stead drew on the conventions of melodrama, Walkowitz points out that his melodramatic vision is solidly lodged in a middle-class male consciousness: the most prominent villains in his narrative are not the wealthy aristocrats who purchase virgins, but the working-class women (and sometimes men) who procure and sell them. Male consumers have been pushed deep into the anonymous background of "The Maiden Tribute," while the "immoral" words and actions of working class women appear in sharp relief throughout the text.

For readers unmoved by the storytelling tradition of melodrama, "The Maiden Tribute" also constituted a male sexual fantasy cloaked as reform tract—*My Secret Life* rendered palatable for the moralist. The report went further than any other mass-distributed text of the era in graphically describing not just the procurement practices associated with late Victorian London's extensive sexual commerce, but also the deviant sexual preferences of clients. In the introduction to the first installment of the piece, Stead suggested that the ensuing report would be received "with a shuddering horror that will thrill throughout the world," describing two affective states that are roughly paralleled by melodrama and pornography. If Stead expected readers to be horrified by scenarios of children "whose lives are passed in the London Inferno," he also expected them to be thrilled by the titillating details whose publication he deemed "necessary" to the cause of reform. To that end, the first installment's subsections suggested hardcore pornographic scenarios even by today's standards: "The Violation of Virgins," "Virgins Willing and Unwilling," "The London Slave Market," "Strapping Girls Down," and "A Child of Thirteen Bought for 5 Pounds." While purity movements attempted to convince men to turn away from vice, Stead's report linked the seemingly contradictory affective states of lust and moral outrage. Rescue itself, it must be acknowledged, is also a powerful sexual fantasy. Furthermore, as Walkowitz notes, in masquerading as a client in pursuit of virgins—instead of a journalist in pursuit of a story—Stead repeatedly flirts with the libertine role, calling into question his own subjectivity and motives while conducting the investigation.[17] At various moments in the text, he confronted girls as their presumed seducer, yet always drew back and appealed to his own reputation as a moral purist at the last moment. Readers are thus invited to vicariously enjoy a sexual fantasy while reassuring themselves of their own moral virtue by identifying with Stead's reformist agenda.

JOURNALISM, COMMUNICATION, AND CLASS IN LATE VICTORIAN SOCIETY

Late nineteenth-century journalists on both sides of the Atlantic lacked ready access to informants who occupied higher social positions. They could more easily make downward or lateral moves. Access and trust were key elements in this context, and when the latter failed, money usually acted as an effective lubricant.[18] Stead would later argue in "Government by Journalism" that high-level officials should avail themselves of journalists at a moment's notice, thereby giving reporters access to institutions and people of power (and in the process elevating the status of the journalist).[19] For his information in "The Maiden Tribute," however, Stead relied primarily on working- and middle-class informants.

Class distinctions were apparent in the labels Stead used to describe his interchanges with informants. They ranged from the intimate (the "conversation"), to the professional (the "interview") and the religious and legalistic (the "confession"). The language used to describe interchanges with people across the British class system revealed much about both the position of the journalist in 1885 and the social status of each informants' authority as possessor of social knowledge. While his middle-class informants were figured as unproblematic experts on the trade, his working-class interviewees are not assumed to be automatically trustworthy. By defining their statements as "confessions" about the underground market of sex and linking their narratives to a sense of penitence, Stead gives their knowledge credence and legitimizes his use of their statements as evidence while maintaining the backdrop of class-based suspicion and affirming his readers presumed attitudes. Stead's one encounter with a politician (a "member of Parliament") was called a "conversation," emphasizing that the interchange was not an official interview but a casual exchange, which had the benefit of suggesting that the editor-reporter had friends in high places and was perhaps gaining equal standing with this man (a longtime fantasy of Stead's). As if to emphasize their parallel status, Stead had no problem in using this anonymous member's words against him and positioning him at the very center of the political problem at hand: Parliament's failure to pass the Criminal Law Amendment Act. Encounters with solidly middle-class members of professions (nascent experts) were deemed "interviews," reflecting a newly developing formalization of relations between police, detectives, rescue workers (future social workers), and reporters.

However, in order "to substantiate the accuracy of every statement contained" in the text, Stead endowed upper-class men with the power of holding secrets and verifying his statements. To prove that his revelations were true, he placed the concrete details of each source, "together with full and detailed explanations" of his methods in the hands of reputable men in Britain's royal and noble heritage, including two archbishops and two earls, as well as one M.P., and the ex-director of the Criminal Investigations Department. The social status of these men guaranteed their reputability and, Stead assumed, would help convince readers that the revelations of "The Maiden Tribute" were true and verifiable while preempting the need to divulge his sources to the public—a primordial characteristic of the aristocratic, journalistic review (63). Yet at the same time that Stead uses aristocrats, he attacks them. They are authoritative but not necessarily innocent.

VOLITION, RATIONALITY, AND TEENAGE PROSTITUTION

The question of volition vexed the text, repeatedly asserting itself—as it does in most discourses of commercial sex that figure women as victims—and not finding resolution until an "unwilling virgin" was procured.[20] Stead's foil, the "well-known member of Parliament," took the position that the girls were willing participants in their exchange: "I doubt the unwillingness of these virgins. That you can contract maids at so much a head is true enough. I myself am quite ready to supply you with 100 maids at £25 each, but they will all know very well what they are about" (66). He added that a few of them might be unwilling, but most "take a very businesslike view of the value of their maidenhead." Where the M.P. saw an unproblematic standard contract that involved a buyer and equally willing seller, Stead saw a sexual slave trade that operated without the girls' consent. He drew on the economic metaphor of slavery and the sexual metaphor of rape to make his case. The M.P. imbued potential prostitutes with calculative agency and downplayed the role of the middleman, while Stead emphasized the procurer or middleman in his account of the economic underpinnings of prostitution.[21] In Stead's view, girls became commodities "quoted like lambs at so much a head," packaged and sold to the highest bidder for the express purpose of sexual violation and abuse. Thus Stead focused in his text on soliciting descriptions of procurement from brothel owners and procuresses.

One reformed brothel keeper suggested that "fresh girls" could be supplied either by seduction, disguise, or reproduction, because a "very simple mode of supplying maids is by breeding them." These girls, "bred and trained for the life," "become merchantable" at the age of twelve or thirteen. This description harkened back to the time of chattel slavery, during which reproduction in some locales became an efficient means of maintaining the slave population.[22]

If Stead sought theories from male informants about the girls' relative willingness or unwillingness to be seduced, from teenage informants he actively sought only personal narratives of either brave escape or ruinous seduction. In arguing for a view of prostitution as slavery, Stead overlooked the language of the girls themselves. However, a discussion of their economic motives inadvertently found its way into his text. In one instance, he procured a teenager who persistently insisted on seduction. In his view the girl was surely "incapable of forming any calculation as to the consequences of her own action." Their subsequent conversation featured Stead trying to "reason" with the girl (a reasoning that was more like fire-and-brimstone moralizing):

> "Now," said I, "if you are seduced you will get £2 for yourself, but you will lose your maidenhead; you will do wrong, your character will be gone, and you may have a baby which it will cost your wages to keep. Now I will give you £1 if you will not be seduced; which will you have?" "Please sir," she said, "I will be seduced." "And face the pain, the wrong-doing, and the shame, and the possible ruin and ending days on the streets, all for the difference of one pound?" "Yes, sir," she burst into tears, "we are so poor." Could any proof be more conclusive as to the absolute inability of this girl of sixteen to form an estimate of the value of the only commodity which the law considers her amply able to deal the day after she is thirteen? (106)

For Stead, the "maidenhead" was a precious commodity to be cashed in at marriage according to Victorian middle-class norms. This rare exchangeable good was "what a woman ought to value more than life" (105). The girl's plea to be seduced was interpreted as ignorance of the cultural and economic benefits conferred by virginity. Stead thus claimed to speak for the poor, but ignored the exigencies and immediacy of poverty that might have made the extra pound seem desirable at that moment. Stead is also blind to the possibility that the greater exchange Stead imagines the girl relinquishing for a pittance may simply not exist. There is also the irony that Stead himself capitulates to the logic of "maidenhead" exchange value, perhaps detracting from his weighty morality. As a short-term economic choice bred of poverty, the girls' desire to have the two pounds for seduction over Stead's one pound to secure salvation looks neither unreasonable nor illogical. And Stead may have been naive to assume she was truly a virgin. Her calculations may indeed have been different than he realized. She may have been one of the "vamped up virgins" Stead claimed were mythical figures on London's streets.

"The Maiden Tribute" acknowledged the existence of willing prostitution but quickly moved on to inflate the problem of teenage prostitution so that it appeared as a dominant form determining the character of other forms of prostitution. This type came to stand in metonymically for the entirety of all urban vice. Stead conflated the social relations and economies that produced vice into a scientific system of coercive procurement that impelled organized rape. Although he sought to frame teenage prostitution as slavery, he had a difficult time containing all the different models of prostitution that emerged during his investigation. Particulars of methods and forms proliferated as Stead wrote up his investigative details, and many of these particulars veered from the sensationalist coercion model, suggesting a multiplicity of occasionally mundane arrangements, strategies, and motives for engaging in commercial sex. While these were rarely as simplistic as a libertarian model might imply, they nonetheless suggested that the paths to vice were multiple and not universally determined by one overarching social logic, though poverty and social class played dominant roles. Despite his rhetoric about the "daughters of the poor," what Stead wanted was for working-class girls to be chaste, for them to exhibit the same alleged morality and calculative rationality as Victorian middle-class girls. Stead's "empiricism" belies his unacknowledged project: to spearhead a social and legal movement to redefine vice, its age limits, boundaries, categories, and broader cultural relevance.

SIGNS OF TRUTH: INTERVIEWS AND SCREAMS

Stead's vice investigation found him traveling between London's East and West Sides, visiting nodes in "the system" of commercialized vice. He sought three forms of evidence: social facts in the form of interviews, aural confirmation in the form of a scream, and embodied proof in the form of an unwilling virgin. His main method of investigation—and the conduit of what Francke calls the "sensory detail" of sensationalism—was the interview.[23] The journalistic device was first used in the United States during the Civil War but did not make inroads across the Atlantic for another twenty years. Publishing an exposé comprised almost entirely of interviews was a radical and unfamiliar act in late Victorian England. When British papers slowly began to utilize the interview, they faced accusations of Americanization, and interviewees were shamed for submitting to conversation with a journalist. Stead, an early adopter of the interview, defended the mode as the "most interesting method of extracting the ideas of the few for the instruction and entertainment of the many which has yet been devised by man." The role of the interviewer "is almost as indispensable as that of an interpreter is to an Englishman in China." He further declared that, despite criticisms, the interview "has a future."[24]

The journalistic interview began in the United States as verbatim renderings of court interrogations in the penny presses.[25] The aim of editors in printing these sessions was to entertain readers with the behaviors of the working classes while informing them about local crimes. As reporters became interrogators themselves, their objectives in conducting interviews veered from the goals of a warden or policeman. Interviews were conducted in private, and thus did not seek to establish guilt or innocence before an already public audience but to replicate a communicative mode associated with intimacy and privacy: face-to-face dialogue. A reporter might hope for a moment of weakness in which a secret might be unearthed. Early reporters strove, not always successfully, to get public officials to consent to interviews, but few would consent because, as the *Nation* suggested in 1873, the conversational style of the interview write-up made even the greatest men look like unthinking fools. The interview was also considered an invasion of privacy that constituted a violation of the interviewees' right to hold certain items in secrecy. These details found their way back into the private sphere through their consumption in the home. Thus George Rider complained in 1882 that the interview was a "latter day nuisance" that comprised "the indelicate and offensive parading of personalities, of appearance, presence, and conversation," doing harm not only to the institution of journalism but to the very "sanctities of domestic life and marriage."[26] Interviewees were often surprised to see their conversations reprinted and made available as public commodities to newspaper readers. Although the popularity of the interview grew throughout the late nineteenth century and into the twentieth century, critical reviews from the era's press offered little in the way of accolades for the genre.[27]

Stead however viewed the interview as a central technique of journalism:

> A journalist is, or ought to be, a perpetual note of interrogation, which he affixes without ceremony to all sorts of conditions of men. No one is too exalted to be interviewed, no one too humble. From the king to the hangman—and I have interviewed both—they need no introduction to the sanctum, provided only that they speak of facts at first hand bearing directly on some topic of the day. That universal accessibility, that eagerness to learn everything that can be told him by any one who knows the facts, gives the editor one great advantage; and another, perhaps as great, is the compulsion that is laid upon him to serve up the knowledge he acquired in a shape that can be read and remembered by all men.[28]

The interview form would later be linked to journalistic objectivity—in particular to the process of getting "both sides of the story"—and to qualitative research methods. In the 1880s Stead turned others' narratives into a heterogeneous text that shifted genres sometimes mid-sentence and opened itself up to a multiplicity of subsequent interpretations and political uses. The evidence he marshaled took the form of verbal statements from people associated with the trade. He positioned himself textually as interviewer, even though we know he was not present for all the exchanges. This dialogical narrative form fed into his reform goals by allowing Stead to position himself first as a skeptic asking probing questions of his interviewees and ultimately as a converted believer forced to face the truth about criminal sexual practices on London's streets. Stead's omniscient voice created the illusion that he had conducted each interview alone rather than having assembled interviews from a number of sources. The journalist's own authority was bolstered by his self-construction as a possessor of "first-hand knowledge" of London's traffic in women.

The interview, a mode in which a questioner elicits unscripted answers, in which interviewees are coaxed, but their answers are neither predetermined nor judged as correct or incorrect, became a literary and rhetorical device in the service of establishing sensationalist knowledge about child prostitution. To gain the trust of his informants, Stead and his team refused to press charges or make information available to London police and took great care to conceal the identities of their informants. Stead asserted that his goal was not to pursue criminal investigation of his interviewees but to elicit a range of information that would ultimately cast the state as the guilty party. Informants were anonymous, referenced only by generic social profiles or signs ("a member of Parliament"), the first letter of their surname ("Mr. N—"), or contrived titles ("Mesdames X. and Z."). Thus revelations were offered, but few specific details were ultimately revealed. Through these pervasive acts of concealment, the reader was placed in the position of detective trying to uncover an exact location or event in Stead's narrative. Rather than a criminal investigation or a gossip column, both of which seek to tie events to specific names and places, readers of the *Gazette*'s exposé were only left with the revelation that "unthinkable" sexual and economic practices existed in late Victorian society, perhaps pervasively.

Stead's investigative process lacked rigor (he often recounted conversations from memory and dictated their results to his staff sometimes days after the interview occurred), and this laxity, together with Stead's fusion of sensationalism and reformism, produced a text that bridged fantasy and social inquiry. However, the investigation exemplified a burgeoning ethnographic method that used participant observation and interviews to understand and reconstruct social contexts.[29] Stead took hold of this method, recognizing its epistemological importance in inquiries of all kinds. The social world Stead attempted to reconstruct was abstract and multilayered; no single informant held more than a partial view of the true nature of child prostitution in the city. Investigators could achieve a faithful understanding of a social context by conducting numerous interviews with variously positioned social actors and cross-checking them for consistency. Thus each informant embodied partial knowledge of London's teenage prostitution racket, and the journalist became the nascent social scientist able to offer a synthetic, universal image of social relations by consulting a cross section of sources.

Stead's successful wielding of the interview was particularly remarkable in light of the state of journalism at that historical moment. In the next century a reporter's status would be measured by his access to powerful sources. However, as the interview technique was being developed, the journalist's status had not been concurrently elevated. Nor were the journalistic techniques we now take for granted deemed legitimate. The interview was not a simple procedure of journalistic objectivity, as it was later understood to be in the 1920s, but a revolutionary style of intervention that held special powers. The interview operated in "The Maiden Tribute" as a revolutionary mode in which affective states were reproduced from informants and produced in readers. Meanwhile, objective truths and details of social phenomena were verified by eyewitness accounts and dialogue with the reporter, and thus given the stamp of legitimacy. As such, the interview in this early context was more obviously a technique for producing truth and sensation simultaneously. While today we assume that truth and sensationalism are at odds (this is an important debatable concept that I return to later), in the late nineteenth century the newness and power of the interview as a means of producing truth overshadowed concerns over its juxtaposition with sensationalism.

Though the interview as deployed by Stead juxtaposes sensation and fact-gathering in a way that would not be acceptable fifty years later, his use of the interview is nevertheless more familiar as an empirical device to us today than his second major truth-gathering innovation. He used an already familiar technique of positing journalists' own eyewitness experience as evidence, but he bolstered the finality and unimpeachability of the truth he found by engaging in a fetishistic quest to experience a particular event: a virgin's scream.[30] The truth that Stead sought to prove by the attainment of this event was none other than the slave status of young prostitutes. Seeking to counter alternative explanations of why young women sell sex, including poverty and rational profit-making, Stead tried to cut through densely matted webs of metaphors, signs, and associations by invoking "a scream" that would frame his report and lay the other theories to rest. Indeed, if the ideas and practices of brothel owners, procuresses, ex-detectives, ministers, and reform workers populate the text, there is a deep silence at the very center of it. The saleable virgins—the very objects of his exposé—are never asked their theories of prostitution. While the text reproduced several conversations with teenage prostitutes, only the details of their seduction were important for Stead's purposes. He omitted, and perhaps did not even pursue, lengthy interviews with his "girls seduced and ruined" that solicited their own understandings of sexual exchange. Instead, he obsessively pursued pre-linguistic evidence of their victimization in the form of a scream. Even if the girls' words might indicate otherwise, the scream signified certain abuse.

Unwilling victims, he reasoned, would surely scream. Why therefore, were cries not heard throughout London? To answer this question, Stead solicited the testimony of self-fashioned experts as assurance that virgins in fact screamed at the moment of seduction. Since the scream constituted the ultimate proof of their resistance, Stead sought help from an ex-detective in answering this perplexing question:

> "But," I continued, "are these maids willing or unwilling parties to the transaction—that is, are they really maiden, not merely in being each a *virgo intacta* in the physical sense, but as being chaste girls who are not consenting parties to their seduction?" He [ex-detective] looked surprised at my question and then continued emphatically: "Of course they are rarely willing and as a rule they do not know what they are coming for." "But," I replied in amazement, "then do you mean to tell me that

> in very truth actual rapes, in the legal sense of the word, are constantly being perpetrated in London on unwilling virgins, purveyed and procured by rich men at so much a head by keepers of brothels?" "Certainly," said he, "there is not a doubt of it. . . ." "But do the girls cry out?" "Of course they do. But what avails screaming in a quiet bedroom? Remember, the utmost limit of howling or excessively violent screaming, such as a man or woman would make if actual murder was being attempted, is only two minutes, and the limit of screaming of any kind is only five. Suppose a girl is being outraged in a room next to your house. You hear her screaming just as you are dozing to sleep. Do you get up, dress, rush downstairs, and insist on admittance? Hardly. But suppose the screams continue and you get uneasy, you begin to think whether you should not do something? Before you have made up your mind and got dressed, the screams cease, and you think you were a fool for your pains." (65)

Stead returned to this question of aural evidence throughout "The Maiden Tribute." The scream was central to ascertaining and verifying interviewees' statements as well as convincing Stead that his preexisting theories were correct. The theme recurred throughout the first issue, with one subsection, "Why the Cries of the Victims Are Not Heard," devoted entirely to the subject. After interviewing a number of brothel owners, "the difficulty again occurred to [Stead] how it was possible for these outrages to take place without detection." In vague exchanges with a midwife and then with the owner of a brothel in West London, he was assured that many brothels had underground rooms where "the girl may scream blue murder, but not a sound will be heard." Stead reasoned that since flogging occurs routinely to both men and women out of earshot, there is little chance that a young girl's cries would be detectable to anyone else, especially when "means of stifling a cry—a pillow, a sheet, or even a pocket-handkerchief—lie all around" (75–76).

Stead pursued synthetic knowledge through his interviews, suggesting that no single person can accurately convey truth (or reserving the position of truth teller for himself). However, in his relentless pursuit of the scream, he sought a piece of irrefutable evidence—through the nonlinguistic vocalization of pain or terror—that teenage prostitutes possessed no agency. If multiple informants are necessary to elicit truth from interviews, only one cry is required to convince Stead of teenage girls' innocence. Of course, this also implied that teenage girls could not simultaneously exercise agency and be worthy of protection. Yet, as the ex-detective suggested, there was only a brief window of opportunity for ascertaining "the truth" conveyed through screams. This might be missed because a girl's cries were too weak and too brief to record. However, Stead's investigative approach, seeking verification directly by participant observation and indirectly by expert testimony, could reveal this truth.

"A PERSONATION OF VILE CHARACTER"

The centerpiece of the exposé was Lily, a thirteen-year-old virgin, purchased by Stead for five pounds. Adopting "a personation of vile character to obtain information" marked a critical and controversial moment in the investigation, in which the reporter goes from being a mere interviewer to an ethnographer, a participant observer of sorts. However, the virgins were not as forthcoming as Stead represented them as being. Three times in the first section of "The Maiden Tribute," Stead closed in on teenage girls and drew back at the last moment for unspecified reasons. In the place of testimony from these girls, Stead substituted the word of a brothel keeper in one instance and a telegraphed promissory note in another. In an exposé in which names and locations were routinely withheld, letters and statements might constitute supporting evidence, but ultimately the text demanded a body.

Rebecca Jarrett, a reformed prostitute collaborating with Stead, conducted negotiations with a local brothel owner who claimed to have "one fresh girl within reach." However, this girl escaped during transport:

> The money was paid, the girl handed over, but something said had alarmed her, and she solved the difficulty of disposing of her by making her escape. My friend who witnessed the whole transaction, and whose presence probably contributed something to the difficulty of the bargain, assures me that there was no doubt as to the sale and transfer of the girl. "Her escape," said the ex-keeper, "is one of the risks of the trade. If I had been really in for square business, I should never have agreed to take the girl from the house, partly in order to avoid escape and partly for safety. It is almost invariably the rule that the seller must deliver the girl at some railway station. She is brought to you, placed in your cab or your railway carriage, and it is then your business, and an easy one, to see that she does not escape you. But the risks of delivery at a safe place are always taken by the seller." (74)

Having lost the first girl by apparently failing to follow protocol, Jarrett found a second brothel keeper who promised a girl "as yet untouched." However, another escape stymied the stunt: "When the woman came for her prey the bird had flown." Throughout "The Maiden Tribute," Stead emphasized that virgins could easily be procured. Despite the journalist's assurances of this ease, he had a difficult time finding a girl who did not escape at the last minute.

Finally, Jarrett met Lily's mother, a "drunken neighbor" of the brothel, described as "poor, dissolute, and indifferent to everything but drink." The mother inquired whether they might take Lily (Eliza Armstrong's pseudonym) instead of the first girl. After negotiations, Jarrett allegedly purchased Armstrong for five pounds. As Stead reported, all discussion occurred "in the open"; both parents allegedly knew their daughter was being sold for prostitution. The father, also described as "a drunken man," "received the news with indifference, without even inquiring where [Lily] was going to" (79).

The "little cockney child" was taken to the midwife-abortionist, who examined her and testified to her virginity. Even the "hardened heart of the abortionist" grew soft at the sight of Armstrong and she expressed pity for the girl (79–80). The abortionist nonetheless offered Stead's assistant chloroform to dull the girl's pain during her seduction. The girl was given chloroform and put to bed at a nearby brothel, where Stead was supposed to visit her. Gazing upon her sleeping body was meant to be the culmination of a process of verification that would constitute the final word on the question of unwilling teenage victims in London. However, the exposé provided more than an unconscious certified virgin. Stead entered to the room to find an alert girl from whom there "rose a wild and piteous cry—not a loud shriek, but a helpless, startled scream like the bleat of a frightened lamb. And the child's voice was heard crying, in accents of terror, 'There's a man in the room! Take me home; oh, take me home!'" (81). The girl and her scream provided the evidence Stead sought as proof that virgins could be purchased and that they did not actively seek seduction.

Stead's representation of the scream attempted to take the reader into the sensory details of the girl's consciousness. Her scream became metonymic for the entirety of unwilling virgins in London. Yet Armstrong was an articulate virgin who could issue commands as well as scream ("Take me home; oh, take me home!"). Stead read her directive as further proof that girls were virtuously protective of their "maidenhoods." But she also broke the silence of girls in the text by foreshadowing the later court battle that exposed Stead's unscrupulous journalistic methods.

This ambitious endeavor rendered Stead an early pioneer of stunt and role journalism. In the process of refining these journalistic techniques, he subjected the girl to potentially painful medical exams in the interest of public knowledge and a broader reformist agenda that conceived of itself as morally righteous. The medical examination also met Stead's desire to legitimate Lily's virginity and insure the sensational credibility of the text through a form of prurient sensationalism in which the abortionist stood as proxy rapist. This simulated rape flew in the face of the original purity campaigns against the Contagious Diseases Acts, which sought to protect prostitutes from state-enforced medical examination.[31] Stead's willingness to send Lily to the midwife was an indication of how far the purity movement had strayed from its earlier, non-repressionist, libertarian emphasis. His "bleat of a frightened lamb" analogy is ironic, given that he turned Eliza Armstrong into a social movement's sacrificial lamb in a journalistic and reformist quest to convey a larger moral truth through a portrayal that was both sensationalist and pornographic.

"WE KNEW WE HAD FORGED A THUNDERBOLT"

If mass-mediated scandals typically result from the exposure of a powerful figure (often attached to an institution) who transgresses a moral or ethical norm, we can view this episode as a surplus scandal: a scandal that became so generalized and generative in its denunciations that its object at times became muddied amidst all the accusations. The scandal expanded from the issue of underage prostitution to the issue of the corruption and immorality that allowed such exploitation to occur, the participation of the elite and nobility in such acts, the tacit complicity of Parliament through its inaction, and, finally, to the immorality of journalists for bringing this matter to public attention by introducing scandalous pornographic literature into the news.

Within a day of its publication, Stead's account dominated public discourse throughout London. Its melodramatic rendering of a taboo topic guaranteed that the text would become a lightning rod for scandal and controversy. Public reaction to the exposé was mixed: alarm over alleged sexual practices on London streets commingled with concern over textual practices in the *Pall Mall Gazette*. The initial public debate was polarized around the issue of teenage prostitution, on the one hand, and pornographic representations, on the other.

The exposé produced an institutional scandal around age-of-consent laws by indicting prominent institutions that refused to acknowledge or address the problem and implicating them in a scandal over sexual trafficking. As Bristow points out, late nineteenth-century reformers linked male lasciviousness to declining national power and the demise of the empire.[32] "The Maiden Tribute" laid the source of a feared national weakness and decline at Parliament's feet. The parliamentary body, a masculine one, had failed to protect female bodies from male abuse, a breakdown of noblesse oblige that threw leaders' moral judgment into question. Women's groups, as well as working-class and religious groups, felt that Parliament's silence in the face of the double standard indicated a broader inability to govern. Elected and appointed officials who could not effectively protect women at home were similarly ill-equipped to preside over an empire in perceived need of strict moral and behavioral guidelines. If male leaders tacitly condoned extramarital sexuality leading to the "degeneration of the race," how could they insure that Britain was prepared for the "age of escalating international rivalry" that was on the horizon? Middle-class reformers in England viewed purity as a "precondition for national preparedness" during this period.[33] Stead's exposé implicated the government, the press, and the church in a conspiracy to allow the nation's moral infrastructure to collapse under the weight of uncivilized practices.

The scandal of ignoring the plight of innocent girls led Parliament to revisit the Criminal Law Amendment Act in the same week that Stead's exposé circulated. The act that passed on August 14, 1885, raised the age of consent to sixteen; allowed brothels to be summarily shut down; outlawed the use of drugs, intimidation, or deception in procuring girls; forbade building owners from permitting underage sex on their property; permitted the court to remove girls from legal guardians who allowed their seduction; and, in a clause introduced late in the proceedings by Henry Labouchere, criminalized public and private homosexual acts. Unlike the legislation that resulted, Stead's approach to consensual sexuality was largely libertarian. Stead had argued against attempts to intensify an already exploitive system in which corrupt police received kickbacks and sexual favors from brothel owners and prostitutes. Yet, in the aftermath of "The Maiden Tribute," the state allowed unprecedented police intervention into vice (and consensual male homosexuality) and mandated extensive crackdowns on brothels. While "The Maiden Tribute" used publicity to achieve specific political results, the actual consequences of the piece were difficult to contain and channel. They unfolded independently of the views of its author and reform-minded supporters of age-of-consent laws.

At the same time that Parliament was reeling from scandal, the lurid nature of Stead's topic and presentation drew vocal criticism from those who similarly felt that the moral order was under attack. In this case, however, it was the circulation of Stead's report that allegedly threatened the integrity of the nation. W. H. Smith and Sons, with its monopoly on railway newsstands, stopped selling the *Gazette* after the Monday installment of "The Maiden Tribute." Smith and House of Commons member George Cavendish Bentinck emerged as early and ardent critics of Stead's journalism. In the House, Cavendish Bentinck questioned the moral judgment involved in the production and mass distribution of "publications relating to objectionable subjects."[34] He denounced the text as obscene and suggested that criminal action be taken against the *Gazette*. His recommendation for legal retribution drew cheers from the audience.

"The Maiden Tribute" had indeed breached a number of barriers in the press, and had done so in a most dramatic way. As Schultz notes, Victorians were accustomed "to sensationalism in the press, but they did not expect that kind of journalism in the *Pall Mall Gazette*. Even papers that did show a lively interest in crime, scandal, and gossip avoided a subject like prostitution; and . . . at this time the *PMG* itself would not print the word 'syphilis.'"[35] Earlier that year, the *Sentinel*, a reform publication, had printed a list of Mrs. Jeffries's high-profile clientele (the inventory of elite names had been angrily read aloud at a Gospel Purity meeting in the wake of the Jeffries trial debacle). As it did with "The Maiden Tribute," W. H. Smith and Sons refused to sell the issue. It was this cover-up, in part, that Stead referred to when he accused the press of a "conspiracy of silence."

As positions on "The Maiden Tribute" coalesced, the *Gazette* began reporting on events inspired by the exposé. On Wednesday, the daily printed its third installment of "The Maiden Tribute," along with stories that detailed the censorship campaign against it and documented other developments attributed to the piece. Provoked by Tuesday's House of Commons session, Stead included a section entitled "A Flame Which Shall Never Be Extinguished." Feigning surprise at the overwhelming response, he wrote, "We knew we had forged a thunderbolt; but even we were hardly prepared for the overwhelming impression which it has produced on the public mind" (109). He went on to challenge the prosecution in the Jeffries case, arguing that a court case "is the thing of all others which those who shriek for silence most dread." While Mrs. Jeffries had pleaded guilty in court "to save her noble and Royal patrons from exposure," the *Gazette* would instead "subpoena almost half the Legislature in order to prove the accuracy of [its] revelations" (110–11). Stead threatened to turn an abstract, diffuse scandal that implicated institutions but not individuals into a concrete, court-based scandal that would name and unseat individual powerful men.

The irony here is that Stead had previously made a resolute statement that he himself would not inform against his sources: "I am an investigator; I am not an informer," he claimed in the exposé's first installment (63). The obvious contradiction here between Stead's protection of his sources and his denunciation of Mrs. Jeffries for protecting her clients (she too "was not an informer"), whom he even threatened to "out" himself, was resolved once again by Stead's invocation of the "conspiracy of silence" model. The madam acts in collusion with powerful figures who commit organized acts to violate innocent, unintelligent, yet ultimately unwilling and unwitting victims, and then collaborates with them in a massive cover-up. Protecting her clients is really just another part of the broader conspiracy. Stead, on the other hand, protects his sources, the bit players in this drama, as part of his pursuit of the greater good of bringing down the powerful henchmen and revealing the truth of vice and its dimensions to the public. In the contrast, one sees the emergence of the powerful journalist, a figure who protects and serves society by revealing truths about social ills, takes on powerful corrupt institutions, and applies ethical standards to protect interviewees, while assuming the powerful responsibility of arbitrating the truth gleaned from a collage of statements, perceptions, and personal experiences.

"The Maiden Tribute" set off a firestorm of debates in which the boundaries of the scandal became uncontainable. From a broad scandal over vice and an underlying dissatisfaction over Parliamentary inaction, the scandal then turned against Stead himself. The journalist found himself under attack for distributing essentially pornographic literature. What began as a battle for public opinion to turn the tide in favor of specific acts by Parliament ended up as a war involving multiple fronts, in which Stead himself served as field marshal, executing strategies intended to redefine the meaning of vice and prostitution, to permanently alter the scope of morally and legally acceptable discourse in mass media, and to reshape the relationships between journalists and institutions of power. His tactics in these battles included jousting rhetorically with competing media and threatening to retaliate against public officials if they dared censor him. Stead himself grew increasingly conscious of the implications of these events for journalism, as he would note later.

NEWSPAPER RESPONSE

The *Gazette*'s circulation, which typically ran between twenty and thirty thousand copies a day, was selling a hundred thousand copies a day during "The Maiden Tribute" campaign (circulation similarly surged during Stead's three months in Holloway Prison). Thus, though London newspaper readers may have agreed with W. H. Smith and Sons and Cavendish Bentinck, they waited until they had a chance to read the articles before moving on to censure the paper. Cut off from the newsstands, "The Maiden Tribute" found its way into readers' hands through alternate distribution paths. The *Gazette* hired child street vendors to hawk the paper. According to Cavendish Bentinck, these newsboys carried "indecent placards" advertising the report. One horrified observer of London that week, H. A. D. Philips, described his disgust upon seeing one placard that read, "£5 for a virgin warranted pure!" and, at another site, overhearing a boy yell to two teenage girls waiting for a bus, "Come on, Miss, 'ave a copy. This'll show you 'ow to earn five pounds!"[36]

Philips's vituperative critique of the Criminal Law Amendment Act appeared in the October 1885 issue of *Law Quarterly Journal*. Philips served in the colonial administration as Justice of the Peace for Bengal, Behar, and Orissa. An adherent of law and order, he felt that, in lieu of a patchwork Criminal Law Amendment Act, England needed stronger laws against adultery, bigamy, and incest. Philips went on to excoriate Stead's crusade for implanting "sensual ideas" in "young minds where they never existed before." He further suggested that Stead harbored illicit sexual fantasies himself and should be subject to the harshest of punishments: "'Our Secret Commissioner' must himself be a veritable Minotaur, and a sentence of penal servitude for life would not be too severe for him."[37]

Throughout the campaign, the demand for papers greatly exceeded the ability of the *Gazette* to produce them. However, the slow and fallible machinery of distribution did not impede the exposé's most eager readers from procuring copies. By Tuesday, throngs of people surrounded the *Gazette*'s Northumberland Street headquarters hoping to circumvent vendors by purchasing a copy at its point of production. Wednesday's crowd was larger and more vociferous than the previous day's, and there were a number of skirmishes outside the headquarters. As the number of avid readers and onlookers swelled, police attempted with little success to control the crowd. By the end of the day, several of the *Gazette*'s windows were broken. That same day the city solicitor banned the sale of the *Gazette* within London city limits. Once again, this attempt at censorship failed; the paper continued to sell out each day, leaving thousands of prospective readers emptyhanded. The following week, presses would commence reprinting a million and a half copies to make up for the inability to feed demand and the effects of the city solicitor's boycott.

The logic of competition among London papers insured that other dailies could neither agree with nor participate in the age-of-consent campaign. Doing so would have been an acknowledgment that Stead was right and an implicit admission of the "conspiracy of silence." While London's citizens were ablaze with talk of Stead's exposé, many of the city's papers were

Figure 2.2. A growing throng outside the *Gazette* office, July 1885. From Estelle Stead, *My Father: Personal and Spiritual Reminiscences* (London: William Heinemann, 1912), 123.

silent, choosing not to contribute to the spectacle and risk catapulting their rival to higher levels of fame. A few papers did chastise Stead for his pornographic imagination. The *Evening News* devoted the most space to its attack:

> The evening organ of Advanced Radicalism has this week succeeded in earning for itself a notoriety of infamy never approached, certainly in English journalism, and which, so far as our experience goes, has never been gained by the most sensational journalism either of Europe or America. We have long been accustomed, unfortunately, to see from time to time some filthy sheet appear in the gutter of London streets, and maintain just a brief existence as a vile insect reared on the putrid garbage of the dunghill. Public decency has been outraged by its presence, and the police have winked at the evil. But that a journal that addresses itself to the most educated classes of the country . . . should descend to the same level, is a new departure which must inspire every decent man with disgust.[38]

In suggesting that the *Gazette* had exceeded even continental and American newspapers in sensationalism, the *Evening News* clearly delighted in a fantasy of its own: its once popular and respected competitor reduced to a "filthy sheet," legislated against, and censored like the paper's nameless, ignoble predecessors.

If officialdom and the London press charged Stead with obscenity and indecency, the religious and provincial print media lavished his crusade with praise and adulation. *The Methodist Times* pleased Stead with its proclamation that "the editor of the *Pall Mall Gazette* has done what we believe Jesus Christ would have done in his place."[39] Stead reveled in the comparison to Christ, a persona that he had toyed with for years and would adopt more explicitly in later journalistic pursuits. The provincial press was also more likely than the London papers to speak openly about the *Gazette*'s crusade, granting it credit for sparking a national dialogue about a critical issue and making newspaper history. While some papers disagreed with Stead's methods, most believed that he was motivated by genuine concern for young girls rather than desire for notoriety or profit. The *Reading Observer* claimed Stead's crusade had "fully earned the right of claiming for itself that it has created the greatest sensation of modern journalism."[40] Unlike the urban press, which did not want to contribute to Stead's mounting fame, the rural papers entertained the notion that the *Gazette* had succeeded in pulling off a historic journalistic stunt. These publications did not compete directly with the *Gazette* and reveled in the characterization of London as a modern Babylon, which made comparatively bucolic pastoral life seem preferable in comparison. The religious press, for its part, did not recoil from Stead's lurid descriptions of sexual immorality but embraced them on the assumption that a broad-based vigilance crusade would gather momentum in the wake of Stead's revelations.

JOURNALISM DISROBED: THE ELIZA ARMSTRONG TRIAL

In July and August 1885, Stead reveled in this newfound notoriety and cultural prominence. In September, abduction charges stemming from his virgin-purchasing stunt derailed what he assumed would be a steady ascension to power. Hints dropped in his exposé about the time and location of Lily's purchase fueled local suspicions that this girl was Elizabeth Armstrong's daughter, Eliza Armstrong. Like the pseudonymous Lily, Eliza left the neighborhood with a stranger on Derby Day. Lily's mother was reported to be a heavy drinker, just like Mrs. Armstrong. Neighborhood speculation and gossip about the now famous virgin led Mrs. Armstrong to file a missing persons report on her daughter.

The crime section of *Lloyd's Newspaper* was the first to seize on the story and its implications for Stead's report. The treasury solicitor prosecuted six people involved in "purchasing" Eliza on charges related to abduction, including taking the girl from her parents without consent, conspiring to commit this act, forcing the girl to take a "certain noxious thing," and subjecting her to an "indecent assault." The committal proceedings prosecuted Stead, as well as Rebecca Jarrett, Bramwell Booth, and Elizabeth Combe of the Salvation Army, Samson Jacques of the *Pall Mall Gazette*, and Madame Mourez, the abortionist who had testified to Eliza's virginity. Booth and Combe were found innocent of all charges during the initial proceedings, while the remaining four were placed on trial.

The details of the dramatic Bow Street proceedings and the criminal trial have been treated in depth elsewhere.[41] However, several aspects of the case pertained to Stead's reporting, illuminating certain journalistic methods that were invisible in the exposé itself. At particular moments, the trial constituted a battle between journalism and the law over which of them had the cultural and institutional power to speak and the legitimacy to construct and narrate reality. Issues of sourcing, quotation, transcription, and memory came up repeatedly. The proceedings demonstrated that nascent techniques of interviewing were not yet embedded in a system of journalistic objectivity and that late nineteenth-century reporters were only beginning to distill a process through which they could rely on the words of others and protect their own credibility in the process.

The trial's focal point was the alleged abduction of Eliza Armstrong, but questions about the value and veracity of the new journalism were woven into statements and witness testimony. The prosecution characterized Stead's reporting as untrustworthy and at times outright fictitious. During the Bow Street Hearings, the prosecution's counsel, Henry Bodkin Poland, introduced his clients' case by calling Stead's stunt "a vile fabrication from beginning to end," a "pure invention." He went on to state that "this performance with regard to this child was a got-up thing from beginning to end, either for the purpose of vamping up a filthy, sensational article, or perhaps from good motives, I care not which, but that it was a got-up thing, I think there can be no doubt whatsoever. . . . You will see for yourself, sir, these witnesses in the box, and whether, for their class in life, they have not conducted themselves as well as respectable persons of that kind can be expected to."[42] Acting in his own defense, Stead countered that his actions on behalf of girls outweighed harms that might have come to an individual girl (indeed, he vehemently denied that Eliza suffered when he took her away from a place "steeped in vice" and put her in the care of the Salvationists).[43] He frequently appealed to the greater good with reminders of the social and political reforms that his work enabled. Stead claimed he had not participated in a conspiracy but "exposed a conspiracy of vice and crime" that cut across Britain's class system.[44]

Mrs. Armstrong, Eliza Armstrong, and their neighbor, Nancy Broughton, the alleged brothel owner, provided verbal testimony during the initial committal proceedings. Mrs. Armstrong and Broughton both stated that they believed Eliza had been offered a "respectable position" as a maid in the country. They claimed Jarrett had approached them with a story of recent marriage, improved economic standing, and physical disability necessitating the help of a "kneeling" girl. It was this story that prompted them to send Eliza away. They denied the open negotiations described in the exposé and asserted that, had they known Jarrett's real (albeit similarly fictitious) motives, they would never have assented to the deal. These women's working-class speech and comportment at times sent the court audience into convulsive laughter, making the criminal proceedings as big a spectacle as the exposé that spawned them had been.

Eliza's behavior on the witness stand was widely noted and praised. As an actual witness to the stunt, her testimony provided a firsthand account of events that had only been knowable up to that point through Stead's text.

Her statement suggests that Stead had indeed exaggerated and even fabricated events surrounding Eliza's purchase. Indeed, Stead got much of his information secondhand, through Jarrett, and both likely engaged in their own embellishments. Eliza told the court that Mourez was cold and silent while examining her, a description at odds with Stead's account of the "hardened heart of the abortionist" growing soft at the thought of the girl's seemingly inevitable seduction. If Eliza Armstrong's telling was correct, then the depiction of withering objectivity was a rhetorical device fashioned by Stead to inflect his piece with appropriate sentimentality. The scream, for its part, apparently occurred but not according to the circumstances described in the text. In "The Maiden Tribute" Eliza screamed when directly confronted with her apparent seducer. According to the girl's courtroom testimony, she heard a man behind a screen while lying in bed with Jarrett by her side. She exclaimed that there was a man in the room, but her addressee was obviously Jarrett: "I said, 'There is a man in the room.' And she put the curtain up, and said, 'Why, there is no man in the room.' I said, 'No, because he was gone out of the room.' She then left the room. She was not away long. When she came back, she said, 'Get up and dress yourself, because there are too many men in the house.'"[45] In her testimony, Eliza Armstrong did not address the reported second half of her statement: "Take me home; oh, take me home!" Whether or not this was a figment of Stead's imagination, he certainly did not support its content by the time the trial occurred; in fact, he hoped to stress that Eliza did not want to be taken home, that her home was not fit for a girl of her age.

In the courtroom Stead demonstrated an ability to rouse the audience as he actively antagonized the magistrate as if to underscore their equal standing. While many of the other witnesses lacked facility with language, and some, like Eliza's father, were illiterate, Stead began his defense by producing a written statement he had composed "in order to avoid making any rash or needless statement."[46] This several-page testament was the first offered in lieu of impromptu speech and likely made the witnesses for the prosecution palpably conscious of their class position. Stead had already used the power of writing against them in his exposé, and now he produced another such document to lay out his version of events in a rhetorically eloquent way that he hoped would resonate with educated and reform-minded Londoners.

However, the magistrate would not allow him to read his prepared speech from beginning to end on the grounds it might contain "outlying circumstances that would not . . . be cognate to the case." Stead responded by pleading that "the prosecution have urged everything and called witnesses. I have cross-examined very little, and I presume you will not be hard on me if, in putting my statement before the court, I stray somewhat from the strictly technical charge." The magistrate averred, but then interrupted his first sentence, calling it impertinent to the case. Stead pleaded with the magistrate again: "For five days the most odious and repulsive charges have been brought against me and published in every newspaper in this land. My mouth has all this time been closed, and I have had no opportunity of explaining how and why it was that I, a journalist, came to be here before you charged with crime. I appeal to your worship, even if it be by the exercise of your magisterial indulgence, to allow me to explain why it is that I am here."[47] The ensuing repartee, with Stead reading, the magistrate censuring, and Stead proceeding again, provided lively drama for the court audience: "Those who have never stirred hand nor foot during the long years through which English girls have been left to [be] the helpless prey of lust and crime . . ." The magistrate interrupted: "Will you have the kindness to remain silent for a moment, Mr. Stead?" Stead: "Certainly." Magistrate: "I cannot allow that." Stead: "Page two ruled out. That is down to the words 'urging the imperative necessity for a parliamentary inquiry.'" Magistrate: "Will you allow me to read it?" Stead: "I think, your worship, that I can read it to you." On it went in this fashion until the magistrate had ruled out Stead's entire written speech. Stead did, however, succeed in reading fragments to the magistrate, the prosecution, and the audience.[48]

At times Stead behaved whimsically in the courtroom, clearly delighting in the criminal case and the publicity it generated. His major strategy was to play the silenced victim role to bolster the case that a conspiracy of silence around criminal vice permeated official institutions, which was why he was being censored in the abduction trial. Stead sought to frame court protocol as a form of broader censorship miring him in irrelevant interpersonal minutiae and preventing him from speaking a more global truth. The irony of Stead's silent role is that he was only truly silent when listening to witnesses. During his allotted time for speaking, he frustrated and confounded the magistrate, and utilized a variety of media to place his own frame around courtroom events. He attempted to use written language in his opening statement and then used it more broadly in the *Gazette*, publishing accounts, transcripts, and interpretations of the trial each day. His silence was performative at best, in radical contrast to the witnesses for the prosecution, who lacked the ability to volley verbally with the magistrate and did not have access to an organ of mass distribution.

Of all the testimony, Rebecca Jarrett's damaged Stead the most. First she revealed that Mrs. Broughton was not in fact a brothel owner but an old friend she met while doing domestic work. When asked whether Stead faithfully reproduced everything she told him about the Eliza Armstrong case, she replied, "I think he has made some slight mistakes. One mistake is where he says the child was bought off a brothel-keeper. Mr. Stead did not write down what I told him."[49] The prosecutor pointed out that this was a problem because the section of Stead's exposé concerning Eliza was the "only vouched statement in the whole article of the 6th." Later in the trial Stead insisted he wrote down everything Jarrett told him, but added that he "did not put it down at the time." He then revealed he had written the piece "about June 30, or somewhere about that time—some four weeks after the conversation [with Jarrett]." Asked if notes were taken, he said, "Certainly not at the time, and I do not remember doing so afterwards." On the discrepancies between his and Jarrett's accounts, he impugned his assistant's memory: "I believe she intends to tell the truth, but her memory seems very defective."[50] The prosecution pointed out that Jarrett's statements did not add credibility to the report of a man who, by his own account, "had been visiting brothels and drinking champagne and smoking, which [he] was not used to, and was very excited."[51]

Another problem that was pointed out in the trial was that Rebecca Jarrett had failed to get (and Stead had failed to ask for) written consent from the mother or the father, and had also failed to get a receipt for the girl. Whereas Stead had provided ample documentary evidence for the girls he ultimately failed to purchase, he was unable to provide such evidence in the case of Eliza Armstrong. When the verdict was read on November 7, 1885, Stead, Jarrett, Mourez, and Jacques were all found guilty of conspiracy to commit abduction.

As Judith Walkowitz and Alison Plowden have both pointed out, class and gender played themselves out in a remarkable way in this courtroom spectacle. Stead was sentenced to three months in prison "without hard labor," Jacques was given one month's imprisonment for his role in transporting Eliza, Jarrett was sentenced to six months' imprisonment without labor, while the elderly Madame Mourez was condemned to a full six months in prison and "kept to hard labor." The punishment proved hardest on the abortionist, who died while serving her jail term. Not only were the working-class women subjected to disproportionately harsher treatment than the middle-class male *Gazette* journalists, but the barrister's closing remarks portrayed the two women in the most scathing and ugly terms, despite the fact that Stead had masterminded the stunt, and the two women were performing a service on his behalf.

Once in prison, the two women experienced harsher conditions than

Stead. Mourez was condemned to hard labor, and Jarrett, suddenly disowned by the movement that had adopted and reformed her, served her sentence in austere and lonely conditions. Stead, by contrast, was treated as a "first-class misdemeanant" and was by all accounts a "joyful convict" at Holloway Prison."[52] He wore his own clothes as a convict and had his meals brought in by his wife and children. Of his time in prison, he publicly recounted, "Never had I had a pleasanter holiday, a more charming season of repose. . . . I had papers, books, letters, flowers, everything that the heart could wish. Twice a week my wife brought the sunlight of her presence into the pretty room, all hung round with Christmas greetings from absent friends, and twice a week she brought with her one of the children."[53]

On some level Stead did relish his imprisonment. It made him a martyr to members of the social purity movement and rendered him more famous than before. He acknowledged his journalistic mistakes but held fast to the idea that his largest mistake was trusting Jarrett to conduct the investigation. But some of his behavior during the trial and purported happiness during imprisonment was for show. In his diary he described becoming sullen and deeply depressed during the trial. Several months after this imprisonment, he acknowledged that the experience had been psychically and professionally damaging:

> I am now about seven months out of gaol. The curious effect it has had on me has been that I have lost to some slight extent the nerve and dash which used to belong to me. This showed itself oddly enough in a certain timidity in getting into a train in motion in the crowd that rushes for the first carriage of the morning train. Before gaol I never cared. More important than this is the slight loss of nerve that makes me less unhesitatingly impudent, if I may use my enemies' phrase, in tackling notabilities, etc. It supplies a palpable excuse for those who wish to evade me. Why should they see me or do what I ask them to do when, to a certain extent, I am my paper are under the cloud of imprisonment and social odium. . . . I shrink from demanding, as an obvious right, interviews, etc., from persons whom I know will have heard the censure and may not know the praise. . . . To live this down I must do something splendaciously, something that will give the silly world some other label to paste against my name than that of criminal convict.[54]

After the trial, Stead's critics feminized him, calling him "emotionally unstable," alleging he suffered from "emotional exasperation."[55] His supporters, however, particularly those in the social purity movement, continued to support him. According to Plowden, they immediately forgave Stead for his shortcomings and promoted the idea that "it was Rebecca Jarrett who'd told all the lies—Stead had just been the victim of his own pure soul."[56]

EMPOWERING THE PRESS

After the simultaneous trial and debacle that was "The Maiden Tribute," the *Gazette*'s publisher pressured Stead to resign from his editorship. Stead's previous campaigns were accordant with the *Gazette*'s own image of itself as a politically engaged intellectual newspaper with a small but influential readership. But 1886 witnessed an unprecedented drop in the paper's original circulation rates, indicating that lurid stories of sex slavery coupled with courtroom revelations of suspect journalistic methods displeased the daily's dependable core audience. The *Gazette* had become synonymous with Stead at a time when readers were increasingly uncomfortable with extreme editorial control.

Stead responded to this institutional crisis by resigning his editorship, leaving daily newspaper work, and founding the *Contemporary Review*, a monthly opinion magazine. Two of the *Review*'s early articles, "Government by Journalism" and "The Future of Journalism," outlined Stead's emerging understandings of reporting, public opinion, sensationalism, and the role of journalism in politics. Both argued that journalism should play a more prominent and formalized role in governance. The call for broader power was seemingly ill-timed: even as reform circles regarded Stead as a social purity martyr, public memory of his imprisonment had damaged his wider reputation. An entreaty to recognize and institutionalize journalism's power published at a time when Stead's own career had forcibly shifted due to his role in "The Maiden Tribute" scandal seemed ironic at best. It is perhaps best to read these articles as recuperative texts in spite of their exaggeratedly triumphant rhetoric. Yet they also offer a glimpse into understandings of the press at a certain moment in its formation and have important connections to later prescriptive theories of the press, such as those of Walter Lippmann, that adopt some of Stead's basic assumptions while promoting a very different political role for journalists (see chapter 6).

Stead had always been attracted to the idea of the journalist as preacher, but while serving his sentence in Holloway Prison, he began to think about the idea of the journalist as ruler. In "Government by Journalism," he argued that the telegraph and printing press had created new democratic-minded citizens "impatient of intermediaries between themselves and the exercise of power."[57] The only legitimate mediator in this context was journalism: "The editorial pen is a sceptre of power. . . . In a democratic age, in the midst of a population which is able to read, no position is comparable for permanent influence and far-reaching power to that of an editor who understands his vocation."[58] An editor-reporter could misrecognize his power, understanding himself only as "an obliging human phonograph" alerting the citizens to public officials' pet legislation, or he could seize this power for himself, bypassing sovereign and elected representatives in the process.[59]

This journalist knew he could preach, "but to rule!—Yet an editor is the uncrowned king of an educated democracy. The range of his power is limited only by the extent of his knowledge, the quality rather than quantity of his circulation, and the faculty and force which he can bring to the work of government."[60] While members of the press were not formally elected, citizens also voted with money, and this consumerist vote equaled readers' acceptance of press sovereignty. However, this sovereignty also elevated citizens because, like sovereigns before it, the press was an extension of the public body: "The Press is at once the eye and the ear and the tongue of the people. It is the visible speech if not the voice of the democracy. It is the phonograph of the world. On its columns are printed the spoken words of yesterday, and it is constantly becoming more and more obvious that the importance of a spoken word depends chiefly on its getting itself printed."[61] Stead recognized the importance of the mass media as an extension of the senses. Print amplified speech, extended the public's range of vision, and gave it a voice.

In his new capacity as extension of the public, the editor-reporter does not abandon the apostolic role altogether. Indeed, his audience is also a "vast congregation" that lingers on his every word. Members of Parliament, by contrast, lacked such a constituency, and would become increasingly irrelevant to the political process. So how would the politician secure power in this envisioned technology-enabled moment? By making himself beholden to the journalist: "Parliament will continue to meet in the midst of this newspaper age, but it will be subordinate. The wielders of real power will be those who are nearest the people."[62] Stead argued that in this new context, "the editorial *we*" would be "the only authoritative utterance."[63] Stead then offered statesmen-in-decline ideas on how to effectively utilize a press-in-ascension: "Instead of denouncing a 'temporizing press,' statesmen would find it more convenient to take its conductors into their confidence, so far at least as the imparting of confidential information necessary to enable them to criticize intelligently a policy which, without such guidance, they might, on the facts open to them, believe they were bound to oppose."[64] Lines of communication between the parliamentarian and the reporter would be pried open, allowing journalists to attain information and speak to their constituencies meaningfully about proposals. This passage, which anticipated sourcing, erroneously suggested that reporters were entering an era in which they would hold sway over elected officials. That the latter could grant access and take it away, rending the journalist-source relationship more balanced—and in some cases rendering the journalist subservient—did not figure into this envisioned scenario.

While the journalist is more concerned with the "vagabond, the landless man, and the deserted child" than the M.P., "he has his Achilles' heel in the advertisements, and he must not carry his allegiance to outcast humanity too far."[65] Stead recognized that emerging communications technologies had produced the mass audience as a new political constituency. But he also recognized that this audience was a commodity, and that editor-reporters walked a fine line between representing the unrepresented and bringing in necessary advertising revenue. It was necessary to speak to a middle-class aggregate about the real or envisioned needs of the working class, but advertising subsidy mandated that the latter could never be the sole audience for such journalistic entreaties.[66]

After "The Maiden Tribute," the idea of investigation was at the forefront of Stead's thinking. How could journalists conduct investigations without breaking the law themselves? Calling the press "the great inspector, with myriad eyes, who never sleeps, and whose daily reports are submitted . . . to the whole people," he called on legislators to sanction press inquiries into all varieties of social institutions, thereby preempting the need to engage in risky stunt reporting:

> The sphere of inspection needs to be enlarged so as to include such official establishments as lunatic asylums, prisons, workhouses, and the like. An editor of a daily paper, or his representative, should be *ex officio* vested with all the right of inspection enjoyed by a visiting justice or a Home Office inspector. . . . It ought not be necessary for a journalist to have to impersonate a tramp to expose a casual ward, to get himself locked up as disorderly to see how the charges are treated at a police station, or to commit a misdemeanor to be able to say whether the "skilly" of prisoners is edible, or whether the reception cells are sufficiently warmed.[67]

This vision of inspection had journalists paying unannounced visits to institutional sites to insure that they were functioning within ethical and legal bounds. It seems to suggest that newspapers would publish these dry reports whether or not an event occurred, or at least always be there to report when something went wrong, thus safeguarding all establishments. Such a role would take journalists into bureaucratic domains, changing the practice of reporting and creating new alliances with the state. In becoming an arm of the state, the press would be protected from such perils as Stead had faced in the previous year, and the role of the journalist would be elevated so that no journalist would again have to suffer such indignities as Stead's prison term.

"The Future of Journalism" returned to issues of authority, offering an elaborate stratagem for achieving political power and laying out an early and sophisticated plan for eliciting and transforming public opinion. An editor, it proposed, could "become [by] far the most permanently influential Englishman in the Empire." However, to attain this "dizzy pre-eminence," it was necessary to "be a master of the facts—especially the dominant fact of all, the state of public opinion."[68] Most editors guessed at public opinion, but Stead laid out an elaborate proposal for actually gleaning it. For Stead, public opinion was not something to follow blindly, but to understand and either follow or transform.

If the journalist had to be connected to the mass of people, via public opinion, he also had to be intimately connected to the elite strata of powerful people "from the Queen downwards." Thus a primary reform was to establish "relations of confidence" with people whose opinions mattered. Within twenty-four hours, a journalist should be able to "ascertain authentically . . . the views of all the Cabinet Ministers and ex-Cabinet Ministers in town—not, of course, for publication, but for his own guidance and the avoidance of mistakes." Stead stressed that "this is not interviewing," but a private phase of the reporter's investigation. If a journalist "betrays confidence, the whole edifice collapses."[69]

In this fashion, an editor moves through the entire social system, intimately connected to everyone within it. Stead did recognize that it would be impossible for one man to enact this role, so he proposed a "system of major-generals and . . . journalistic travellers" connected to the newspaper and dispersed throughout the country. These editorial "alter egos" would keep the central figure abreast of everything occurring in each district. Such a model, Stead argued, was distinct from that of the reporter/correspondent dyad, because these "voluntary unpaid associates," content to help the newspaper govern, would report directly to the editor without publishing reports themselves. These journalistic satellites would help in "ascertaining facts, in focussing opinion, and generally in assisting the editor to ascertain the direct views of his countrymen."[70] Stead envisioned a system in which a politician advanced a program or made a statement, and then that statement would be sent to all the associates in the country, who were to ascertain its truth for that area and report back to the editor—essentially an early model of the public opinion poll, without statistics, surveys, or the technological means of communicating with each and every citizen. Remarkably, Stead also predicted the tiered model of public opinion, in which there are, in each sector, opinion leaders and opinion followers. Stead's ideas about public opinion leaders foreshadowed the work of foundational thinkers in the field of communications research in the early and mid-twentieth century, from Walter Lippmann to Paul Lazarsfeld. Stead went on to suggest that eventually his major-generals would "be entrusted the further and more delicate duty of collecting the opinions of those who form the public opinion of their locality."[71] The system would be held in place by "peripatetic apostles of the new journalism," journalist travelers, who would preach the importance of the associates' work across the country. Stead saw it as his duty not only to report but to build institutions and movements, and he envisioned this plan resulting in "the greatest spiritual and educational and governing agency which England has yet seen."[72]

Stead wrote at a moment when the various communications fields were still in formation. Communication in the 1880s was characterized by an undifferentiated social field in which journalists informally and usually unwittingly served as all-purpose experts, social scientific investigators, pollsters, reporters, consultants to public officials, and public relations specialists. This was an early attempt to devise a plan for assessing public opinion so that it could be altered. Stead's characterization of the various communicative roles the press might play is a very early expression of the mitotic division in knowledge production that was under way at the time but would not come to fruition until the twentieth century. Thirty years later, the roles and duties Stead hoped the singular figure of the journalist would inhabit and undertake were occupied by distinct communications and knowledge professionals: the public relations specialist, the pollster, the expert, and the social scientist. The reporter's job would not be to operate in the vanguard of each of these arenas, or as their overseers, but to report the findings and beliefs of these professionals.

Both "Government by Journalism" and "The Future of Journalism" reflected Stead's growing awareness of the news media's power in an era of mass distribution and rapid diffusion. Newspaper crusades against a traffic in women were central to these developing understandings. Such campaigns and their political effects in fact became a social laboratory in which new formulations of the public, public opinion, governance, and the power of the press were developed. Stead began to theorize his power and position differently in the aftermath of "The Maiden Tribute," an exposé that he felt made him the most powerful man in England. Of course, his vision of the new journalist's role in social movement formation and governance was grandiose; he imagined a far greater role for journalists in the political sphere than they would ever actually possess.

While Stead's proposals concerning journalism would never be enacted, his experience in spearheading a national vigilance movement, forcing Parliament to enact new laws, and achieving notoriety through a prison sentence contributed to his belief that the editor-reporter held an unprecedented and extensive form of power that no public citizen (not elected, and not sovereign) had previously possessed. This power was perhaps illusory and fleeting, but in the immediate context of the sex trafficking scandal, it was a genuine reflection of the journalist's potential. However, this power was not available to all journalists because it depended on the ability to launch a sensationalist story at the precise moment that democratic governments would feel threatened enough to respond. The audience, moreover, had to be responsive to the journalist's claims, or the story would dissipate without making a mark on governance.

CONCLUSION

The publication of "The Maiden Tribute" marked a turning point in the history of the international social purity movement. The episode demonstrated the power of journalism to direct and intensify public awareness and action around specific issues. In this period, politicians found themselves on the margins of a powerful new mechanism and strategy for shaping public opinion and influencing legislation in democratic regimes. Aided by the telegraph, the press had reached an unprecedented level of saturation. There still was no national media, but a well-timed sensationalist scandal like that surrounding "The Maiden Tribute" could command national and even international attention.

Within days of each signal event in "The Maiden Tribute" episode, news of the textual/sexual scandals surrounding the exposé reached other continents through the period's rapidly expanding communication system. American newspaper readers voraciously consumed reprints of Stead's work as well as journalistic accounts of the editor's subsequent trial and imprisonment, and American newspapers debated the implications of Stead's methods. The earliest campaigns in the United States against sex trafficking and white slavery were modeled after this episode in England and encouraged by key British social purity reformers like William Coote and Josephine Butler.

Though Stead offered readers "facts" based on "personal knowledge," he routinely emphasized that the issue transcended facts, demanding a form of engagement that stood above issues of verification. If, in Stead's rendition, the typically detached abortionist could not maintain emotional distance between herself and Lily, neither could the journalist report dispassionately about the subject. For Stead, the trade in unwilling virgins was a subject "upon which even the coolest and most scientific observer may well find it difficult to speak dispassionately in a spirit of calm and philosophic investigation." In this statement we already find a link between science and detached knowledge that develops in journalism more fully in the next century. Yet between 1885 and 1910, sex trafficking repeatedly became the litmus test that measured the limits of objectivity on both sides of the Atlantic. It did so not because of any objective features related to sex trafficking or sexuality but because the scandals inflamed public debates that transgressed the conventional boundaries of mass-mediated discourse and journalistic professional behavior. As we see in the case of Stead, the debate and trial over virgin abduction became a debate and trial over pornography and journalistic ethics and objectivity. This debate transformed public perceptions of journalism, Stead's own conceptions about journalism and the public, and, ultimately, the professional expectations and demeanor of the entire field. The following chapters trace the development of sex trafficking journalism through its different stages to show the centrality of the topic to the development of journalistic techniques, attitudes, and procedures in American journalism as well.

CHAPTER THREE

The Journalism of Reform and the Reform of Journalism

> But it is no question of aristocracy or democracy. Here in America, for instance, we have a democracy. We also have quite as fine an assortment of vices as the *Pall Mall* reveals. We don't go bragging about them. We don't publish "disclosures" and undertake to "thrill the heart of the people." But we try to make the best of a bad job and say that, after all, we are no worse than our neighbors.
>
> —*New York Herald*, 13 July 1885

> The journalistic spirit is almost the finest in the world—keen, kind, progressive, and humanitarian. Take away the hallucination of nicotine and the craze of alcoholic dreams, and you would have remaining an incomparable set of brother-hearted men, whose glimpses of God would be not at all infrequent. Anchor alongside these chivalric-natured experts, women as gifted as themselves, and free from drug delusions; then, in one quarter century, you will have driven pugilists and saloon keepers, ward politicians and Jezebels from the sacred temple of journalism, and the people's daily open letter from the great world shall be pure as a letter from home.
>
> —Frances E. Willard, *Glimpses of Fifty Years* (1889)

During the nineteenth century, the expression of concern over prostitution in the United States shifted from intermittent and isolated brothel riots and other violent confrontations to more organized and persistent moral crusades.[1] "Social purity" campaigns took root in cities after the Civil War, arising out of a broad-based coalition of religious groups and women's moral reform organizations that opposed mounting efforts by medical practitioners, policemen, and public officials to regulate commercial sex. Modeled after programs in continental Europe, "regulationist" organizations like the New York Society for the Prevention of Contagious Diseases had advanced legislation to license prostitutes and subject them to medical inspections. The initial experiment in continental-style regulation was launched in St. Louis in the early 1870s, but social purity activists' nationally organized protests successfully ended the program. Regulationists advanced similar legislation in San Francisco, New York, Chicago, and Philadelphia throughout the 1870s and 1880s, but each attempt was soundly defeated by organized social purity protests.[2] By the end of the 1880s, abolitionist forces could claim multiple key victories, having effectively defanged formal attempts across the nation to license, tax, and examine prostitutes.[3]

Written to produce political effects in England, "The Maiden Tribute" illuminated new objects of inquiry, exposure, and reform in the United States as well. Stead and his supporters in England offered American anti-vice activists a new perspective on prostitution. Prostitution was not a sinful economic arrangement between "fallen women," lustful men, and brothel-owning madams. It was instead a physically coercive relationship involving innocent women and girls, abusive men, and profiteering slaveholders that had more in common with chattel slavery than with other commercial endeavors. The analogy forged in "The Maiden Tribute" between slavery and prostitution resonated with American evangelicals, many of whom had been participants in or were sympathetic to the antebellum abolitionist movement and readily appropriated the symbols and rhetoric of the earlier movement to underscore the urgency of the new moral crusade fought on behalf of female "white slaves" ignored by the Thirteenth Amendment.

British activists played a central role in forging the connection between prostitution and chattel slavery in the US context. After the social purity successes in England, wrought in no small part by Stead, Josephine Butler toured the Northeast and the Midwest to promote a new international abolition movement against prostitution as slavery. She spoke to reform-minded audiences about an international traffic in women similar in scope and dimension to the slavery of blacks that was spreading invisibly and unchallenged throughout the country. Her "Appeal to the Women of America" identified the United States as the primary destination for this traffic. Appealing to the increasingly linked Gilded Age sentiments of nationalism and nativism, she suggested that while "people in Europe speak with indignation of the traffic in negroes," they have no concern for the exportation of white slaves from their own countries. In the United States these "youthful victims" could be found "descending the Mississippi . . . to New Orleans and Texas," while others were "taken on to California." Poverty and lax moral codes directly implicated southern and eastern European immigrants in this new manifestation of the slave trade: "You in America are happily free from the State regulation of vice; but undoubtedly there is an extensive traffic in white slaves in your midst, and a constant importation of poor foreigners to your shores who are destined to moral and spiritual destruction."[4]

As the emotionally charged conceptualization of prostitution as a modern slave trade took center stage in the coalition's worldview, the social purity movement entered a new phase. The social purity activists' goal had always been to eradicate prostitution and usher in a generalized moral awakening, but the quest gained urgency as metaphors from the earlier period of chattel slavery began to populate social purity speeches, sermons, reform tracts, and newsletters. The late nineteenth century's most popular women's temperance organization, the Woman's Christian Temperance Union (WCTU), joined the anti-trafficking campaign in 1885 and thereafter couched its movement goals in emancipatory, abolitionist rhetoric. The group's president, Francis E. Willard, told WCTU members at an annual convention, "There are three sets of slaves that we are working to emancipate. They are white slaves, that is, degraded women; wage slaves, that is, the working classes; and whisky slaves, that is, the product furnished by brewers and distillers."[5] Prostitution became the paradigmatic case of slavery that enabled Willard to link the WCTU's diverse campaigns into a more unified agenda. The *Philanthropist*, an umbrella social purity periodical, likewise used the idea of prostitution as slavery to speak of a future in which men and women were emancipated "from a degrading bondage to abnormal passion and sensualism."[6] Moral reformers made the broader case that physically chained women and girls were not the only victims of this form of slavery; its psychic bonds enslaved and degraded men and women throughout the nation.

This second phase of the social purity movement that began in 1885 held the indelible imprint of journalism and transatlantic media flows. In the wake of Stead's exposé, a handful of sympathetic general newspapers began asserting the existence of regional prostitution-trafficking routes along the East Coast and in the upper Midwest. The Republican *Chicago Daily Inter-Ocean* and the *Detroit Free Press*, two urban dailies that had forged strong connections with the woman's evangelical temperance movement, printed disturbing stories of abduction and physical violence in the upper Midwest, while female evangelicals conducted investigations into the phenomenon and agitated for the creation of municipal and state laws to punish white slavers. These papers' stories of regional trafficking were reprinted and com-

Figure 3.1. Frances E. Willard. From Anna Adams Gordon, *The Life of Frances E. Willard* (Evanston, IL: Women's Christian Temperance Union, 1912), 153.

mented upon nationally, but the response failed to reach the fevered pitch that reactions to Stead's work had in England. Nonetheless, a dialectic of sensation and scandal similar to the one that characterized the London episode would occur on a smaller scale as these regional controversies over accusations of sex slavery inspired moral reformers and worried state officials who feared symbolic or material connections between their political administrations and prostitution.

This chapter traces the beginnings of reform journalism around white slavery in the United States. It tells the story of how British mass culture reshaped the landscape of American moral reform movements in the late nineteenth century. These movements would take on a complex national form as they developed in dialogue with American journalism, which they increasingly came to influence during this period. The central argument is that Stead's exposé transformed American journalism through a circuitous route: it inspired the growing numbers of female evangelical reformers—especially in the industrializing areas of England, New York, and the Midwest—to direct a number of their reform activities at the press itself. In the late 1880s and early 1890s, women temperance and social purity activists helped shape press content and worked tirelessly to transform the "masculine" culture of secular journalism. This chapter considers the relationships fostered among the Gilded Age press and women's moral reform movements and the role these interactions played in forging particular narrative styles, objects of inquiry, and the character and constitution of media audiences and practices to come. In particular, it focuses on the role that gender politics played in aligning the press with reform and paving the way for the rise of national, socially conscious, investigatively focused magazines in the following two decades.

As they were in the 1830s, women, the majority of them middle-class Protestants, were on the front line of this convulsive phase of the anti-vice movement.[7] Neo-abolitionist women challenged a system that condoned men's infidelities yet placed women under heavy sexual surveillance. They campaigned to raise the age of consent and establish criminal penalties against procurement and pandering in the United States in the 1880s and 1890s. Groups like the WCTU envisioned a purer polity modeled on the ideal middle-class Protestant family. Emerging out of the demise of the 1873–1875 Women's Crusade that pitted evangelical Ohio women against saloons and other sites of masculine culture, many of the WCTU's most prominent members believed that women were purer and keener conduits of God's will. Under the leadership of Frances E. Willard, the WCTU's goals expanded to encompass every aspect of "home protection," from censorship of "impure" literature to suffrage and the abolition of white slavery.[8] Willard promoted a "do everything" approach to politics with an eye toward eventually "dissecting out the alcohol nerve from the body politic."[9]

The notion that women's position in the home endowed them with a natural moral authority underlay much of the group's rhetoric and reform work. Willard argued that through "equal suffrage women will help to protect both the external and internal interests of the home."[10] Political institutions should welcome women, not because women have the same capabilities as men but because they "bless and brighten every place" they enter.[11] The WCTU drew heavily on the conservative Victorian ideology of separate spheres, privileged domesticity, and religiosity at every juncture and therefore did not directly threaten what many late nineteenth-century men and women perceived as a natural gender divide. Because the WCTU's domestic and Christian inclinations dovetailed with a prevailing ideological order, the group's membership greatly eclipsed that of staunchly political organizations like the North American Woman Suffrage Association (NAWSA).[12] Under Willard's assiduous leadership, the WCTU expanded from twenty-seven thousand to two hundred thousand members in the 1880s alone.

Groups like the WCTU and NAWSA were not only concerned about relations between "the sexes" and securing rights for women. The movements that emerged after the Civil War increasingly framed their appeals for women's rights in racist and nativist terms. The native-born, middle-class women who constituted the membership of these organizations often considered themselves members of a superior race. Carrie Chapman Catt, head of the NAWSA, suggested that former slaves and members of immigrant groups had been enfranchised "with ill-advised haste" and argued that giving the vote to white women would neutralize the north's "ignorant foreign vote" and forfend against the South's black male vote.[13]

Prostitution itself became a flashpoint issue in the late nineteenth century for both social and cultural reasons. Social purity activists regarded the abolition of prostitution as a means to curtail and contain extramarital sex and promote abstinence and marital stability. The nineteenth century had in fact witnessed a marked and discernible increase in prostitution both in urban centers and western frontier towns.[14] Men's extramarital affairs sometimes resulted in incurable venereal diseases passed on to wives and children. Female anti-prostitution crusaders also viewed the regulation of prostitution as an expression and institutionalization of an inexcusable sexual double standard. Efforts like England's Contagious Diseases Acts and America's municipal programs were seen as immoral attempts to license and impose health standards on prostitutes with the goal of insuring men's safe access to "public women." But social purity perspectives were also grounded in a fear of importing perceived foreign practices and modes of government and a belief in Anglo-Saxon moral and racial superiority.[15]

Barbara Epstein has described nineteenth-century American society as "a culture in which sexual difference became intertwined with questions of morality, . . . in which what were seen as masculine and feminine principles were placed in combat."[16] The direct infusion of morality into sexual difference, aligning one sex with a set of strict moral practices and beliefs and the other with the transgression of those rules, suggests why prostitution became middle-class women's foil *par excellence* in the late nineteenth century. Prostitution constituted an often painful reminder of class differences among women during a period when essentialized notions of virtuous femininity functioned to assuage the increasing class stratification that accompanied rapid industrialization.[17] An occasionally public commercial endeavor and visible sign of extramarital sexuality, it threatened the era's separate-sphere ideology: the notion that women's position in the domestic sphere—as opposed to the public world of commerce—and their almost ethereal distance from carnality guaranteed them a natural moral superiority. At the same time, the Civil War glamorized male heroism and established intimate connections among men that were played out in the era's burgeoning institutions and professions.

Middle-class white women used reform movements and Victorian gender ideology to gain access to a formal political sphere that had included most white and some black men but excluded women of all races and economic backgrounds. Legitimized and emboldened by the cult of femininity, middle-class female reformers sought to impose moral standards on the working poor by rescuing "fallen women" and otherwise domesticating unruly late nineteenth-century urban spaces.[18] Activists like Willard were able to exploit the association of women with care and nurturance, as well as their culturally granted moral superiority, to make political claims through moral reform societies and moral crusades.[19] These activities enabled women of faith to carry their religious and social message out of the home and onto urban streets. They also politically empowered these women by creating limited access to otherwise inaccessible community, professional, and governmental institutions.

The cultivation of mass culture—a complex process in which a variety of actors and groups sought to create, recruit, and marshal mass audiences—was nascent in the 1880s. Seemingly marginal controversies over prostitution and white slavery were in fact central to this process. To understand the story of mass culture and national reform in the United States, we need to look again at Stead, this time not for a story about one person's influence, but for glimpses of changes in audiences, their constitution, their scope, and their scale. The post–Civil War local press, increasingly politically independent but dependent on advertising, chronicled many of these struggles, took sides in some, and even initiated a few.

THE PRESS AND RELIGIOUS REFORMERS IN THE 1880S

As literacy rates across the country rose during this period, general, specialized, and foreign-language newspapers became the main channels through which Americans kept abreast of local and distant events.[20] The number of periodical publications and their overall circulation rates exploded in the two decades after the Civil War because of the increase in literacy, the affordability of papers, and the rapidly growing population. While there were fewer than five thousand dailies and weeklies in 1870, there were more than fourteen thousand in 1890. In 1870, 2.5 million households subscribed to a daily paper, and that number nearly quadrupled by 1890.[21] This rapid growth in newspaper production was unique to the United States. The 1880 census suggested that the press experienced industrialization as acutely as other economic sectors, reporting that the "rate of growth of the news industry seemed unparalleled in any other country of the world and hardly equaled by any other phase of industrial development in the United States."[22] Accompanying this growth was a transformation in the nineteenth century from what David Paul Nord has labeled an associational press that catered to distinct interpretive communities linked to civic and religious associations to an informational or entertainment-based press that competed for general readers by producing seemingly less ideological news of local, national, and world events thought to be of common interest.[23]

The associational papers that brought narrowly identified communities together were increasingly sidelined by more politically and religiously fluid publications that started attracting more readers as early as the 1830s. By the 1880s, the majority of mainstream commercial papers privileged information and entertainment over moral instruction or social relevance.[24] The content of these publications seemed worlds away from the tone and perspective of the religious press that had played such a formidable role in the early and mid-nineteenth-century print marketplace.[25] If religious publications preached sobriety, devotion, and restraint, secular publications emphasized hedonism, danger, and titillation through their mainstay sports columns, crime stories, and gossip pages. As America urbanized and industrialized, the urban press, which was itself experiencing these demographic shifts as a novelty, paraded a daily feast of stories about urban fortunes and misfortunes before its readers. General readership papers in 1880s New York offered daily lessons in the many ways one could die. Headlines like "Crushed Under a Car," "Threw Herself Over a Cliff," "Salvationists Attacked by Roughs," and "Slain by a Dynamite Blast" from the *New York Herald*'s front page on January 7, 1886, were typical of this genre. Following each headline was a sentiment-free, visually rich depiction of the crime committed or the method of death—free of moral commentary and recrimination.

The ascendancy of the information- and entertainment-based press incited a backlash among believers like evangelical Christians, for whom these publications signified a secularism growing like kudzu throughout American culture. Yet even disapproving readers found it difficult to ignore the number, ubiquity, and increasing influence of the commercial print publications that had emerged after the Civil War. Commentary on press items in evangelical publications suggests that believers avidly if grudgingly read general newspapers along with their own media. These organs directed them toward bountiful objects in need of religious instruction and intervention—especially abject social types like the prostitute or the drunk made visible in urban crime coverage. At the same time, mainstream newspapers also directed evangelicals toward the daily paper itself as a central object of moral reform.

Late nineteenth-century evangelical women reformers correspondingly worked to combat "sensationalism" in the press, which they defined as detailed portrayals of criminality and deviance. Concern about the negative effects of crime stories—what Illinois WCTU member Anna Garlin Spencer called their "disgusting particularities" of criminal acts and "minute photographs of those who committed them"—prompted collective action against newspaper content.[26] Spencer was responding to the level of fascination shown by daily papers like the *National Police Gazette* and the New York descendants of the penny press for crime coverage. Evangelicals felt that such stories corrupted youth and celebrated non-Christian behavior; during the late 1880s they sought to change journalistic content to reflect their own moral framework. In 1887 Spencer called on other WCTU members to "begin with the public tastes [*sic*] which forms the popular daily newspaper, and reform it!"[27]

Of course, the press itself had its defenders and detractors. Against claims that "newspapermen" are "impudent, conscienceless intruders" who are "capable of any act whereby a sensational 'beat' may be secured," M. Y. Beach responded that a reporter was in fact a "gentleman . . . pursuing a perfectly legitimate business" and was "entitled to the respectful consideration of the people he approaches."[28] James Parton, the editor of an urban daily, on the other hand, was cynical about the degree to which business interests dominated Gilded Age newspapers. He advised young men of intellect to avoid newspaper work: "The most respectable and honorable part of a daily paper is the one which the 'ordinary reader' seldom looks at. It is the page of market and shipping news. What a relief to turn to its honest and painstaking reality from the agonizing sensations of the other parts of the paper, with heartless headings that make us writhe in torment before our time."[29]

The activist women of the WCTU took this critique of sensationalism one step further by advancing a gendered analysis of secular print culture that attributed its perceived immorality to masculine vices. The group symbolically equated officialdom, journalism, and saloons—all sites of male culture that WCTU leaders' felt had veered from Christian doctrine and created a tight-knit network of men that allowed innumerable sins against women and families to be perpetuated with impunity. In the 1880s the WCTU formed its own Department for the Suppression of Impure Literature, a division that fought numerous censorship battles against publishing companies and crime-story papers, in particular the *National Police*

Gazette and the sites where it was read and sold.[30] The organization also started its own Press Department and established superintendents of press in each state with a WCTU branch.

Underlying the WCTU's activities concerning the press was a deep suspicion of the motives and biases of male editors and journalists. WCTU president Willard invoked her signature rhetoric of home protection, familial virtue, and temperance in arguing that women should enter the growing field of journalism. Describing all-male newsrooms in almost Gothic terms as impure and sordid associations, full of "cobwebs in the air and brain" and "alcoholic ink," where journalists put drunken hallucinations on the printed page, Willard suggested that "newspapers need women more than women need newspapers." The presence of women would transform "sensationalistic" crime and sports columns that exuded a "beery mental flavor" and "a bitter gall" into something virtuous and pure. American journalism, like other primarily male institutions in need of women members, would then begin to approximate the ideal family form: "newspaperdom is a camp and not a family circle—a half sphere and not a whole one." Willard spoke as one who had previous experience in journalism herself, for a time editing and publishing her brother's *Chicago Post and Mail* before that endeavor failed and she devoted herself to full-time activism and evangelism.

The civic-mindedness of the religious women reformers of the 1880s often put them at odds with corrupt political machines and the daily papers that had long looked the other way. Although privileged, these women lacked full rights as citizens and were often denied entry into the new professions (including journalism itself). Though women in the 1880s were often paid to supply stories to newspapers, aspiring women journalists were typically excluded from the masculine culture of newsrooms. The 1890 Census reported only 888 women journalists out of 21,847 in the profession, or about 4 percent. As a result, many women who would have become journalists found an outlet for their vocational inclinations and their dissatisfaction with a male-centered, Gilded Age culture in the era's reform movements. The WCTU, for example, replicated what its leaders felt were purer versions of male-centered institutions by establishing its own governing board and publishing house, which produced the organization's temperance reform tracts and manuals, as well as its flagship weekly newspaper, the *Union Signal*. The WCTU also partnered with the nascent Illinois Women's Press Association, which was linked to the WCTU through membership, to shape and alter press representations of women's issues and WCTU conventions. The WCTU participated in such initiatives because the organization had "suffered many things at the hands of reporters," whose "ignorance of [the WCTU's] methods of work [made them] unable to become sufficiently *en rapport* with it to report it satisfactorily."[31] The WCTU believed women journalists would offer more knowledgeable, sympathetic reporting.

In 1885, when Stead's story broke in London, the secular informational press and the evangelical associational press expressed starkly different attitudes about prostitution and other forms of vice. The diverging responses to the tale of sex slavery in "The Maiden Tribute" underscored how little mainstream editors and journalists had in common with evangelical social purity leaders.

REVELATION BY WIRE

Many Americans first encountered Stead's revelations through telegraphed accounts in their own daily papers. New York newspapers reported on the London sensation with fascination and a jocular curiosity, but were not initially eager to embrace his topic, methods, or conclusions. Nonetheless, newsfeed from the transatlantic cable enabled nationally dispersed readers to experience "The Maiden Tribute" and the controversies surrounding it within days of their publication. Stead mentioned "telegrams from the United States begging for telegraphic information as to the progress of the great exposure" in the July 13 installment of his exposé: "The purest journals in the great American Republic have reproduced our revelations in full, and the perusal of our narrative has, we are told, silenced the adverse criticism based on imperfect information, and convinced the American public that no other method would have availed to rouse public attention to the vital necessity of remedying the existing abuse."[32] Stead did not exaggerate the immediate market for telegraphic information about the story, but he did misrepresent the degree to which US public opinion embraced the report's content and welcomed its revelations as truth. Most newspapers and journals covered the events in London only briefly and in a tone of detached fascination. Other papers printed information-based stories on the censorship effort surrounding Stead's revelations without taking an editorial stance on his methods.

A deal brokered in the late 1860s between the New York–controlled Associated Press and Western Union guaranteed that New York dailies were always first to access news from Europe.[33] Because they controlled the wires, New York papers were the first to comment on "The Maiden Tribute." The New York of 1885 was teeming with vice, yet the city's press refrained from comparing New York to London. The bulk of New York papers treated the revelations as high entertainment. James Gordon Bennett's impudent *New*

York Herald opined, "Revelations of this sort tickle gross minds and sell a few papers; but the world knows as much of them as it cares to know."[34] Three days later, in a story entitled "Obscene London" about Parliament's response to "The Maiden Tribute," the same paper editorialized, "Really, really, we cannot help laughing. The prudery of London is too ridiculous."[35] By July 10 the *New York Herald* had dismissed the story as pure melodrama and suggested that the public "is merely buying the *Pall Mall Gazette* as it would buy cheap editions of the poems of Rochester or the plays of Mrs. Aphra Behn."[36] The heralded New York daily speculated that American papers would never undertake such a project because of their sensible practical nature and their disinclination toward reforms. It concluded that American papers do not seek to "thrill the heart of the people" by "bragging" about urban vice.[37]

The *New York Sun* and the *New York Daily Graphic*, the two New York papers that came closest to embracing Stead's account, appeared as outliers in the mostly negative reviews. The *New York Sun* stood by the veracity of Stead's story but insisted that its plot was a distant one: similar conspiracies and abuses could not occur in the United States, where "the huge machinery of justice can be set in motion at any time at a touch from the humblest citizen."[38] The paper printed direct excerpts from "The Maiden Tribute" on July 11 and 12, providing American readers with their first account of the exposé. This descendant of the penny press, which solidified its reputation by covering the infamous Helen Jewett murder in the 1836, defended its decision to print the "horrid details" by equating it with public actions undertaken to prevent cholera: "To reproduce those pictures in this country is to put our people on guard against the growth of like abominations here."[39] Other papers and journals might have been critical of the decision, but on July 13 the *Pall Mall Gazette* singled out the paper, thanking it for endorsing its virgin slave trade revelations, an honor the *New York Sun* reveled in the following day.[40]

The illustrated *New York Daily Graphic* exclaimed in a similar vein that "the newspaper is the proper reformatory agency, and all honor to the *Pall Mall Gazette* for its courage in undertaking the work!"[41] The *New York Daily Graphic* did not have a reputation for reform up to that point but was riveted and inspired by "The Maiden Tribute" saga, perhaps seeing in it a way to boost circulation. The following day, it declared in response to the *Herald*'s sarcastic dismissals, "It is not the yearning for obscenity that makes this honest, courageous paper sell. It is a desire to get at the truth and to secure the reform which the publication of the truth makes necessary."[42] The *New York Daily Graphic* hinted at a forthcoming "series of stories" on the "social life" of Washington, DC, that "will create as great a sensation as the *Pall Mall Gazette* articles," though, for whatever reason, the earth-shattering series never appeared.[43]

The *Nation*, a later champion of investigative journalism, saw in the revelations a certain didacticism and obscenity masquerading as reform. It predicted that a reader of the "beastly publication" would have "his horror of vice somewhat lessened and his ideas of the vicious possibilities and opportunities somewhat enlarged." On the possibility of American journalism taking up such a political role for itself, the *Nation* stated that Stead "evidently thinks that he has opened up a new and glorious field for 'journalism.' . . . That some of our contemporaries are quite ready for such a job we have no doubt, . . . and there are others which we have no doubt consider this a most mortifying 'beat.'" The article surmised that numerous reporters were willing to "do the scavenger work of modern society" by "describing its foulness and indecency" and sarcastically suggested that Anthony Comstock should join the faculty in "one of those 'schools of journalism' which we hear every now and then that some puny college is thinking of setting up."[44]

THE SOCIAL PURITY RESPONSE

If American commercial newspapers gazed upon the proceedings in London with fascination and disdain, anti-vice reformers viewed Stead's journalistic *tour de force* as a turning point in the national campaign for social purity that had worked to eradicate prostitution in the decades after the Civil War.[45] Frances Willard described reading Stead's exposé in 1885 as a veritable spiritual experience. She described the *Gazette* disclosures as a "moral cyclone" that "cleared the air and broke the spell, so that silence now seems criminal and we only wonder that we did not speak before." They "so stirred the heart of womanhood" that, "were the hidden life of our great cities known," the knowledge would spawn a similar movement in the United States.[46] Willard and other reformers came to idolize Stead for his courage in undertaking "The Maiden Tribute" investigation and for his example of what journalism in the hands of spiritually guided practitioners could be.

For the next several years, the WCTU's battle against white slavery coincided with its broader call for temperance. "The Maiden Tribute" inspired Willard to incorporate anti-trafficking and age-of-consent activity into the WCTU's regular operations. In late 1885, Willard established the Suppression of the Social Evil department, which in March 1886 would become the

Department of Social Purity (DSP), as a special WCTU branch. Stead's disclosures also served as catalyst for a heightened level of interorganizational communication and action in the American social purity movement. Within months of Stead's exposé, social purity advocates formed new groups, such as the Episcopalian White Cross Society, modeled after the one in England, to advance male purity. On December 13, 1885, the *Union Signal* reported that the new crusade had united women's and men's groups alike:

> Our elder sister, the Woman's Suffrage Association, moved by the same spirit, has taken the same stand and the two great organizations will work for the same object. Other organizations of women are wheeling into line; we hope that soon the womanhood of America will stand in an unbroken phalanx for the protection of her girls. . . . In this work we are nobly aided by the best manhood in the nation. The Society for the Prevention of Vice and the White Cross League are both our loyal coadjutors, working in directions and from vantage ground from which we cannot command.[47]

As an anti-trafficking agenda coalesced among diverse social and political reform organizations, English social purity missionaries like Josephine Butler and William Coote traveled the United States offering tactical and strategic advice to a newly energized movement.

Supporting these developments was a growing network of associational print media through which reformers kept abreast of the national and international fronts on which social purity battles were being waged. Reform publications alerted adherents to rallies, mail-in campaigns, boycotts, and other strategies for advancing the purity agenda. The practices and content of movement publications and the types of political actions employed evolved during the 1880s to accommodate new technologies and ascended to a new level of organization. The social purity and temperance press began to use its own media as vehicles not only to convert others but to press for reform, coordinate national actions, and stay abreast of local issues pertaining to social and moral purity.

The most prominent women's evangelical periodical was the WCTU's *Union Signal*. The *Union Signal* was founded in 1883 with the merger of the *Signal*, an Illinois-based temperance paper, and *Our Union*. The WCTU had editorial control over the *Union Signal*, but until 1903 the publication was owned by the Women's Temperance Publishing Association (WTPA). With a circulation of more than a hundred thousand by 1890, the *Union Signal* was the most heavily read late nineteenth-century women's weekly. The paper was an admixture of short updates pertinent to temperance or WCTU members, state and departmental reports, temperance-related short stories and essays, didactic games and puzzles for children, letters from members, and reports debunking the latest scientific defenses of alcohol. Matilda Carse, the owner of the WTPA, oversaw a staff of 111 employees, the majority of whom were women. In 1885, Carse reported at the WCTU annual convention that her publishing house had "published over thirteen million pages of temperance literature, besides the *Union Signal*. These leaves have been scattered abroad for the healing of our nation."[48] Throughout her tenure as WCTU president, Willard served as editor-in-chief of the *Union Signal*. She considered the publication one of her organization's finest achievements. She reflected in 1895 as her tenure drew to a close: "It is doubtful if any of our reform newspapers published on the globe has earned greater respect or made for itself a home with a larger number of our 'best families'—those in which husband and wife are one, and that one is husband and wife."[49]

While the *Union Signal* predated the WCTU's campaign against white slavery, another social purity publication, the *Philanthropist*, was formed in direct response to the London revelations. The monthly newsletter's first issue in January 1886 was dedicated to "the promotion of social purity, the better protection of the young, the suppression of vice, and the prevention of its regulation by the state." Founded by the New York Committee for the Prevention of State Regulation of Vice and edited by Aaron and Anna Powell, the publication served as a clearinghouse for transnational reform news from the American White Cross Movement, the English Vigilance Association, and the WCTU.

The *Philanthropist*'s inaugural issue was devoted entirely to Stead's exposé and imprisonment, and their reception in the general press. The first page carried the transcript of Josephine Butler's speech at Exeter Hall, where supporters held an all-day prayer meeting for Stead during his imprisonment. The periodical reported that Butler called Stead a "good and true man" who "was trained by God for this great work."[50] The inaugural issue also reprinted a letter to the *New York Tribune* by Powell defending Stead against that newspaper's charges. Powell did "not endorse Mr. Stead's detective methods," but argued that his story "was essentially true" and aligned Stead with the US abolitionist movement by calling him "the 'John Brown' of these white slaves of the legalized and illegal brothels of Europe." As Powell explained to the *Tribune*, "the farce and injustice of his imprisonment, while real criminals under the law in question are allowed to go free of punishment, will serve to emphasize the urgent need of a thorough, conscientious public awakening upon the subject."[51] All subsequent 1886 issues of the *Philanthropist* apprised readers of the status of American general newspapers' coverage of Stead. Aaron Powell instructed social purity reformers to send letters to daily newspapers defending Stead's journalistic integrity. The *Philanthropist*'s editor took his newfound role as American liaison and public relations spokesperson for Stead seriously; he directly contacted all New York newspaper publishers and editors, including Whitelaw Reid, editor of the *New York Tribune*, seeking the opportunity to engage in face-to-face discussions of Stead's life, work, and accomplishments.[52]

CAMPAIGNING AGAINST AN IMPURE PRESS

As Nord has argued, late nineteenth-century urban papers "provided their audience with a limited, organized, common frame of reference, so that diverse city dwellers could communicate with each other—communicate in the sense that they could think about the same things at the same time and thus share a vision of social reality."[53] While the argument that the nineteenth-century urban press constructed social reality, fostering community understanding in the absence of face-to-face relationships, has had much analytical purchase over the years, it is also apparent that many readers did not accept the press as an accurate map of social reality. Temperance and social purity activists in the 1880s frequently found in the pages of the daily paper an affront and direct challenge to their moral paradigm. Nonetheless, they recognized that the general mass media were central to any effective crusade to alter public perceptions. Willard understood journalism's ability to shape public opinion and felt that the WCTU's efforts would be lost if the organization failed to harness this power: "The history of the reformer, whether man or woman, on any line of action is but this: when he sees it all alone he is a fanatic; when a good many see it with him they are enthusiasts; when all see it he is a hero."[54] She therefore sought to "extend [the WCTU's] sphere of influence" by using its own press as well as by using a number of strategies to influence the commercial press.[55]

With a clear understanding of the importance of influencing the press, she modeled the WCTU's press strategy after the one initiated by the Fabian Society. She hoped all temperance activists would communicate the WCTU agenda to the general press. Each new member was sent a list of local papers and clear instructions for writing pro-temperance and social purity letters to the editor. She also created the positions of national and state press superintendents; these people were responsible for providing news copy focused on temperance and social purity to local papers, a practice that began in the early 1880s.[56] The state superintendent of New Hampshire reported in 1883 that she "copied and sent articles to thirty . . . papers every two weeks." She went on to state that "the reason two editors gave for refusing space may be interesting. One said his paper was devoted to politics, and he has never taken part in temperance or any other ism, the proper place for them was in the religious papers. The other said his paper was not such a one that would be likely to aid our cause, and therefore, 'for the good of the cause, etc.' he must decline."[57] In 1885 Esther Housh, the national WCTU press superintendent, sent out fifty-four thousand bulletins and sent circulars to more than seven hundred general, religious, and agricultural journals.[58] Housh's efforts were particularly effective in Ohio, which had been heavily influenced by the women's crusade a decade earlier. In 1885 and 1886, 125 Ohio papers carried stories originally written by the WCTU.[59]

Underscoring the degree to which Willard believed that influencing the general press was central to her group's mission, she repeatedly argued that the WCTU should have a paid press superintendent, even though other key positions, including her own, were held by unpaid volunteers. She began making this argument in late 1885, the same year Stead published "The Maiden Tribute": "The vagaries of the partisan press must be replied to in their own columns whenever possible. Poison cannot be counteracted save where it is imbibed. To refute the *New York Tribune*'s falsities in the columns of the *Union Signal* is to reach only those who need no antidote. Our superintendent must be salaried, furnished with files of all leading papers, aided by clerks, and instructed to reply in our name to these misleading statements in the very columns where they appeared."[60] For Willard, the WCTU was in direct competition with the minds of readers with masculine interests like organized sports: "The baseball club asks for a journalistic hearing and succeeds; the pugilist asks it, and bloody-nosed and bloody-handed as he is, succeeds—to the shame of the reading public be it spoken. With as much energy in our good and great cause as he has in his bad and bestial one, we might succeed as well as he."[61] She continually set higher goals for the WCTU in its battle with masculine journalistic culture. In 1889 she proposed sending out news bulletins to five thousand papers a week and issuing regular Associated Press dispatches to alert papers to prohibitionist and social purity activities.

Similarly, the *Philanthropist* attempted to shape news copy and reward reform-minded papers through its weekly "Greetings to the Philanthropist" column, which directed reformers to general newspapers proven friendly to social purity causes. These "greetings" noted papers that positively referenced the *Philanthropist*, the *Union Signal*, or other social purity publications; respectfully quoted members of the movement as authoritative sources on moral issues; or took a social purity perspective in one of their stories. The first "Greetings to the Philanthropist" listed the *Central Times* of New Jersey, the *Louisville Southern Journal*, the *Washington American*, and the *Los Angeles Weekly Censor* as papers in the process of attaining social purity credibility. Activists were urged to reward these papers with their readership and family subscriptions.

Women journalists, who were busily organizing regional press associations in the latter half of the 1880s, also mobilized against a perceived masculine bias in general-readership papers that was conveyed through "sensationalist" reporting. In 1893, the Pacific Coast Women's Press Association's petition to end sensationalism gathered twenty thousand signatures. The petition claimed, "We believe it is a minority of your readers who demand sensational, personal, or immoral details, rather than the clean statement of facts and truth. There is a minuteness of detail in the reports of crime, wickedness, and sensuality, which can gratify only prurient and vulgar curiosity, or awaken such curiosity in innocent and inexperienced minds." The petition was sent out to papers across the West Coast. In a letter to the *Women's Journal*, one woman journalist considered the action a great success: "One of the two most offensively and enterprisingly sensational of our dailies told me that since this movement he and his kind were under special instructions to treat their details in a restrained and cleanly manner; notably in a peculiarly revolting murder case in which he had reported"[62]

These crusades against the press allowed evangelical reformers to exercise their power as representatives of desirable middle-class audiences to pressure the press to adopt a stronger, moral, feminine-identified focus. In the months after its initial publication, the *Union Signal* increased its advertising space from one to three pages. By the end of the 1880s, the temperance weekly routinely carried more than four pages of ads. Carse's deft handling of her publishing company and her strong relationship with Chicago businesses contributed to the paper's success in generating ad revenue. The *Union Signal* often promoted itself as a valuable medium for advertising. One article spoke directly to potential advertisers, claiming that the weekly was "one of the best advertising mediums in the country. . . . Its patrons are just the people that bona fide and judicious advertisers wish to reach, being mainly refined and intelligent Christian ladies, mistresses of their own homes, with plenty of means to buy such goods as are brought to their notice by advertisers in this, their own paper."[63] The paper pointed to the class status of its readers as evidence that they were of the purchasing class. There was no contradiction between religious or temperance publishing and commercial capitalist endeavors. In fact, readers of the *Union*

Signal were highly desirable, valuable readers, a fact that the general press, which allegedly catered to the generic public but really oriented its news coverage to men, had not yet discovered on a broad scale.

The WCTU was continually at war with its representation in much of the secular press, and its commentary about the press stepped up in the months after the publication of Stead's report. One issue of the *Union Signal* cheekily wrote that "there is nothing like being informed on topics concerning which you write. A leading city Daily says 'The WCTU has moved its headquarters to New York. There is nothing like being on the spot.' If this measures said Daily's knowledge and accuracy, we need not feel badly about the flings and stabs it is continually giving us."[64]

THE PROLIFERATION OF A GENRE

Even as newspapers came under fire for sensationalism, they were indispensable to a number of the campaigns that purity reformers engaged in. The city paper reflected a range of urban problems back to reformers, constructing the city as an unstable, unruly, and godless space in dire need of domestication, containment, and purification. Many of the issues that members of the WCTU and the New York Society for the Prevention of Vice crusaded against came straight off the pages of the newspaper. Reports of urban prostitution and disorderly conduct in saloons were often not experienced or witnessed by reformers firsthand, but delivered to them in orthographic, secondhand form, compliments of these papers. The secular paper often highlighted, signaled, and provided the coordinates for a vice-related occurrence. Reformers intent on intervention typically followed the newspaper's lead to the episode's epicenter.

In 1887 a handful of newspapers began writing of domestic trafficking routes that moved women between New York and Newark and from Chicago to Michigan's Upper Peninsula. That year the *Philanthropist* was able to print a story that relied almost entirely on mainstream press accounts of girls trapped against their will in "dens of infamy."[65] While at first glance it might appear that general-interest commodity papers were simply borrowing the "white slavery" genre from Stead or responding to an objective increase in domestic sex slavery, the story is more complex than either narrative diffusion or realism would suggest. "The Maiden Tribute" did provide the critical discursive opening that allowed both moral reformers and daily newspapers to speak in increasingly open terms about prostitution, which they proceeded to do at great length. However, the adoption of the sex trafficking story by daily newspapers is at least partly due to the pressure placed on the secular press by a reinvigorated social purity alliance that used its own reform journalism and the promise of economically stable middle-class readers to influence general papers. Using direct pressure as well as write-in campaigns, these men and women encouraged papers to feature journalistic reports on organized prostitution and its methods: the trickery, kidnapping, and bribery that were seen to enable it, as well as the abuses suffered by trafficking's victims.

It may seem a curious contradiction for groups to rail against "sensationalism" while promoting a topic that—at least in England—had already lent itself to so much sensationalism. We have already examined how Stead considered sensationalism as a weapon in the journalist-editor's arsenal to be wielded in the service of a larger moral agenda. However, in the late nineteenth-century United States, the meaning of the neologism *sensationalism* was not defined against objectivity, as it currently is. The WCTU in particular helped to establish the sex trafficking exposé, bolstered by an investigation of the "facts" as a fixture of US journalism and a central tool in social purity campaigns against prostitution.[66] The WCTU and its evangelical allies strove to align sex trafficking stories symbolically with fact-based investigation and an enlightened interest in social ills, and to oppose it to sensationalistic reportage and a prurient interest in sports or crime. In other words, discrete stories detailing prurient or violent events purely for informational or entertainment value constituted sensationalism. Morally guided exposés of social ills such as alcoholism or prostitution that were oriented toward abolition and informed by facts did not constitute sensationalism. More simply, if a news story contained details that the evangelicals or WCTU disapproved of, and the article did not promote their agenda, it was sensationalism.

In January and February 1887, a small number of US papers began experimenting with the new "white slavery" genre. These stories of girls "decoyed into dens of vice" were met with the great approval of and vindication by social purity activists across the country. Trafficking stories satisfied newspapers' desires for sensational coverage and simultaneously satisfied neo-abolitionists' strong belief that white slavery was a significant problem that cut across the urban/rural divide. Interestingly, while big cities like New York and Chicago were represented as sites of procurement in these initial stories, in each narrative the "dives" to which city women were taken were located in smaller regional cities and towns. Big urban dailies in the 1880s appeared unwilling to assert the presence of entrapped women in their own cities and thus set off the inevitable investigations that such allegations would incite. Instead, papers like the *New York Sun*, the *Chicago Daily Inter-Ocean*, and the *Detroit Free Press* focused on other municipality's trafficking problems.

The two midwestern dailies dabbling in trafficking coverage happened to be the papers that had cultivated the closest relationships with the WCTU. The *Chicago Daily Inter-Ocean* had earned the accolades of the WCTU in 1883 when it published an exposé on the liquor traffic. Between 1883 and 1890, the paper's owner, William Penn Nixon, and editors occasionally appeared at WCTU-sponsored events and devoted space in the paper to WCTU news. Willard and the *Chicago Daily Inter-Ocean*'s news editor sometimes headlined together at public lectures, including one sponsored by the Illinois Women's Press Association, whose membership overlapped considerably with the WCTU. The news editor and Willard each spoke as experts in the field of journalism, representing the "masculine" and "feminine" perspectives, respectively.[67] While the *Chicago Daily Inter-Ocean* was the WCTU's staunchest ally in the world of mainstream journalism, the *Detroit Free Press* had also reached out to WCTU members as early as 1885 by purchasing *Union Signal* advertising space.

In reporting on trafficking, such urban papers as the *New York Sun*, *Detroit Free Press*, and *Chicago Daily Inter-Ocean* benefited from the attention that such reportage garnered while shielding their host cities from scrutiny and at times describing citizens of big cities as victims of trafficking rings. The *New York Sun* had also developed a relationship with social purity reformers in New York. While the daily had lauded Stead's handiwork in 1885, it insisted that nothing like Stead's account of virgins bought and sold could happen in the United States. But after Powell's prodding, the paper began to dabble in trafficking narratives itself. A brothel murder in Newark in early 1887 led the paper to print "startling revelations" that were "truly hideous" but "should be most beneficent," adding that "nothing more potent in exciting [attention] than the exposures made two years ago in the *Pall-Mall Gazette*." While other New York papers were treating the incident as an everyday murder, the *Sun* pointed to deeper causes, suggesting that the brothel's madam was involved in "nefarious traffic." The *Sun* also went further than other papers by alleging a conspiracy, saying that the woman systematically brought "Germans and Jewesses" from New York to Newark for ten dollars apiece. Such coverage, from the perspective of the *Philanthropist*, confirmed the existence of "a regular systematic trade carried on in young girls, a brokerage of vice" in the United States.[68]

Alongside the "Newark horror" came the "shocking story of the infamous dens of the lumber camps of the upper Peninsula of Michigan" in the *Detroit Free Press* that also captured the attention of *Philanthropist* and

Union Signal readers. Claiming that "what is published is but a hint of the life of these dens of infamy, the details being too revolting for publication" the *Detroit Free Press* declared that women and girls were systematically lured to the Upper Peninsula from Detroit, Chicago, and elsewhere with the promise of employment. Upon their arrival, these women found themselves enslaved under lock and key and prevented by bloodhounds from escaping.[69] Over the next two years, numerous stories featuring young women, bloodhounds, stockades, physical abuse, and even murder in the pine forests of northern Michigan and Wisconsin circulated throughout the Midwest. Social purity activists embraced these newspaper reports of girls held in captivity even as they assailed "blood and thunder" crime and sports stories. They praised depictions of trafficked women and attested to their veracity while calling crime coverage sensationalist, prurient, and immoral. What began as a narrative deflection of attention by journalists from their own locale came to be interpreted as trafficking stories—stories that were reified, amplified, and served as templates for a broader conceptual model of a widespread social evil.

The representations of prostitution routes from New York City to Newark or Chicago to Michigan's Upper Peninsula amounted to a new way of describing prostitution for the mainstream press. In previous urban crime coverage, the commercial sex trade had typically been depicted as spatially fixed—located in brothels, at particular intersections, or in specific districts—whereas this new representation emphasized passage from one locale into another. The movement or traffic of women was seen as central to the harm the trade was perpetuating.[70] The impetus for such representations was as much the American legacy of chattel slavery and the transcontinental slave trade as it was any discernible increase in sex trafficking between 1885, when papers were saying the phenomenon was isolated to Europe, and 1887, when they began reporting on domestic trafficking. In addition to covering the pressure from evangelical crusaders, journalists covered public events in the social reform milieu that reinforced the domestic trafficking framework.

The early sex trafficking reportage was regional, but nationally organized abolitionist groups had a hand in circulating these stories far beyond their geographic scope. In response to local stories, the *Philanthropist* predicted that there were trafficking rings on par with those in New Jersey and Michigan in every locality in the country, especially in urban areas: "In all our large centers of population there is too much reason to fear there is being continually carried on, hidden from the general view, but often with the knowledge of the police authorities, this hideous traffic in girlhood and womanhood to meet the purchasing demands of sensual men."[71] The urgency that ensued upon hearing of "real" cases of white slavery led social purity groups like the WCTU, not content to allow only recently converted secular newspapers to handle these reports, to visit the sites of alleged white slavery, fund and conduct their own inquiries into the phenomenon, publicize the results in their publications and public lectures, and use their findings to agitate for stricter laws against prostitution.

THE WISCONSIN AND MICHIGAN STOCKADES

The WCTU's Department of Social Purity remained without a head for its first year in existence. In taking stock of the department's activities for 1886, Willard declared that the year had been spent studying Stead's revelations along with the Criminal Law Amendment Act and the White Cross Society, with the goal of enacting similar developments in the United States. At their annual convention in late 1886, WCTU members decided to group their purity work into three broad categories: preventive, reformatory, and legislative.[72] In 1887 Willard recruited another Illinoisan, the devout Methodist physician and missionary Katherine Bushnell, to serve as National Evangelist of the Purity Department of the WCTU. Bushnell's previous social purity work among Chinese prostitutes in Denver provided her with critical rescue-work experience. Back in Chicago, she and a team of volunteers established a number of programs aimed at saving women trapped in systems of vice. Bushnell and her assistants turned to the daily papers and police records to find names of women caught up in the "social evil" who might be open to support and counseling.

Immediately after establishing rehabilitation and training programs in Chicago, Kate Bushnell scheduled a nationwide lecture tour to introduce audiences to the WCTU's social purity activities. Like other commentators in this post–"Maiden Tribute" moment, Bushnell remarked on the candor with which she could suddenly discuss prostitution: "Women are speaking and audiences listening to the discussion of a side of social life concerning which the whisper of a sentence a few years ago would have been considered a breach of the rules of propriety."[73] As she traveled across the United States, Bushnell read the stories in the *Detroit Free Press* and the *Chicago Daily Inter-Ocean* alleging the existence of white slavery in the pine forests of northern Michigan and Wisconsin. The reports described the brutal conditions under which women and girls were lured to the area with the promise of employment and instead forced into prostitution to service the Canadian, German, and Polish laborers in the region's lumber camps. One report in the *Chicago Daily Inter-Ocean* told the story of twenty-two-year-old Hattie Nathan, a well-educated "prepossessing and refined" girl whom the brothels of Marinette, Wisconsin, had driven insane. According to the report, the girl had committed an early "indiscretion," after which she "drifted to a dive" near Marinette. Once there, she was "made a prisoner with the other unfortunate women in the place." After the abuses of her first night, she escaped by scaling a high fence, but as she ran down the road, she heard the "baying of hounds" and was ultimately forced back into the brothel, severely beaten, and "locked in her room." Her next escape was successful: she made it to a brothel in Chicago, whereupon she became insane and lived in a trunk, "trembling with the fear of imaginary hounds."[74] Similar stories circulated about the pine forests of northern Michigan, though the *Chicago Daily Inter-Ocean* spent more time describing conditions near the northern Wisconsin town of Marinette. The WCTU immediately called on the governors of these states to take action against the alleged brutalities.

Allegations of Upper Peninsula trafficking came just months after Willard had visited the region to lobby for the passage of a Prohibitory Amendment. The *Union Signal* had represented the passage of Michigan's amendment as a near-certainty and expressed shock and outrage, particularly at the press, when the measure did not pass as expected in April 1887. Significantly, the analysis of Upper Peninsula lumber camps began at this point, and so did the region's contentious relationship with the WCTU. In "A Week in the 'Upper Peninsula,'" Willard described being duped by ostensible social purity allies who staged a debate in Marquette, Michigan, in which she represented temperance, while they (two attorneys and a lumberman) argued for "practical temperance." Willard described not being allowed time to rebut her opponents and feeling outnumbered. She concluded that Marquette is "an aristocratic city of the Upper Peninsula. Here, in luxurious homes, live the lumber, iron, and copper 'kings.'"[75] Once the amendment failed, Willard claimed that the battle was one between a false press and a righteous pulpit, exclaiming, "Woe unto you Scribes and Pharisees, hypocrites! was the refrain that echoed in my ears for the first time in my life, as I followed their terrible words stenographed in the Detroit press and industriously spread throughout the nation."[76]

After Michigan's initial skirmish with the WCTU over the Prohibitory Amendment, Wisconsin and Michigan officials were not eager to embrace Chicago-based allegations about prostitution abuses in their states, especially so close to an election year. In late 1887 and early 1888, both Wisconsin Governor Rusk and Michigan Governor Luce ordered investigations into the abuses to see if bases existed for the "rumors." Governor Rusk also ordered raids on two "dives" near Marinette, but the officials arrived to find them already deserted.[77] He also dispatched a special investigator, James Fielding, to determine whether the newspaper claims had any merit. In the face of non-indigenous assertions, the *Milwaukee Daily Journal* and the *Milwaukee Sentinel*—archenemies on most other issues—rallied around Rusk and Fielding. The *Milwaukee Daily Journal* provided a laudatory account of Fielding's "Journey Through Northern Wisconsin" and lambasted the "dime-novel sensationalists who painted the matter in lurid colors, distorting and embellishing facts" and the "newspapers in various parts of the country [that] copied these cheap narratives, and found silly people to believe them." Fielding, his detective, and the Milwaukee papers did not dispute the existence of prostitution in the northern territory but argued that there was no evidence of abduction or abuse, except excessive debt for clothes or drink on the part of the women. After allegedly visiting several northern Wisconsin brothels as an undercover agent and talking to the women living there, Fielding concluded that "there was no truth in the stories about the north containing prisons where women were made slaves to the passions of brutal men."[78]

Bushnell became skeptical when she read the *Milwaukee Daily Journal*'s account of Fielding's refutation of the newspaper reports and decided to conduct her own investigation of the stockades. What ensued was a yearlong battle between Bushnell, Fielding, the Wisconsin legislature, and the Milwaukee papers over the veracity of the stories of abduction and forced prostitution in the camps. Bushnell and members of the WCTU put their stock in the papers that reported on Wisconsin's white slavery as fact. In a *Union Signal* article, "Another Maiden Tribute," they drew parallels between Stead's work in London and the reportorial allegations of white slavery in the Midwest. WCTU member Bessie Cushman's article figured women readers as supremely rational, capable of readily discerning truth from sensationalism, yet not inclined to advertise this ability. It asserted that "the modern Babylon" is not confined to London or even big cities but occurs even "between the lumber districts of the upper Peninsula of Michigan and American and Canadian cities." While the "wires had grown hot" with details of lumbermen, hounds, high board fences, and kidnapping, the general reception of the revelations on the whole disappointed the social purity wing of the WCTU. The problem was encapsulated in an illustrative encounter between a generic husband and wife, John and Mary, who, between sips of coffee, read out loud a story of midwestern prostitution. John remarks, "The papers couldn't live without a little spice of this sort once in a while," and Mary soberly but understatedly replies, "But wouldn't it be horrible if it should be true?" The following week, their paper prints a story in which a saloon keeper assures the reporter that an erstwhile kidnapped girl knew "just what she was going to do up there." John takes the saloon keeper's assessment as truth, saying, "Here's a denial of that kidnapping canard I was reading you a couple days ago." The fictive Mary defers to John, saying, "I'm glad there's no truth to it," while the third-person narrator comments wryly, "The ripple in moral sentiment of heart and home and community is smoothed away. It is pronounced an exaggerated account of an every day occurrence."[79]

The question for members of the WCTU came down to whom one chose to believe: the male saloon keeper; or the male investigator, who treats the bar owner as an authority on prostitution; or the testimony of the women themselves and those few male journalists who claim to speak for or on behalf of them. John identified with the masculine authorities, while Mary's initial instincts told her that these unthinkable abuses could actually happen to women in the United States. As we have seen, the WCTU and other social purity reformers sounded plenty of warnings about press sensationalism themselves, but for these activists, the new "white slavery" stories were strictly off limits to such charges. Through this genre, the WCTU sought to challenge a social order in which Mary had to withhold her superior sentiment on women's issues rather than risk disrupting male domination. Bushnell, an unmarried and therefore unencumbered version of the fictive Mary, conducted her own investigation into the lumber-camp towns of upper Wisconsin and Michigan with a firm belief that her mission was guided by God and that, as a woman, her investigative skills and inclinations were superior to those of men.[80]

After securing permission from Willard and funding from the Wisconsin WCTU, Bushnell traveled to Wisconsin in the spring of 1888. She went to Wisconsin with a deep conviction that "women were led away by conspiracy rather than by inclination" and a deep suspicion of male detective work, which saw it as permissible to "simulate criminals" and "to feign crimes" in order to attain evidence—practices that she found "hardly consistent with Christian spirit."[81] Her own extensive investigation spanned four months, during which she and a group of WCTU women took the histories of 577 prostitutes and interviewed brothel owners, saloon keepers, and religious leaders about abuses around the lumber camps. In a lecture to the Milwaukee branch of the WCTU, she charged that Fielding's investigation was a sham and claimed that he and his detective had never actually visited the stockades that his report exonerated, calling "the statement [that] he made the trip an infamous lie" and alleging that his investigation was "an imaginary one." She went on to detail a set of associations that implicated three wealthy Marinette men and a local judge in a conspiracy to entrap, detain, and physically abuse women. So central was vice to the town of Marinette's livelihood that she personally "saw telephone lines connecting these dens with the livery stable, the stores, etc., in the town."[82]

The Milwaukee papers immediately attacked Bushnell and her charges. The *Milwaukee Daily Journal* called her work "purely emotional" and recommended that she take her skills to Chicago, where "she could get more material in . . . one day's walk than she could get in a month in northern Wisconsin."[83] A week later the same paper offered an unflattering character sketch of Bushnell that referred to her "Homely Face" and "Angular Figure" in its subheading. Particularly threatening, from the perspective of the paper, was her planned lecture tour to eastern states "to tell tales of the state's immorality." Bushnell was cast as an ambitious crusader conducting missionary work in Wisconsin while ignoring vice in her native city. Reviewing her background of missionary work in China, the paper slipped in this backhanded compliment: "[Bushnell is] a remarkable woman in many respects besides her appearance, which is not what one would call an artist's dream, unless the artist had lunched on mince-pie and pickles before going to sleep on a rail bed."[84] These comments betrayed the level of hostility that the Wisconsin press had for the woman reformer, but also indicated the presumed masculine readership of the paper. The same day the *Milwaukee Sentinel* printed a story under the headline "Resented by All: Kate Bushnell's Slanders on Wisconsin," saying that the legislature felt pressured by "sensational reports impugning the character of the people of Wisconsin . . . that have been circulating lately in the metropolitan dailies of this country" to call another state investigation into the accusations.[85]

When Bushnell visited Madison to take part in the legislative proceedings, her mutually libelous relationship with Rusk's investigator, Fielding, began to further deteriorate. As she and fellow WCTU members again charged that he had faked his inquiry into the Wisconsin stockades, Fielding retaliated, telling Bushnell about a malicious story impugning her virtue that was being repeated throughout Marinette. The repetition of this lore caused the women to call for his arrest for "using obscene and abusive language towards Bushnell, an unmarried woman." The case was eventually thrown out of court, but the hostility to Bushnell continued in Wisconsin to the point where she needed police protection to attend a meeting of the Wisconsin legislature.[86] After Wisconsin undertook its second investigation under a new governor, the legislature passed a bill against the procurement of prostitutes that colloquially became known as the "Kate Bushnell Bill," though she played no role in drafting it. Bushnell was even invited to address the legislature after the passage of the bill.

Although the Michigan WCTU did not conduct extensive investigations into Michigan's lumber-camp brothels, its members waged a campaign to end the traffic there. They held regular mass meetings to encourage Governor Luce to curb white slavery in the state, including a much-publicized one at Detroit's Grand Opera House. In Lansing, Michigan, the legislature passed a bill for the suppression of vice that made "all persons keeping or resorting to such houses" subject to five years' imprisonment or a thousand-dollar fine (or both).

Despite Willard's and Bushnell's attempts to popularize the issue of forced prostitution and produce legislation in the United States similar to England's, the notion of white slavery did not become a national flashpoint issue in the late nineteenth century. Agitation surrounding Stead's exposés led to three international conferences on the traffic in women. William Coote organized the first of these conferences, which was held in June 1899. The proceedings primarily emphasized the trafficking of European girls to the Middle East and Argentina. While representatives from the United States were present at this conference, no one suggested that there was a domestic white slave trade. Henry Chase, a delegate from Boston, stated in his report that "we have in the United States, so far as I am aware, no organized system of white slavery."[87]

SHIFTING ALLIANCES: PRESS AND REFORMERS

Using the *Union Signal* and allied media, the WCTU attacked the American print media, which they felt was complicit in the masculine saloon and prostitution culture they sought to overturn. Inspired by Stead's example and key social purity victories in England, US reformers challenged the secular news media in three ways: (1) they created their own national network of print media to serve as an organizing tool and lobbied the general-interest media to adopt social purity issues and concerns; (2) they funded their own investigations into sex trafficking and published the results in their media organs; and (3) they mounted protests against sensationalism in the press while simultaneously offering print dailies something in return: the sex trafficking story, a new way of discussing sexuality and prostitution.

A number of conclusions can be made about the WCTU, women's movements, and social movements more generally as they relate to media. Prior to organizing, women in the United States at this time lacked influential access to news and other print media. Nor did the news media seek them out as readers by printing material that would be of special interest to them. Moreover, women remained politically disenfranchised, having neither voting rights nor legislative influence concerning matters like vice and community integrity that concerned them. The rapid rise of a variety of organizations such as the WCTU, suffrage organizations, and the social purity movement more generally gave women access to the political sphere and to mass media on all of these levels. In order to understand major currents in news media at the dawn of mass culture and later, we must understand how social movements engaged the media strategically, discursively, and as media audiences. The WCTU mounted a media campaign that would be considered sophisticated even by today's standards. They challenged the relevance and veracity of media accounts, they assigned relevance to and redefined new issues, and they drew attention to themselves as valuable audiences. They also conducted their own social-scientific investigations and published alternative media. In doing so, they had a transformative effect on mainstream media content and practices.

With the rapid expansion of local daily and weekly newspapers after the Civil War came the need for these papers to distinguish themselves to both readers and advertisers among an ever-increasing field of diverse print media. As reformers agitated to make the press more receptive to social purity messages, newspapers were beginning to discover that capturing the sizeable middle-class evangelical audience might just be a viable economic strategy. In a decade that saw major economic slumps and downturns, labor strikes, and high unemployment, some papers saw the value of appealing to these already collectivized, middle-class, largely female communities of believers who also had the resources to buy their advertised goods. The press responded to the increase in the number of women readers throughout this period, gradually toning down its blatant "sensationalism." However, it found new ways to produce sensationalist stories as the domain of relevance shifted to topics favored by the moral reform movements.

As discussed in chapter 1, a rethinking of sensationalism is needed to understand it as a process and engage its various uses. The WCTU lavishly criticized mainstream media for "sensationalism" in its day-to-day crime coverage. Here they used the more familiar negative connotation of sensationalism as dismissive critique. The WCTU attempted to delimit the range of allowable discourses and topics in mass media, essentially demarcating certain issues as being socially irrelevant and even potentially harmful. However, they also deployed sensationalism in the same way Stead did, as a means of demarcating issues as being worthy of the public's attention. While they targeted as irrelevant the details of specific crimes and sporting events not connected to a larger moral agenda, they designated the crimes of sex trafficking and intemperance as being part of broader social evils. They were in a sense imposing a nomothetic standard that became the shibboleth of sensationalism.

Thus sensationalism as a positive process must be seen as a strategy deployed in contests over cultural relevance and salience that occur on the battlefield of mass media. By defining what is relevant and promoting its promulgation in mass media, the social purity activists and the WCTU sought to redefine meanings, assign relevance to them, and increase the cultural salience of such narratives through media saturation. In this deployment one is struck by the overwhelming positivity of sensationalism that is belied by the WCTU's rhetoric, in keeping with the more traditional use of "sensationalism." The WCTU strategically modeled its strategy after Stead's, but failed to acknowledge its positive use of sensationalism, as Stead had so self-consciously done. The WCTU to some degree succeeded in achieving its goals. They initially utilized only the narrow, negative version of sensationalism, but they only really gained traction when they used it positively, as Stead had, producing their own sensational product and offering mainstream media an attractive alternative to the products they attempted to displace. Yet they failed to recognize this as a key to their successes; hence, an apparent contradiction persisted between their simultaneous rejection and transparent use of sensationalism.

As the pages of the *Philanthropist* and *Union Signal* make clear, evangelical reformers slowly came to accept mainstream journalism as an ally in their crusades against vice. We see a gradual increase in acceptance of the press as reformers conducted letter-writing campaigns and printed positive and negative reports on purity reform in various newspapers. In 1886, publications like the *Union Signal* and the *Philanthropist* commonly described the general-readership, informational press as salacious and sensationalist, but by 1900 they often referred to the press and purity reform as partners working in tandem to reform urban governments and promote social purity. An 1889 issue of the *Union Signal* defends the press against a letter-writer's claim that "virtue might be more easily preserved if the press were subjected to the censorship of women at her [*sic*] best." The editor's reply signals this shift in WCTU attitudes toward the press: "While our contributor is doubtless right in his strictures of a portion of the press, we are glad to believe there are many honorable exceptions in the ranks of journalism."[88] During this brief span of time, reporters gradually began to take on a greater activist role and show more subjectivity as publishers began to rely on collectivized reform movements as audiences for their publications.

It is also true that some papers in the late 1880s heard from evangelical reformers and steadfastly refused to listen. The *New York Tribune* mocked the gentleman who "wears a white cross badge and complains of the offensive stories he is compelled to listen to" and suggested that the best way to avoid such "impure stories" was to "take his hat and retire."[89] However, other members of the press establishment began to take social purity activists' allegations about the press seriously or at least catered to them as an attractive audience. In a public address, H. K. Carroll, of the *New York Independent*, identified with reformist efforts and labeled even "respectable" newspapers "sheets of the slums" that "circulate extensively beyond the gutter population." He drew a sharp distinction between the moral instruction offered on the editorial page and the "dangerous" news columns. The common newspaper "industriously gathers the details of salacious events, of brutal sports, and of revolting crimes as though it were a purveyor, not to decent people, but to the disreputable classes."[90]

By 1893, editors were trying to defend the press by trying to redefine the term *sensationalism* in a positive light. Louis Megargee, writing for *Lippincott's Magazine*, described an occasion in which his newspaper uncovered the story of an illicit trade in cadavers that were sold to the local medical school. Laws were changed as a result of his reporter's work. He wrote to "teach a lesson to those who cast aside a kaleidoscope of the world's doings in the previous twenty-four hours without one thought of the wizard-like genius which has unrolled the panorama before them at the price of a pauper's blessing." And he argued that "the 'newspaper sensation' has almost invariably as its object and effect the righting of a public wrong."[91]

Representations of trafficked women in the late 1880s failed to induce action on a national level. Not only was the federal government notoriously weak and unresponsive to a host of problems during the Gilded Age, but the United States, struggling with its status as a unified nation after the Civil War, still lacked mass audiences sufficient to support a mass-mediated national controversy in which hypothetical readers from the eastern states to the western territories might be focused on the allegations of one or a handful of newspapers. A truly mass-mediated national controversy around the traffic in women would not occur until the first decade of the twentieth century, when muckraking magazines revived stories of trafficking in a new political environment, one ripe for the kind of legalistic excess that claims of sex trafficking had inspired in England two decades earlier.

CHAPTER FOUR

George Kibbe Turner, Muckraking, and the Brief Reign of Piteous Facts

In a 1910 collection of essays by prominent white slavery activists, the Chicago Reverend Ernest Bell rejoiced in the power of mass distribution. He praised nationally distributed magazines for alerting the public to the daily atrocities committed by those who profit from the bodies of white slaves. Referencing an October 1908 article in *Woman's World*, which printed a total of "50 million pages on the topic," Bell declared magazines to be foot soldiers in "the war on the most shameful crime of debauchery [that] exploits the youth of both sexes."[1] Bell invited readers to share his awe that the monthly claimed more than two million subscribers and to imagine the power of this vast audience once it had organized itself on behalf of the nation's trafficked girls. Indeed, after 1907, many anti-vice activists had come to consider popular magazines as active participants in political reform, actors in the social arena.

Between 1890 and 1907, sex trafficking was not viewed as a significant social problem in the United States. Even the Committee of Fifteen's 1900 report on prostitution in New York City argued that forced prostitution was the exception rather than the norm.[2] During this period members of the American Purity Alliance harnessed their efforts to a growing international campaign against white slavery, sending representatives to a series of international conferences organized to encourage suppression of the international traffic in women. This multinational agitation led to a 1904 agreement among thirteen European countries to assist each other in curbing trafficking (the United States ratified this agreement in 1905). The immigration acts of 1903, 1907, and 1910 prohibited the importation of women for "immoral purposes." The 1907 law established an Immigration Commission to investigate the relationship between immigration and prostitution. The commission, chaired by Senator William P. Dillingham, produced two seminal reports on prostitution. Its 1909 report focused largely on the relationship between international immigration and prostitution, while its 1910 report, *Importation and Harboring of Women for Illegal Purposes*, considered trafficking in a number of US cities.[3]

Progressive Era magazine coverage of domestic sex trafficking began in 1907 in *McClure's*, the era's preeminent muckraking magazine, and migrated from there to dailies, books, stage, and cinema. George Kibbe Turner's "The City of Chicago: A Study of the Great Immoralities" (1907) and his "The Daughters of the Poor: A Plain Story of the Development of New York City as a Leading Center of the White Slave Trade of the World, Under Tammany Hall" (1909) helped shift concern from international trafficking to the role of new immigrant populations in domestic prostitution rings.[4] Turner's Chicago piece inspired some of the city's top legislators, religious crusaders, and activists, including Bell, Jane Addams, Clifford G. Roe, Edwin W. Sims, and Congressman James R. Mann, to conduct local and federal campaigns against white slavery. With the exception of Stead's internationally influential "The Maiden Tribute" in 1885, Turner's 1907 and 1909 sex trafficking exposés circulated on a scale unseen in 1880s and 1890s America.

Once *McClure's* established sex trafficking as a grave domestic social threat in American cities, the mandate to curb it led to a propagation of formal responses on both the local and federal levels, including the election of anti-trafficking candidates to governmental office; the funding of police investigations into the phenomenon; the proliferation of commissions to study white slavery and vice; the implementation of their recommendations, including the formation of special vice units as subgroups within municipal police forces; the passage of such national legislation as the Mann Act to curb white slavery; and the expansion of the Bureau of Investigation (the precursor to the FBI) to enforce this act.[5] All of these responses played a major role in shaping the way the United States dealt with illegal interstate commerce, the use of corroborative testimony and street-based informants, the legal definition of intent, and definitions and proof of conspiracy.

While the WCTU/*Chicago Daily Inter-Ocean* anti-trafficking crusades against the Michigan and Wisconsin lumber camps had received scant national attention, the *McClure's* pieces were read and responded to as important objects of local and national concern. The early twentieth-century crusade against sex trafficking did not originate from associational movements and literature but from the rising national media itself. If reform advocates a generation earlier in both the United States and England influenced publishers to initiate media crusades, Progressive Era activists seized the opportunity afforded by mass distribution and a reform-oriented news field to link their own efforts retrospectively to these more popular forms. The period thus witnessed a shift from news as a response to activist groups to media-generated investigative work.

Why had the work of evangelical organizations like the WCTU failed to galvanize a national consensus to use legislation and law enforcement to curb the traffic in women, while the investigative pieces published in *McClure's* achieved for a time the legitimacy and state-sanctioned mandate that had eluded Francis Willard, Katherine Bushnell, and other Gilded Age anti–white slavery activists? This chapter considers this question, arguing that the key to the early twentieth-century panic around sex trafficking was the rise of a national media, in the form of nationally distributed magazines, that could produce a sense of large-scale, collective vulnerability via stories of sex trafficking. This national and generalized response allowed for a shift away from the regionalization of trafficking scandals and toward direct discussion within cities about their own vice problems as part of a larger national problem. This was particularly the case in Chicago, where local publicity and intense activism in the years after Turner's exposé led to the creation of the federal White-Slave Traffic Act (also known as the Mann Act). Turner's Chicago vice exposé generated new meanings regarding prostitution and inspired an intensity of public activism concerned with white slavery, while the New York City piece created a political firestorm that ultimately led to a media backlash. For reasons that I explore in this chapter, Turner's Chicago piece generated belief in sex slavery, galvanizing activists and legislators to act on behalf of white slaves, while his New York City exposé engendered intense skepticism in the form of a surplus scandal that had a transformative impact on journalism.

MUCKRAKING MAGAZINES AND PROGRESSIVE ERA REFORM

By the end of the 1880s, many general-readership newspapers had adopted a new commercial strategy of actively courting middle-class women and children as readers and toning down their discussions of drink and depravity in favor of family-friendly and women-oriented features. As the trade journal *Newspaperdom* suggested in 1892, the period's readers "want something more than the mere news in their daily paper. The women and children are newspaper-readers, and there must be stories, and poems, and fashion articles, and correspondence, and illustrations, sermons, and biographies, and holiday specialties, and serials."[6] Part of this strategy involved hiring more women to write news from a specifically feminine perspective.[7]

At the same time that women and children were being courted by informational newspapers, previously icy relations between the press and anti-vice moral reformers began to thaw. When Willard and her army of WCTU members campaigned against the sensationalist press in 1885, it would have been difficult to imagine an American general-interest publication achieving financial dominance by printing fact-based articles on social and political corruption. The possibility that these publications could bring new participants into activist movements, prompt publicly and privately funded investigations into malfeasance, and force local and national legislative change would have seemed equally remote. But these features are what national investigative muckraking magazines like *McClure's* began to market and deliver after the turn of the century. The magazines covered an array of political topics that fell outside the scope and concern of some moral reformers and struck some as being too radical. Nonetheless, the emergence of specialized reporter-reformers on the American cultural and political scene marked the beginning of a convergence between the interests of national news magazines and moral entrepreneurs that began in 1907, peaked in 1909 and 1910, and toppled with the economic collapse and cultural demise of muckraking magazines, which had all but disappeared by 1915.

After 1902 the new "cheap" magazines of the late 1890s began to sponsor politically engaged investigative journalism grounded in data and hard facts.[8] Monthlies like *McClure's* and *Cosmopolitan* distinguished themselves from newspapers and other magazines with their politically and socially relevant nonfiction, capital-intensive investigation, and careful editorial vetting.[9] The long-form journalism of exposure practiced by Ray Stannard Baker, Ida Tarbell, Lincoln Steffens, Theodore Dreiser, David Graham Phillips, Upton Sinclair, George Kibbe Turner, and others between 1902 and 1915 was grounded in social and political reform, but found its unique identity in the distinction between impetuous, prefigured conclusions and cautious, painstaking research.[10]

Investigative journalists would occupy a central position in popularizing and focusing the movements for political and social change that came to characterize the Progressive Era, authoring pieces on urban poverty, southern lynching, corporate malfeasance, political corruption, voting irregularities, unsafe food and medicine, government payoffs, and other social problems. Deploying methods and narrative forms derived from fiction, history, documentary evidence, and interviews, they chronicled and provided frameworks for understanding the seismic demographic and economic shifts transforming the nation after the turn of the century. While popular with middle-class, civic-minded audiences, their work sometimes crossed the line between calling for incremental reform and advocating more sweeping social transformations.[11] The label *muckraker*, widely used to describe these journalists, embodies this ambivalence. Theodore Roosevelt first applied the name to the period's investigative journalists two months after the publication of Upton Sinclair's *The Jungle* and David Graham Phillips's "The Treason of the Senate." In his 1906 "Man with the Muck-Rake" speech at the House of Representatives, he denounced the "wild preachers of unrest and discontent, the wild agitators against the existing order, . . . the men who preach destruction without proposing any substitute for what they intend to destroy, or who propose a substitute which would be far worse than the existing evils."[12] Drawing an analogy to the muck-rake figure in Paul Bunyan's *Pilgrim's Progress*, who was singularly focused on the dirt and excrement below, oblivious to the celestial beauty above, Roosevelt warned that the journalist who "never thinks or speaks or writes, save of his feats with the muck-rake, speedily becomes, not a help to society, not an incitement to good, but one of the most potent forces for evil."[13] Many Progressive Era investigative journalists interpreted Roosevelt's critique as a gauge of their own cultural authority and proudly adopted the label.

As the first nationally distributed news form, muckraking magazines constituted the perfect venue for the production of stories linking prostitution in distinct localities to a national and even transnational commerce in white women. While daily newspapers were often distributed and consumed outside their nominal territorial boundaries, they nonetheless interpreted national and international news through a local filter. As powerful political and civic institutions, the period's urban dailies struck an uneasy balance between reporting on urban strife while simultaneously presenting a positive image of the city to urban readerships. Ray Stannard Baker recalled working as a young reporter with the *Chicago Record* in the 1890s. During that time Baker witnessed and participated in the World's Columbian Exposition of 1893, Coxey's march of the unemployed on Washington in 1894, and the Pullman strike of the same year. Observing these historic events led Baker to writerly excess. He wrote "three or four times as much everyday as the *Record* could or would publish." The *Chicago Record*'s city editor heavily edited his work, excising much of it on the grounds that the paper could not "make Chicago look as though everyone was starving or homeless."[14] Baker left the *Chicago Record* because its investment in regional interests had a silencing effect on writers who felt compelled to describe the Gilded Age city in less favorable terms. He sought employment with magazines and was eventually hired to write for *McClure's*. Reflecting on his experience in writing for both media, Baker concluded that the news-oriented, mass-distribution magazine was "better adapted to the accurate and thorough-going presentation of the new world" than the newspaper.[15]

Possessing no local referent, magazines interpellated readers as members of a broad national audience. Because magazines were less dependent on territorially bounded audiences, advertisers, and urban institutions, their coverage of cities and municipal institutions could more easily take on an indicting tone that led to legislation at the federal level to regulate misdeeds at the local level.[16] Exposés, of course, were neither new nor limited to magazines.[17] Newspapers with large urban circulations had been commissioning small-scale investigative reports since the 1880s, and these served as a prototype for Progressive Era, magazine-based muckraking. However, crusading newspapers like the *New York World* were exceptional among the era's daily papers, and the geographic scope of their crusades and stunts tended to be limited. What made the turn-of-the-century literature of exposure unique was what Richard Hofstader called "its reach—its nationwide character and its capacity to draw nationwide attention, the presence of mass muckraking media with national circulations, and huge resources that went into exposure."[18] The Progressive Era muckraking magazine's national platform emboldened it to take on special interests and corrupt political machinery, and also rendered it the greatest threat. In his 1932 study, Will Irwin claims that muckraking exposed not only municipal, state, and federal corruption, but also the "lack of a national journalism" in the United States.[19] National distribution also afforded magazines the resources to conduct major investigations. As one literary scholar puts it, while on assignment, *McClure's* writers were given the "equivalent today of generous multiyear foundation fellowships."[20] Although its features were often antagonistic toward big business, in 1905 *McClure's* brought in more advertising revenue than any other periodical.[21] By this time, the most popular reform magazines had a combined monthly circulation rate of more than three million, thereby gaining a true mass audience not bound to any local identity.[22] The large revenues that these publications generated allowed them to commission research-intensive investigations (which often invoked research methods akin to the nascent social sciences) and enabled greater independence from local political groups and businessmen.

THE FORGOTTEN MUCKRAKER

In 1893 Samuel S. McClure and John Phillips founded *McClure's Magazine*. McClure's upbringing and education were steeped in evangelism, abo-

Figure 4.1. S. S. McClure. From S. S. McClure, *S. S. McClure: My Autobiography* (New York: S. S. McClure, 1914).

litionism, and temperance. After graduating from Knox College, he went into publishing, initially serving as American literary agent and syndicator to Robert Lewis Stevenson, Arthur Conan Doyle, Rudyard Kipling, Mark Twain, William Dean Howells, H. G. Wells, Richard Harding Davis, and Joel Chandler Harris. When he started *McClure's*, his literary connections allowed him to print high-quality fiction in the magazine and resell it to book publishers and newspapers for additional profit. Initially, *McClure's* featured quality fiction and autobiographical accounts of famous figures, but by 1901 McClure and Phillips had decided that there was an untapped audience for serialized, research-based pieces that represented and explained the obstacles to democracy and progress in the form of special interests. Thereafter *McClure's* funded and published many of the period's famous exposés, including Tarbell's "History of the Standard Oil Company" and Steffens's work on municipal corruption in "The Shame of the Cities."

Despite *McClure's* commercial success and solid reputation, Phillips left the magazine in 1906 to start another magazine, taking Tarbell, Steffens, Baker, Finley Peter Dunne, and William Allen White with him.[23] McClure, in need of a new urban crime and politics reporter, hired George Kibbe Turner away from the *Springfield Republican*. Turner was born in Quincy, Illinois, and graduated from Williams College in 1890. He was a fiction writer and journalist whose first novel, *The Taskmaster*, and a number of short stories had been published by McClure. Despite his low profile today, Turner was one of the most influential and controversial muckrakers of his generation. His articles on municipal conditions and political organizations in Galveston, Chicago, New York, Cincinnati, Boston, and Des Moines were wildly successful. Turner's popularity was both augmented and tempered by controversy. McClure persistently stood by Turner, defending his work against critics. As he wrote to a colleague, Turner's one flaw was that he rarely documented his sources: "If Turner has any defect in writing, it is a defect that almost all writers lean toward; that is a certain distaste toward documentation." McClure went on to say that when "a writer himself knows the facts he does not realize how important it is to put the reader into possession of the same convincing proofs."[24]

Turner's first assignment at *McClure's* was to investigate rumors of an "enlightened" form of municipal governance that had sprung up in Galveston after the disastrous hurricane that killed 20 percent of the city's population. Turner's article, "Galveston: A Business Corporation," represented the city commission model instituted in Galveston as a foolproof alternative to corrupt ward politics and urged its replication elsewhere.[25] Seattle and Topeka requested thousands of reprints. Philadelphia distributed the article as a pamphlet, and Des Moines ran excerpts in two of its newspapers. Civic leaders and reformers across the country read Turner's article, and a number of municipalities copied Galveston's experiment after 1906.[26] In 1907, the same year he published "The City of Chicago," Turner secured the confession of assassin Harry Orchard, who in 1905 had killed Idaho's former governor. "The Confession and Autobiography of Harry Orchard," edited with an introduction by Turner, was published in the May issue of *McClure's*.[27] Through Turner, *McClure's* attained exclusive rights to publish Orchard's life story and confession in book form.[28] Turner's 1909 critique of the US Navy's lack of preparedness angered Theodore Roosevelt and prompted the president to greatly expand that branch of the military.[29] After the decline of muckraking, Turner spent much of the 1920s and 1930s writing fiction and screenplays for such films as *The Tip Off* and *Those Who Dance*.[30]

After the success of the Galveston article, Turner was sent to Chicago. McClure had been clipping stories of crime from the local dailies and was shocked by the number of Chicago murders, burglaries, and suicides in 1906. He instructed Turner to present Chicago as the anti-Galveston and write a follow-up to two earlier *McClure's* pieces: Josiah Flint's underworld series linking Chicago police and criminals, and Steffens's 1903 article on successful attempts by reformers to rid the city of crime and corruption.[31] The new story was to be called "Chicago as Seen by Herself," and the catalog of the newspaper clippings would speak for themselves, augmented by a preface from Turner.[32] Turner produced instead a detailed account of vice in Chicago's First and Eighteenth Wards that exposed linkages between new immigrants and elected officials.

Muckrakers are often characterized as the era's most vocal enemies of monopoly capitalism, but individual journalists' political sympathies were more heterogeneous than this representation suggests. While Turner's articles condemned industries that profited from vice, he felt that the Carnegies and Rockefellers played an important and positive role in a democratic society, a stance that distinguished him from *McClure's* earlier staff. Turner believed the accumulation of great wealth through monopolies was a logical outgrowth of capitalism. Breaking up trusts would lead to an unnecessary duplication of efforts.[33] Government wastefulness and corruption was a far greater threat than monopolies. The greatest economic threat to American society lay in the businesses of "dissipation"—liquor, prostitution, and gambling—and in the complex system of payoffs and joint ventures between breweries, ward bosses, saloon and brothel keepers, and the policemen who condoned and encouraged unrestrained vice. Turner's definition of good and bad profit seemed to turn on which ethnic groups were profiting in a given endeavor. The majority of monopoly capitalists were native-born Protestants, but vice districts were located where the city's poorest people lived, which, after the turn of the century, meant near the tenements where new immigrants clustered and in the neighborhoods where African Americans settled. While earlier *McClure's* writers like Baker and Steffens had produced some well-researched, insightful work on new immigrant groups and racial injustice, Turner's vice reports provided grist for a growing xenophobia that was finding its expression in political and scientific discourse at the time.[34] His nativist and racialized narratives of white slavery gave expression to deep-seated fears of new immigrant groups and African Americans, positing these populations as enemies of "Anglo-Saxon society."[35]

Turner singled out Jews, in particular, as active leaders of underworld vice. Prior to 1890, Jews represented only a small portion of the US population and went relatively unnoticed within American racial discourse, which to that point had focused largely on blacks and the Irish. In the 1890s Jews fleeing repression in eastern Europe began to arrive in the United States. At the same time, racial discourse around Jews began to shift. Native-born Americans linked the Jew to commerce and urbanization while representing this new racial group's seeming drive for financial success in ambivalent, often contradictory terms. According to Eric Goldstein, competing images of the Jew (mercenary, on one hand, and industrious and modern, on the other) found their expression in the opposed figures of the Jewish white slaver and the faithful protector of Jewish women.[36] Turner's exposés forged the former stereotype of the Jewish trafficker. Cast as radically other than the presumed native-born *McClure's* reader, Jews were portrayed as cunning and mercenary masterminds operating at the very center of vice economies.

DESCENT INTO BARBARISM: TURNER AND THE CHICAGO VICE TRUSTS

By 1907, Chicago had changed considerably in the twenty years since the WCTU's white slavery crusade. The city's population had tripled, surpassing two million in the year Turner arrived to document conditions there. Many of the new immigrants were from eastern and southern Europe. The eastern European Jews, Italians, Lithuanians, Czechs, Greeks, and Poles who moved to the city were widely discriminated against and viewed as racially inferior to more established and wealthier German, Scandinavian, and English immigrants. New arrivals clustered in tenements that occupied a belt stretching from Old Town in the northwest to the Bridgeport neighborhood in southwest Chicago, while the rapidly growing African American migrant population was forced into the "black belt" on the city's South Side.[37] After the turn of the century, Chicago's red-light districts and these South Side African American neighborhoods increasingly overlapped. Reformers were often as concerned about the black/white social interactions that occurred in these areas as they were about vice itself.[38]

During his investigation, Turner noticed the single, working-class women living in the city who were employed in the low-paying garment industry, as clerical workers, and in retail sales positions. The journalist claimed that these "low-paid employees of department stores and factories" provided the majority of the "English-speaking" prostitutes in Chicago.[39] Turner's observation was astute. An ideology of dependency that kept women's wages below subsistence level had created a high demand for women's labor. Employers acknowledged these low wages but argued that the income women earned was invariably supplemental. In fact, however, self-supporting women of all backgrounds and ages lived in Progressive Era Chicago, often in extreme hardship.[40] Many young, working-class women drifted in and out of the red-light districts, one of the few places they could earn a living during this period. According to historian Joanne Meyerowitz, "to avoid poverty, some women adrift, especially young women, chose to work in the one sector of the female labor force where an unskilled woman earned adequate wages—what might be called the sexual services sector."[41]

While some anti–white slavery activists viewed low wages as a factor driving women into prostitution, others disregarded economic forces as an explanation, arguing instead that prostitutes were victims of deception and trickery at the hands of new immigrants. Brian Donovan calls these differing explanations for white slavery "environmental" and "nativist."[42]

Many of the saloons, brothels, and gambling houses in 1907 were located in Chicago's notorious First Ward, which ran along Lake Michigan from the Chicago River down to Twenty-ninth Street. This ward encompassed Chicago's oldest red-light districts, the Levee and Little Cheyenne, as well as the Tenderloin and Custom House Place, which had sprung up to accommodate visitors to the World's Fair. In 1907 Democratic aldermen "Bathhouse John" Coughlin and Michael "Hinky Dink" Kenna held a tight rein on the First Ward. Brothel operators were forced to pay monthly tribute to Coughlin and Kenna; failure to pay typically resulted in a police raid. The police received bribes to look the other way when periodic waves of reform swept through the red-light districts. Saloon and brothel operators in this ward were required to purchase tickets to Coughlin and Kenna's annual campaign fund-raiser, the First Ward Ball, a debaucherous "who's who" of Chicago (and occasionally New York) vice that grew so large by 1904 it was relocated to the Chicago Coliseum. In addition to serving as alderman, Kenna ran the Workingman's Exchange, a saloon that also offered free lunches to the poor. In a 1904 interview, he told Jules Huret, "This is where we make voters. They drink 12,000 glasses of beer a week in my place."[43]

Turner's exposé took note of the shifting immigrant population, women's inadequate wages, and rampant corruption in the First Ward. Steeped in Spencerian evolutionary thought, the article portrayed a society pulled in two directions along a barbarism-civilization continuum. The exposé located organized prostitution and its profits within a national crime wave gripping Chicago, Pittsburgh, and San Francisco, and promised to expose the forces "dragging [these cities], according to the record of their own press, into a state of semi-barbarism."[44] For Turner, urban pockets of neobarbarism threatened to pull the entire nation into a state of savagery. The "European peasant" and the "vicious negro from the countryside of the South" were the primary sources of "savage crime" in Chicago (580). The actions of these "criminal" populations were a direct threat to an Anglo-Saxon civilization that had built "up painfully . . . definite, orderly rules of life—work, marriage, the constant restraint of the gross and violent impulses of appetite" (576).

Turner's Chicago piece drew on episodic accounts of crime in daily newspapers but absorbed these isolated incidents into a larger institutional frame, tracing the existence of "an elaborate organization—financial and political—for creating and attracting and protecting the criminal" (575). A vast business in "dissipation" had grown up around the "rough and hairy tribes which have been drawn into Chicago" (578). Deliberately easy access to liquor, drugs, gambling, and prostitution created conditions under which murders, robbery, and suicide flourished. At the center of the conspiracy were the brewing interests that encouraged every immigrant with two hundred dollars to open a saloon. Fierce competition among saloons insured that only those with side businesses in prostitution and gambling survived, leading to "a high and successful premium on the criminal saloon" (579).

The report turned to prostitution after carefully detailing the profits made by the largest liquor interests. According to Turner, four large interests had a stake in prostitution: hotels, brothels, dance halls and saloons, and "the men—largely Russian Jews—who deal in women for the trade" (581). While the small establishments "cater[ed] to the demand for ruining young girls," especially the English-speaking ones, most of the new prostitutes were Jewish, supplied by "a loosely organized association extending through the large cities of the country." These women were cheaper than native-born prostitutes, subject to what is now known as debt bondage, and unable to profit from the trade because they gave "a large share of their earnings" to the men who supplied them. Prostitutes' life expectancy ran from "five to ten years," and they often "acquired some drug habit" toward the end of their careers. Cocaine was the drug of choice in Chicago, even though it caused "various acute hallucinations—the most characteristic of which is the belief that worms are crawling just underneath the skin." Users of cocaine "often slash their skin with a knife in an attempt" to rid themselves of these worms (582). Turner's two-page discussion of Chicago prostitution concluded with the following summation:

> The chastity of woman is at the foundation of Anglo-Saxon society. Our laws are based on it, and the finest and most binding of our social relations. Nothing could be more menacing to a civilization than the sale of this as a commodity. To the average individual woman concerned, it means the expectation of death [in] under ten years; to practically all the longer survivors, a villainous and hideous afterlife. There is great profit in this business, however. Chicago has it organized—from the supplying of young girls to the drugging of the older and less salable women out of existence—with all the nicety of modern industry. As in the stockyards, not a pound of flesh is wasted. (582)

"The City of Chicago" proved to be *McClure's* biggest commercial success of 1907. Though its portrayal was dismal, papers like the Republican-leaning *Chicago Daily Tribune* largely embraced the exposé's representation of the city, in part because the article appeared in the same month that Fred Busse, the city's new Republican mayor, was inaugurated. The daily expressed great certainty that Busse's administration would take on corruption, putting an end to Chicago's reputation as the center of bossism and a haven for criminals. The paper said that, though it was important to "disprove or confirm" his facts, Turner's characterization was apt. Portions of the exposé seemed "exaggerated," but there was still "much truth in the statements made in *McClure's* about evil conditions in Chicago." The paper concluded by championing a vagrancy act to drive "criminals and the hobos" out of Chicago and the formation of a grand jury inquiry into corruption in the First and Eighteenth Wards.[45] The *Chicago Daily Tribune* returned to the topic the following week. "A 'Bad City'" stated that "the article, which has stirred up so much ill feeling among our esteemed contemporaries, seems to us to be largely founded in fact." It lambasted the city for allowing criminals and vagrants to lodge, eat, and drink more cheaply in Chicago than in other cities, expressing embarrassment that the itinerant and poor "look upon Chicago as a luxurious city [in which] to live." Finally, it called for the creation of photographic records of criminals so that they could be identified and "driven out of town."[46]

While this initial commentary might suggest that Turner's "The City of Chicago" was read as a text focusing on crime and vice broadly construed, Turner's narrative was ultimately taken up and deployed by other writers and reform movements as primarily a text about prostitution. His vice exposé helped consolidate a number of Chicago-based anti-prostitution efforts into a more streamlined campaign against white slavery. Committee of Fifteen President Clifford W. Barnes later wrote that "it was during the summer of 1907 that Chicago was startled out of her usual attitude of indifference toward commercialized vice by a series of shocking revelations, which indicated that our city was the center of a well organized traffic in women, a very real white slave market."[47] A number of Chicago anti-vice reformers went on to build careers around the fight against sex trafficking. As concerns about domestic white slavery intensified in subsequent years, the city produced some of the nation's most prolific anti-trafficking prosecutors, legislators, and publicists.

Clifford G. Roe was assistant to the Illinois State's Attorney when Turner's revelations broke. In 1906, Roe had prosecuted two cases that left him wondering whether the use of physical force and coercion to lure women into brothels was common in the red-light districts. One such case was that of twenty-year-old "Agnes," who claimed she had been drugged by a man she accompanied to a dance hall. When she woke up, she found herself in Panzy Williams's brothel. Williams, described as a "negress madam," brutalized her, holding her under threat of force until she worked off a contrived debt. Roe successfully argued Agnes's case, and the judge declared Williams guilty. This verdict, according to Roe, was deeply unpopular with the "babbling throng" outside the courtroom, which concurred with the defense attorney that Agnes had fabricated a sob story.[48] Roe, however, firmly believed her story and began to wonder whether she was one of many women in Chicago with similar tales to tell. Roe asked, "Were these isolated cases, or were they specific instances of a well defined traffic? They had aroused in me a suspicion that a slave traffic in girls had been secretly developed and was being carried on, hidden from public notice."[49] Roe's question was in part answered by "The City of Chicago" and its account of organized prostitution, which provided a larger framework for his efforts.

Roe went on to become a tireless prosecutor of trafficking cases and the period's most prolific author of white slavery books. Financial backing from a group of five wealthy Chicagoans in the summer of 1907 allowed Roe to work exclusively on prostitution cases. After Illinois passed the nation's first pandering laws in 1909, Roe convicted hundreds of alleged white slavers as a private attorney.[50] In 1911 he conducted a year-long undercover investigation into white slavery in New York City that was funded by John D. Rockefeller Jr. Roe's books, *Panders and Their White Slaves*, *Horrors of the White Slave Trade*, and *The Girl Who Disappeared*, tell of his exploits as a criminal attorney, recount victims' stories, chronicle the history of the Progressive Era campaign against white slavery, and urge continued action on behalf of the largely native-born white girls whose stories he tells.[51]

Among the other Chicagoans who became anti-trafficking crusaders and white slavery publicists after 1907 was Hull House operator Jane Addams, who wrote *A New Conscience and an Ancient Evil* in response to the system of white slavery in the city.[52] Of all the white slavery books that emerged from Chicago during this period, Addams's is the most nuanced, exploring the social and economic conditions that lead to forced prostitution and focusing on the lives and experiences of new immigrant populations rather than marking them as intrinsically criminal. Unlike Roe, Addams believed that several factors might lead a woman into prostitution, and that each case was different. Some women entered sex economies because of low wages in other economic sectors, while other women desired excitement and economic independence. A portion of women had been coerced into the trade, and a segment of prostitutes had been sexually abused by male family members when they were children. This multifactorial understanding of prostitution led Addams to endorse a variety of approaches to curbing it, including women's suffrage, curfews, surveillance of places of amusement, better wages for women, and stronger criminal laws against panderers.

Another Chicagoan who rose to prominence during the white slavery episode was Ernest A. Bell, superintendent of the Midnight Mission, a converted brothel on Clark Street that served as a rescue home for prostitutes. A proselytizer by night and anti-vice organizer by day, Bell edited the best-selling white slavery book of his generation, *Fighting the Traffic in Young Girls*, a five-hundred-page tome that sold more than four hundred thousand copies.[53] The book featured essays by key members of the abolition movement, including religious leaders, attorneys, and physicians. The collection sits at the intersection of shifting sites of cultural authority; essays recounting the Midnight Mission's efforts to bring young men traveling through red-light districts into the arms of Christ appeared alongside medical chapters describing the effects of syphilis on the body.

Fighting the Traffic was also engaged in a significant battle over the cultural meaning of the urban landscape. It attempted to recast sites of potential pleasure, including dance halls, movie theaters, ice cream parlors, and candy shops, as places of potential peril where procurers sought unsuspecting girls. In this sense, it mapped out an urban geography of danger for young women. Moral reformers like Bell viewed these bright, tempting urban spaces as sinful, enticing youth into an ugly world of vice. One illustration featured a shadowed man escorting a pretty young woman into a dance hall with a sign adjacent to its entrance advertising hotel rooms "by day or week." The caption read: "Dangerous Amusements—The Entrance to Hell Itself."[54] This illustration suggests that the modern city was a simmering, Babylonian inferno.

The pantheon of Chicago-based white slavery publicists also included Jean Turner Zimmermann. Physician, missionary, and president of the Chicago Rescue Mission and Women's Shelter, Zimmermann produced the pamphlet *Chicago's Black Traffic in White Girls*.[55] She did not conceal her preference for Anglo-Saxon stock in this anti–white slavery tract. Her prefatory remarks excluded all other "races" from the category American: "White Slavery, as it exists to-day in Chicago, is almost entirely under foreign control. . . . Almost without exception the Levee and White Slave resorts in the segregated districts are under the direct ownership of the moral and civic degenerates of the French, Italian, Syrian, Russian, Jewish, or Chinese races—once in a great while you may find a German or Swedish whoremaster, but very seldom. An American or Englishman conducting such a business is almost entirely unknown."[56] Zimmermann went on to become a leading author, writing on so-called yellow slavery and publishing the virulently racist *White or Yellow? A Story of America's Great White Slave Trade with Asia* later in the decade.[57]

ILLINOIS LEGISLATORS AND THE LEGAL RESPONSE TO WHITE SLAVERY

For readers of *McClure's* in Chicago and elsewhere, news of organized prostitution confirmed that moral degeneracy and turpitude had finally overtaken Chicago. Several regional and national strategies to contain the alleged traffic in women were initiated, and some had unanticipated and far-reaching effects. On June 12, 1909, Illinois passed the nation's first pandering act, which criminalized the "cadets" who used threats and other coercive means to entrap women in the sex economy. The new law made white slavery convictions easier to obtain. Those found guilty of pandering spent up to a year in prison for their first conviction and up to ten years for their second.[58] Chicago's anti-vice reformers viewed the passage of this law as a critical victory in the campaign against prostitution and white slavery.[59]

In the same year that the pandering act was debated and passed in the Illinois House, federal legislation to curb domestic white slavery was proposed in the Senate by Illinois Congressman James R. Mann, a moderate Republican who had been instrumental in creating the Pure Food and Drug Act of 1906. Mann had just been appointed as chairman of the Committee on Interstate and Foreign Commerce when he was encouraged by US District Attorney and anti-trafficking crusader Edwin W. Sims to sponsor and draft a bill that would use the federal government's authority to regulate interstate commerce to crack down on sex trafficking. The White Slave Traffic Act, also known as the Mann Act, was signed into law in 1910 and proved to be one of the twentieth century's most repressive domestic laws. This legislation prohibited the transportation of unmarried women across state lines for "immoral purposes" and established the maximum punishment for such an act to be a fine of five thousand dollars and imprisonment for five years. The vague reference to "immoral purposes" expanded the range of possible Mann Act convictions. For decades, all that was needed for a successful Mann Act prosecution was an unmarried man and woman, a state line, and an allegation by federal authorities that the two intended to commit "immoral" acts at the destination point.[60]

The need to investigate and prosecute Mann Act charges led to the formation and rapid expansion of the Bureau of Investigation, precursor to the FBI. To enforce the Mann Act, the bureau initiated the first attempt to establish a national database on segments of the citizenry. In 1911, the nascent bureau devised a plan, first unveiled to a broad constituency of anti-vice crusaders and only later to Congress, to create a central file of known prostitutes working in the country. This scheme led to the bureau's rapid growth, extending its reach across the United States and formalizing it as the first national policing institution. These early data-collection strategies related to white slavery ultimately primed the agency for the ascendance of an obsessive record-keeper like Hoover.[61]

Abolitionist organizations, whose early support had been key to establishing the Bureau of Investigation, expressed initial skepticism about the prostitute census plan. Stanley Finch, the bureau's special commissioner for the suppression of the white slave trade, appealed aggressively to these reformers, speaking at conferences and writing for their journals, eventually assuaging fears that the bureau's plan diverged from the broader goal of abolishing prostitution. Finch's public relations efforts ultimately won the support of the nation's two largest social purity organizations by convincing them that the importance of providing information about missing white slaves outweighed concerns that the census plan tacitly condoned prostitution.

By 1912, the plan was under way in Baltimore, Washington, DC, and Richmond, Virginia.[62] A handful of agents set out to identify local brothels and enlist madams in what was presented as a heroic effort to track the movement of prostitutes across the United States. Madams were expected to complete forms detailing the "departure of any girl" and her presumed destination. The cards additionally asked for the name, age, and description of the departed girl, as well as the "street number and house where she first practiced prostitution, a list of sporting houses where she has lived for the past year, a list of all the cities where she has been an inmate of sporting houses, and length of time in each city."[63] Finch next appealed to Congress for hundreds of additional agents to expand the cataloguing scheme to all cities with populations greater than four thousand. The American Vigilance Association and the World's Purity Association responded by organizing a monumental letter-writing campaign on the bureau's behalf.

The prostitute census plan enabled the bureau to grow from an enfeebled agency with a small centralized staff to a formidable organization with 10 full-time employees and 220 local "white slave officers" stationed in cities across the United States. A synergy between print journalism, federal bureaucrats, and anti-vice reformers in the early twentieth century helped reconstitute relations between localities and the federal government. The Mann Act and the Bureau of Investigation shaped and transformed sexual geographies on a national scale. But far from cracking down on prostitution's middlemen, those who enforced the act used it as a pretext to prosecute a range of practices, including political radicalism, adultery, and interracial relations. One example of the indiscriminate and discriminatory application of the Mann Act was the conviction of African American boxer Jack Johnson. In 1913, Johnson was charged with violating the Mann Act after crossing a state line with his future wife, Lucille Cameron, who was white. Cameron refused to testify against Johnson, and he was acquitted of all charges. Determined to get a conviction, bureau agents next charged Johnson for having crossed state lines with another white woman, Belle Schreiber, in 1909—before the Mann Act had passed. Schreiber testified against Johnson before an all-white jury, which found Johnson guilty. Johnson, who fled the country after his conviction, served a year in prison in 1920.[64] The Mann Act gave state borders new meanings while materially regulating the movement of women and criminalizing interracial couples. It was used strategically to prevent racial mixing and as a political tool against radicals like Charlie Chaplin. Furthermore, the Bureau of Investigation's intensive efforts to survey prostitutes did not result in measures that protected women, but amounted to a ratcheting up of surveillance and policing of their activities.

How did "The City of Chicago" differ from Stead's "The Maiden Tribute"? Stead's work on sexual slavery was directly involved with Parliament and pending legislation, and thus was both strategic and aimed at producing specific institutional effects. Muckraking pieces like Turner's were strategic only in a pecuniary sense, using populist rhetoric to arouse concerns over a variety of vice issues in a mass audience. Turner and McClure hoped to produce a mass effect and invoke a scandal that was neither aimed specifically at the federal government nor meant to achieve the passage of specific legislation. Rather, they sought to reach a national audience that would come to identify itself as such. They thus evoked nativist and anti-Semitic sentiments together with anti-monopoly populism to create an image of enemies working in concerted manner to threaten white women. The white female body came to stand in for national identity and served as a trope of the threatened nation. In this sense, Turner's and McClure's deployment of sensationalism was only strategic in a business sense of attracting audiences and advertising revenue; unlike Stead's, it was not intended to produce specific political changes. (The only targeting was the demonization of specific ethnic groups.) The ultimate effect of Turner's Chicago piece came not from the story itself, but from the response it elicited in Chicago and elsewhere, which centered on local and national vulnerability and resulted in the expansion of institutions that were themselves deployed diffusely and not necessarily against the original object of concern.

Illinois was the center of such early legislation to combat white slavery. The pandering act and the federal Mann Act were both spearheaded and championed by legislators, attorneys, and reform organizations in the state. Between 1907 and 1909, when they were first proposed, there was little scrutiny of white slavery claims—certainly not in Chicago, where earnest reformers had different views about the causes of white slavery but largely agreed that it was a problem of great scope and severity. "The City of Chicago" did not produce consensus, but it did generate an ephemeral experience of nationalism that was grounded in perceptions of collective victimization. This feeling of vulnerability stretched beyond the alleged female victims and helped shore up national boundaries and strengthen state institutions by ratcheting up security. However, challenges to the very existence of white slavery began to arise once *McClure's* turned the muckraking spotlight on organized prostitution in New York City.

TURNER AND NEW YORK CITY'S DAUGHTERS OF THE POOR

If "The City of Chicago" represented prostitution as part of a vice triad that consisted of sexual commerce, gambling, and liquor, the report's reception in Chicago and elsewhere convinced McClure and Turner that prostitution was a key means of inciting scandal. *McClure's* revisited the topic of vice in 1909 with three strategically timed articles on political corruption in New York City. The first, "The Control of New York by Professional Criminals: A Study of a New Period of Decadence in the Popular Government of Great Cities," appeared in April. In this exposé Turner described how the Irish, who had traditionally controlled Tammany Hall, had adapted to the influx of Jews and Italians to the city. He described new alliances that had developed between Tammany and the new Jewish and Italian criminal organizations that controlled prostitution in the city. Once again, Turner placed the Jew at the center of moral decline: "Out of the Bowery and Red Light districts had come the new development in New York politics—the great voting power of the organized criminals. It was a notable development, not only for New York, but for the country at large. And no part of it was more noteworthy than the appearance of the Jewish pimp, a product of New York politics, who has vitiated, more than any other single agency, the moral life of great cities of America in the past ten years."[65]

The exposé also described the annual St. Patrick's Day celebration, portraying one adored Tammany leader, Timothy "Big Feller" Sullivan, as surrounded by "a grand march of a thousand pimps and thieves and prostitutes" who sang "to the blatant crying of the band: 'Sullivan, Sullivan, a damned fine Irishman!'"[66] While "The Control of New York by Professional Criminals" focused on obstruction of the popular vote through the deployment of "repeaters," criminals who cast multiple votes for Tammany politicians, *McClure's* October 1909 follow-up piece focused exclusively on organized prostitution. Hoping for a publishing success and political scandal, *McClure's* ran advertisements in other monthlies announcing Turner's "The Daughters of the Poor." An ad in *Collier's* promoted the piece as "the most startling and important article published in years—a plain story . . . of how the White Slave Trade in American girls developed in New York under Tammany Hall and has spread to every large city of the United States."[67] This exposé, accompanied by McClure's "Tammanyizing of a Civilization," went into circulation a week before the city's general election, forcing the issue of white slavery into the mayoral campaign. Tammany candidate William J. Gaynor sought to distance himself from Turner's charges, but the other candidates, William Randolph Hearst and Otto Bannard, vowed, if elected, to take immediate action against white slavery.

An ancillary of the Democratic Party in New York City, Tammany Hall had ruled the city intermittently since the 1840s by establishing a system of bribes and payments in return for votes. By 1850s it was fully enmeshed with saloon culture, deriving its political base from these primarily male establishments. Saloon keepers, in particular, wanted to insure that their businesses were safe from temperance reformers, so they allied with Tammany in exchange for protection. Tammany used intimidation as well as electioneering to win elections for the Democrats. With the help of saloon keepers, who wanted to keep operating costs down and ensure that reformers would not mount successful campaigns to shut them down, Tammany was able to organize gangs of voters and ballot-stuffers, as well as to engage in organized campaigns of intimidation. In the 1870s it seemed that Tammany had been crushed by reformers, including anti-vice vigilance committees. However, the organization gained strength in the 1890s. Republicans and Fusion Party members made some inroads after 1894, when the Lexow Investigation went public with the results of its inquiry into corruption and vice in the city, but a Tammany Hall Democrat, Robert A. Van Wyck, was elected as mayor in 1889, undoing many of the reforms put in place by the previous governor. The Committee of Fifteen published its famous inquiry into prostitution and vice in New York City in 1901. The publicity surrounding the committee's findings helped assure Republican Seth Low's mayoral victory in 1902. Tammany suffered only temporary defeat, however; Democratic mayors ran the city for the next ten years.[68]

Unlike "The City of Chicago," "The Daughters of the Poor" was international in scope, historical in approach, and focused exclusively on the business of prostitution. It asserted that there were three centers of white slave activity: Lemberg, Paris, and New York. Turner offered a history of the procurer ("cadet"), tracing the emergence of this figure from the Middle Ages to the present. He argued that until 1850 prostitution existed in New York "without having attracted the business management of men to securing and exploiting its supplies." The first group to prey on immigrant women in New York's slums was the "French *maquereau*," but each successive wave of immigration led to an increased organization of the trade and a shift in who controlled the city's sex economy. The French *maquereau* was not adapted to conduct the business in the self-governing American municipalities because he "had no direct political influence, and obtained his right to break the law simply by payments of money." Not until the 1880s—amid a wave of Austrian, Russian, and Hungarian Jewish immigrants—would the trade be established on "its present firm footing." Initially, Jewish procurers found supplies of women in small industrial towns along the East Coast. As the population of New York City increased, the size of the trade did as well, so that by 1907 most of the girls were coming from "the tenement districts of the East Side."[69]

Weaving together an elaborate story of "slum politics" in New York, the article implicated Tammany Hall and the New York Independent Benevolent Association, a Jewish group dealing in funeral arrangements, in a widespread prostitution operation. According to Turner, the Independent Benevolent Association trained cadets in Newark, New Jersey. Once properly trained in the skill of procuring, these men were imported to New York City, where they served the double function of generating funds for city coffers and constituting a pro–Tammany Hall voting bloc. Tammany Hall, in turn, funded its programs and favors for the poor with profits from prostitution. As the business boomed, not only was the East Side "producing its own supplies"; it was also "exporting them" to such countries as Argentina and South Africa, where "fortunes were acquired" and reinvested in New York gambling houses and "Raines-law" hotels.[70] With the rise of the Jewish cadet, New York became the epicenter of the global sex trade, a business without boundaries: "After South Africa the New York dealers went by hundreds to the East—to Shanghai and to Australia; they followed the Russian army through the Russo-Japanese war; they went into Alaska with the gold rush, and into Nevada; and they have camped in scores and hundreds on the banks of the new Panama Canal. However, the foreign trade was not large compared with the trade with the cities of the United States, which was to develop later. The demand was naturally not so great."[71]

After Tammany Hall was temporarily defeated in the election of 1901, "Jewish operators" relocated from New York to cities like Philadelphia, Chicago, San Francisco, and St. Louis. With each move they "secured their supplies of women—largely young immigrant girls—from New York, and retrained their New York cadets" (51). Turner made the bold claim that every urban, prostitution-related scandal since then had resulted directly from this exodus of Jewish traffickers from New York (52).

After describing at length how the demise of gambling led to the ascent of organized prostitution, Turner moved to a discussion of the East Side immigrant girls themselves. In the past the girls had been predominantly German and Irish, but now "the odds in life are from birth strongly against the young Jewish-American girl." Jewish girls, according to Turner, were at a disadvantage because their sole purpose in the Jewish family was to contribute to the education of their brothers. At the same time, there was "an acute horror among the Jews of the state of being an old maid" that made "swindling of Jewish women under promise of marriage particularly easy" (54–55). According to Turner, much of the procurement of girls—especially German, Polish, and Italian girls—occurred at East Side dance halls. Calling New York "the national center of the procurer," Turner concluded his piece by describing a discussion he had with a ward politician at a Raines-law hotel, in which the Tammany supporter described the advantages to the poor of voting Tammany: "When a widow's in trouble, we see she has her hod of coal; when the orphans want a pair of shoes, we give it to them." Sitting in the hotel, however, gave the author a glimpse of how these benevolent acts were financed: "The procession of the daughters of the East Side filed by the open door upstairs with their strange men. It was the slum leader's common transaction. Having wholesaled the bodies of the daughters at a good profit, he rebates the widow's hod of coal" (60–61).

McClure's "The Tammanyization of Civilization" accompanied Turner's piece. This article provided a history of how Tammany Hall had corrupted the American political system. McClure characterized Tammany as a primitive, anti-civil organization, not steeped in the civilized manners of deliberative, representative democracy that had been cultivated in England.

The organization had tried for fifty years to "degrade the population," but the acceleration in the rise of cities had contributed to its greater success.[72] In this process of dragging the nation from civilization to barbarism, the traffic in women was the lowest point and the most significant achievement of the forces of barbarism. For McClure, Progressive Era America comprised two broad social groups: the civilized ones, largely hailing from Germany and England, and the uncivilized intruders from "primitive" societies and races, which included southern and eastern Europeans, Jews, and "negroes." The primitives were unable to grasp the fundamental immorality of trafficking in women. McClure asserted that civilized people would experience "a deep-seated and instinctive disgust . . . for this transaction." The traffic in women was by far the worst scourge in the history of civilization because it aimed "at the disintegration and degradation of a civilization, and the social training of centuries—set in the bones and marrow of the race—revolts against it."[73] McClure blamed Tammany Hall, urbanization, and universal male suffrage for the threatened disintegration of civilized society. Extending "manhood suffrage" to primitives opened the possibility of using vice as a means to secure and maintain power. The inherent and unsublimated desire for alcohol and sex allowed Tammany to take advantage of these pliable male populations.[74]

The success of muckraking magazines depended on sustaining the myth that media institutions fused the power to disseminate information on a broad scale with an unyielding commitment to knowledge and truth, creating products that were necessarily put into the service of social betterment. It was in this spirit that *McClure's* commented on the political significance of Turner's exposés. In October 1910, the magazine described "The Daughters of the Poor" as "one of the most notable things that the magazine ever published. . . . [The piece was] largely instrumental in causing legislation dealing with the 'white slave' traffic to be passed in many States."[75] This encomium appeared in print just before a diverse group of private and public interests—including newspaper editors, threatened business leaders, and members of Tammany Hall—began to push back on the vice-trust narrative in an attempt to frame white slavery as more a question than a reality.

Indeed, Turner's April and October articles succeeded in inflaming Tammany Hall, especially "Big Feller" Sullivan, who controlled most of the Bowery. Angered by Turner's scandalous portrayal of Tammany, Sullivan threatened the journalist during an otherwise teary-eyed speech delivered on October 31 at the Miner's Bowery Theater:

> There's something here written by a gentleman named Turner. He's not so bad even if he has been writing horrible stuff, but I can't say as much for the people who have been paying him. I've been looking Turner up. He's got three children and a wife, and they might have been starving. A man who is starving will do anything.
>
> In an article he wrote last April about the Lawrence Mulligan Ball he said that in the grand march the women were of questionable virtue and the men worse. I've got right here in my hand a list of one hundred couples in the march. It ain't no phony list, and the reporters can take it and look up the names and I'm here to say that they will find that every woman is a virtuous woman, and every man a decent man.
>
> Now we come to the last of all, the white slave talk. My God, they have put me in between thieves, and I'm not the first man who has been pilloried between thieves; I've been living here all my life and I never knew a man engaged in this business, and I won't stand for this; I'm not going to say anything, but this man Turner had better keep out of this district.[76]

In the months that followed, *McClure's* found itself blindsided as a debate over the trade's very existence began to take place not only in Tammany meeting places, but also in daily newspapers, criminal courtrooms, and in a New York grand jury inquiry into Turner's claims.

CONCLUSION

This chapter has described a shift from attacks on vice initiated by social movements to attacks originating in the mass media. The advertising and subscription revenues generated by national magazines in the early twentieth century for the first time allowed for the commissioning of large-scale investigative reports. The rise of national news magazines signaled a shift from a local and regional focus to a national one. *McClure's* and other muckraking magazines reported on localities as geographic segments of the nation as a whole, and they brought in national audiences and advertisers. Their national-scale operations allowed writers to discuss problems within specific municipalities as national social ills, reflecting a broader tendency toward the concentration of power and wealth at all levels. At the same time, muckraking coverage for the first time turned the national gaze on problems occurring in particular cities and regions.

While magazine-based investigative journalism was immensely popular in the first decade of the twentieth century, there were tensions between disparate segments of the audience for muckraking productions. Rather than fostering social movements, muckraking relied on political and moral reform movements as preconstituted audiences. This meant that they had to appeal to a limited number of tropes, like anti-monopolism, in order to bring together diverse readerships. With "The City of Chicago," McClure and Turner hoped to produce a mass effect by invoking a scandal built around national identity and exploiting anti-immigrant and anti-monopoly sentiment. Whereas Stead's work was strategic and directly aimed at influencing the passage of existing but languishing legislation, this exposé was only strategic in the financial sense: the magazine hoped to generate as large an audience possible for the issue in which "The City of Chicago" appeared. Any specific political or legislative consequences were welcome but not planned.

The response to the 1907 exposé included the rise of a powerful anti–white slavery movement among a variety of social activists in Chicago, the formation of a committee to address prostitution in the city, the passage of the pandering act, and increased coverage of white slavery in city papers. This exposé and the concern over white slavery that it triggered in Chicago also set the wheels in motion for federal anti–white slavery legislation in the form of the Mann Act and, eventually, the formation of the Bureau of Investigation. The response to Turner's 1909 articles focusing on New York City could not have been more different. Turner and McClure insinuated themselves into a municipal election, were subject to the scrutiny of the city's vast newspaper establishment, and became the objects of a grand jury investigation to determine the validity of Turner's claims about vice trusts.

How do we account for the strikingly different receptions that Turner's 1907 and 1909 pieces received? First, Turner did not write the Chicago article before an election but just after one in which the reform Republican won. The 1909 article, however, not only preceded an election, but it directly implicated Tammany Hall and specific politicians running for office, raising suspicions that *McClure's* had primarily political motivations in publishing the piece. The juxtaposition of the two articles in relation to local elections helps to explain some of the local differences in their reception, but does not explain why the response to the New York piece was so expansive.

In Chicago, Turner's work catalyzed the rise of preexisting social actors and movements to higher levels of prominence and power as they coalesced into a more organized social movement. The association between Turner and the new white slavery activists brought them prestige on both regional and national levels. By late 1909, however, the Mann Act was already being debated in Congress, and domestic white slavery activism was more common. Vigilance work against white slavery had a stronger foothold than it did in 1907 and did not necessarily need an inspirational piece like Turner's to goad it on. Instead, "The Daughters of the Poor" offered bald-faced politicking and racism that offended many and raised concern among immigrant groups and Jews, not to mention Tammany Hall politicians, whom it directly implicated. For business leaders and monopoly capitalists, for whom muckraking journalism had been anathema for some time, Turner's 1909 piece would ultimately provide a straw man that helped to discredit the entire endeavor of exposure journalism.

In "The City of Chicago," Turner made regional claims that resonated nationally. His statements about prostitution, however, were rather modest. Turner's broader depiction of the corruption of local politicians did not generate controversy. His claims about graft were already well established and even a source of pride among ward bosses. However, in "The Daughters of the Poor," Turner made claims on a global scale and linked them in a conspiratorial network that reached down to the local level. His allegations were far-reaching and unsubstantiated. Rather than creating a national identification of vulnerability and threat, the claims collapsed into a local political scandal and national media backlash.

The *McClure's* New York exposé incited a controversy involving diverse and unexpected institutions and actors. With the exception of scandalizing Tammany officials, the various responses that these exposés generated did not flow from the text, nor were the resulting changes instantiated as part of Turner or McClure's broader project or agenda. Particularly unanticipated was the surplus scandal that ensued after the New York piece. As chapters 5 and 6 demonstrate, the reappearance of claims of sensationalism in the muckraking era under a totally different rubric demonstrate that sensationalism and scandal are not based in, nor do they respond to, a type of form, but instead are processes that are at once discursive, strategic, and historically situated.

CHAPTER FIVE

Authorizing Skepticism: The *New York Times* and the Demise of Muckraking

> New York, the first in the development of this European trade in America, remains its center, and its procuring interests are the strongest and most carefully organized of all. The young cadet has his beginning, as well as the women he procures. These boys learn in the primary schools of the farther East Side, from the semipolitical gangs in the dance halls; step by step, as they grow in the profession, they graduate into the Third Assembly District, the chief "hangout" place of the procurer in the world. In all the East Side districts of Tammany Hall these youths have representatives who look out for their interests; but here two-thirds of the active workers are or have been interested in markets of prostitution.
> —George Kibbe Turner, "The Daughters of the Poor" (1909)

Until October 1909, the *New York Times* paid little attention to prostitution and even less to domestic sex trafficking. In 1906 the *Times* printed only three stories on prostitution-related issues, none of which referred to trafficking. In 1907, it ran a total of seven articles on prostitution, two of which mention white slavery. Two of the four stories printed on prostitution in 1908 dealt with the European white slave trade. Coverage in the *Times* dramatically increased after the 1909 publication of George Kibbe Turner's "The Daughters of the Poor," which turned the muckraker gaze on New York City's white slavery problem. Turner claimed that the city was the domestic epicenter of white slave trade activities and that top city officials were conspiring with the New York Independent Benevolent Association, a Jewish organization, to perpetuate the social evil. Appearing just prior to the city's municipal elections, Turner's allegations transformed white slavery into a front-burner issue in the race.[1] With a local election drawing near, the *Times* stepped up its coverage of trafficking and vice. A majority of its twenty-nine stories on prostitution in 1909 referred to white slavery. The paper's coverage of trafficking peaked in 1910 with ninety-four articles. Eighty-eight of these appeared between January and June of that year. By 1911, interest in the topic had run out, and the *Times* carried only eleven stories on prostitution.

After the 1909 election, the paper initially wrote about white slavery as a "real" phenomenon, but by June 1910 the editorial page began to take a skeptical stance toward muckraking allegations. Following Barbie Zelizer's suggestion that "over time, narrators are able to reposition themselves vis-à-vis original events, thereby reconfiguring their authority," this chapter examines how the daily's critical stance developed diachronically, and how the paper backtracked on its earlier endorsement of white slavery claims.[2] The *New York Times* wielded considerable influence among the social and political elite at the time the controversy occurred and played a starring role in the history of twentieth-century American journalism. According to Kevin Stoker, "The success of the *Times*, combined with its position as a trendsetter for the US press, helped validate objective reporting."[3] Among media historians, New York papers were widely considered to be the "bellwether of American journalism."[4]

While the *Times* had a smaller circulation relative to other New York dailies in 1909, the paper wielded a great deal of cultural authority among the city's upper classes.[5] Unlike *McClure's* or many of its local competitors, the *Times* sought a highly specific elite audience capable of purchasing the high-end products the paper routinely advertised. Whereas muckraking magazines were forever trying to expand the size of their audiences in order to attain maximum impact and advertising rates (and used anti-monopolistic rhetoric as one strategy to bring in mixed audiences of middle-class, general-interest readers; labor and anti-vice activists; fiction readers; and others), the *Times'* strategy was not to endlessly enlarge its audience, but to maintain the small audience it had. The paper achieved maximum impact not through mass distribution but by catering to an audience that wielded a disproportionate amount of economic, social, and political power—an audience for which select advertisers were willing to pay dearly.

A premise of this chapter is that the *New York Times'* stories on white slavery demonstrated a heightened level of recursiveness. The paper told stories about trafficking that both reflected elite concerns about the potentially disruptive role of the muckraking press in a capitalist democracy and promoted the paper's own status as a prestigious and accurate source of news. Much as Stead's work and its ensuing scandal caused major transformations in the media in both England and United States, influencing the acceptance of interviews in England, new understandings of sensationalism on both continents, and the rise of muckraking in the United States, so too did the controversy over muckraking and white slavery as portrayed in the *Times* generate subsequent debates that greatly shifted the credibility of news genres in favor of objectivity and away from muckraking. Because the ensuing scandals over media were distributed and consumed on a national scale through mass media, they were capable of producing large-scale effects, and they precipitated debates that led to widespread transformations in media practices and understandings.

The conflict described in this chapter between the *New York Times* and *McClure's*, fought out on the bodies of so-called white slaves and their procurers, was not necessarily over audiences, because *McClure's* and the *Times* were not competing for the same audience. It was, however, over dominance. One group threatened by muckraker accusations—monopoly capitalists and other business leaders—was not thrilled by Turner's characterization of white slave rings as "vice trusts."[6] Indeed, after eight years of investigative exposés targeting big business, many elites were interested in reasserting "moral, political, and intellectual leadership within [the] social system."[7] Coverage of white slavery in the *Times* both shaped and responded to the concerns of local and national elites. Stephen Reese asserts that journalism "has an interest in preserving the larger liberal, capitalist system by helping maintain the boundaries of acceptable political discourse." A paper written for an elite audience would necessarily struggle with this tension in its representation of white slavery.[8]

THE 1909 ELECTION

Turner's allegation that New York City was the epicenter of the white slave trade provoked responses from diverse quarters. The question of white slavery's truth or falsity shaped the ensuing controversy. Tammany leaders themselves promoted this framework. "The Daughters of the Poor" hit the stands a little more than a week before the municipal election, enraging members of the political organization, who feared Turner's claims would severely compromise Tammany candidates. Between October 25 and election day, Tammany officials went into public relations overdrive to publicly defame Turner, question his motives, and challenge his report's veracity. New York papers eagerly covered the battle that suddenly erupted between Tammany leaders and Turner. When Charles Murphy, Tammany Hall's leader, issued the following statement on the *McClure's* charges, the *New York Times*, *New York Sun*, and *New York Tribune* printed it in its entirety:

> It has remained for a man who is almost a total stranger to New York, but who speaks as if from intimate knowledge of a lifetime to make a statement which reeks with falsehood and is entitled to no credit whatever, save such as would be given to any other grossly exaggerated partisan campaign story published on the word of a hired slanderer in the columns of a muckraking and filth-throwing magazine reputed some months ago to be on the verge of insolvency, and desperately turning in every direction for something which would attract circulation and readers to it.[9]

Murphy provided a list of "historical facts" meant to prove that the muckraker's claims were self-interested and slanderous, not only to Tammany but to the entire city:

> That the territory referred to was filled all this time with representatives of the great Churches—Catholic, Protestant, and Jewish.
>
> That the great civic bodies, with all the reformers and sensation hunters, were in full blast.
>
> That the city is full of daily newspapers second to none in the world for enterprise, ingenuity, and ability.
>
> That Hearst, the second greatest sensationalist of the age, was publishing every day dozens of issues of his various papers.[10]

According to Murphy's logic, a vast and entrenched organization of white slavers would have difficulty operating outside the gaze of the city's moralizing churches, zealous reformers, and sensationalistic papers, a veritable urban, moral, industrial complex that kept the region under close surveillance.

That William Randolph Hearst himself—an interested party who was competing in the election against Tammany—had not produced similar exposés of Tammany's role in white slavery conspiracies is here presented as evidence proving Turner's account false. Here we see an interesting argument figuring the sensationalist local press (Hearst's *World*) as vigilant watchdog versus the muckraking national press (Turner) as self-serving slanderer. Any compliment here to Hearst is cleverly backhanded, as the clear implication is that Hearst would go to any length short of lying in using his publishing powers to malign his opponents. While the *Times* was not pro-Tammany, the paper undoubtedly found the castigation of Hearst's sensationalism and the portrayal of *McClure's* as a "muckraking and filth-throwing" magazine-in-decline quite hilarious. For the moment, Tammany and the *Times* had overlapping enemies.

The Democratic mayoral candidate, William J. Gaynor, tried to avoid making public claims about Turner's allegations, leaving that duty to the likes of Murphy and "Big Feller" Sullivan, but reporters, eager to inflame more controversy, hounded him for a response. His first statement on Turner was prefaced as follows: "None of your newspapers has my permission to use this without saying you asked for it. I am not volunteering it. You asked for it." As reported by the *New York Sun*, he went on to call Turner a "dirty fellow, whose own morals are below par," and then mused over the muckraker's name: "George Kibbe Turner. I do not know him, but how pretty his name. Just the kind of a name that does such things. No plain John Pearson or William Murphy ever knows all these refinements of viciousness." He called Turner a "mere political and racial bigot" who had an ignorant, superficial, and reckless "propensity to falsify which are the characteristics of the Hearst writers and which people have got on to at last." He went on to say that Turner was "a vulgar bigoted fellow trying to make political capital out of the fact that there is female prostitution in the city of New York, as there is everywhere in the world."[11] The following day, Gaynor proclaimed the article libelous.[12]

For the *New York Times*, at least, Tammany leaders successfully cast doubt on Turner's article. Following their lead, the paper conducted its own inquiry into Turner's investigative process. "White Slave Story False, Says Guide" quoted Turner's escort to New York City dance halls, described as an "honest" dance-academy owner. After visiting several dance halls, Turner reportedly grew frustrated over the paucity of overt vice occurring in these establishments. He eventually gave up on eyewitnessing the traffic in women and said, "Let's get to Tammany Hall; I'm sure I will get what I want there." When Turner and his guide arrived at Tammany Hall, they saw "a thousand couples attending a masque ball in honor of a Jewish festival," which further agitated the muckraker. Turner claimed a conspiracy to cast doubt on his piece was afoot because of his article's potential to sway the election away from Tammany, an institution "whose foundation is laid upon a variety of crime, the choicest among which is the sale of unfortunate women."[13]

In the days leading up to the November 2 election, Tammany Hall officials busily refuted "The Daughters of the Poor," while members of the opposition Fusion Party suggested that Turner's implication of Jewish organizations in white slavery was "bigoted," but that his identification of sexual trafficking as a social evil plaguing the city was largely accurate.[14] Jewish members of the Fusion Party embraced the anti-Tammany thrust of the muckraking article, but encountered a dilemma in addressing Turner's allegations. They had to defend themselves against anti-Jewish conspiracy theories while publicly committing themselves and their members to combat the trade whenever possible in order to demonstrate the sincerity of that defense.[15] Tammany, in turn, stepped up its rhetoric and called upon Turner and *McClure's* to produce proof of the trade's existence.[16] In addition to election wrangling, a number of groups mobilized to affirm or deny claims that white slave rings had proliferated under Tammany Hall. The Women's Municipal League conducted its own investigation, concluding that the city's employment agencies were complicit in directing young immigrant girls into the clutches of traffickers.[17] An umbrella organization representing more than three hundred Jewish groups signed a resolution in protest of *McClure's* charges.[18]

Despite Tammany's campaign to debase Turner and more general expressions of incredulity in the *Times*, the muckraking exposé likely succeeded in linking Tammany Hall and organized prostitution in the minds of the electorate. Gaynor, who had campaigned tirelessly, won the election handily, but the Fusion Party swept the lower posts, including controller; president of the Board of Alderman; the borough presidents of Manhattan, the Bronx, Brooklyn, and Queens; and district attorney.[19] It cannot be established with certainty that "The Daughters of the Poor" was responsible for the mass ouster of Tammany officials. However, *McClure's* white slavery charges dominated the press in the days leading up to the election and blindsided Tammany Hall, sending it into a desperate public relations tailspin. The considerable attention paid to white slavery surely had some bearing on the election's outcome.

THE RHETORIC OF REVELATION: THE *NEW YORK TIMES* (DIS)COVERS WHITE SLAVERY

The specter of white slavery endured after the November election. Turner's article had left many New Yorkers concerned that official corruption had hidden the existence of organized trafficking from public view. During the campaign, the Fusion Party had embraced Turner's claims and vowed to rid the city of white slaves. The popularity of the new district attorney, Charles S. Whitman, stemmed in part from his vocal pledge to cleanse the city of white slave rings, which he alleged placed all the area's women in grave danger. In October, Whitman had told voters that Turner's article, chronicling "an unspeakable, vile, and horrible condition," was accurate. He promised, "If I am elected, and if there is sufficient evidence brought to me, I shall . . . follow the thing up."[20] Armed with a check for twenty-five thousand dollars, Whitman set out to find these unfortunate victims in New York and prosecute their traffickers. Whitman's reputation rested upon this vow to rid the city of white slavery, but his election placed him in the unenviable position of having to find these dealers in white women.

Whitman first had to find evidence of criminal activity, a potentially difficult task, given that invisibility was a publicized hallmark of the traffic. If a white slave trade did exist in New York at that point, it was taking place outside the glow of the city's lamplights. The signs that tend to incite criminal investigation—the murdered body, the battered face, the vial of "knockout drops" carelessly left near the crime scene—were absent. In their place were endless trails of media accounts illuminating, to the public's horror and fascination, elaborate underground vice syndicates that preyed on society's most innocent members. Such widely circulated cultural representations as the *McClure's* exposé and other spin-off productions served as evidential touchstones and guidebooks for local investigators in pursuit of white slavery.

As *Times* coverage turned increasingly toward Whitman's local investigation, a number of changes in the way white slavery was represented, understood, and made visible to a mass audience occurred. In April 1910, the district attorney's office held a press conference announcing that the first phase of his inquiry into the sexual slave trade was complete. The first article in the *Times* series on this investigation, "White Slave Traffic Shown to Be Real," detailed the arrest of two presumed leaders in the trade. Readers learned that the district attorney had solicited the help of two undercover college women, graduates of Radcliffe and Smith, to track down traffickers in the city. These agents managed to outwit two of New York's most cunning criminals. Equipped with notepads, the investigators spent months in the city's seamiest vice district gathering information on the shape and extent of New York's white slave trade and searching out suppliers of white women. The women were described as possessing "character and experience," as suitably dressed for their role, and as being "skilled in investigation, but unknown in New York."[21] According to the district attorney's statement, their skills gained them the trust of Tenderloin denizens, and they eventually managed to hammer out a deal with ringleaders in the traffic. Their negotiations led to the purchase of four alleged white slaves and the capture of two major figures implicated in a white slavery ring linking points in the Northeast to destinations as far west as Seattle and Anchorage.

As reported by the *New York Times*, these central figures were Harry Levinson (a.k.a. Harry Shapiro and Harry Druckman), and Belle Moore, a self-proclaimed manicurist described in the article as a "light mulatto."[22]

The rhetorical force of the story, however, derives from a description of the white slaves whose freedom the undercover investigators allegedly purchased. The hard-crime genre mingles with the sentimental as one girl is described as "disconsolate over the loss of her teddy bear," while another is said to have "brought nothing with her except a tattered doll . . . [that] was dearer to her than anything else in all her unlovely world."[23] Such markers of youth acted to settle a debate over the girls' ages: they claimed to be eighteen; Belle Moore contended that they were slightly younger; while the district attorney (DA) stated definitively that they were "only 15." Yet as the series developed over time, the doll and teddy bear came to figure ironically, as manufactured props in a sham production. Notions of free choice, age, and agency eventually intruded into the narrative of innocent girls in bondage, just as the connotations of *white slavery* itself became increasingly problematic.

Read in the context of previous *Times* coverage of white slavery, this article revealed a distinct ambivalence about the very terms it used to describe white slavery: its framing of the problem as one of reality versus fiction and the repeated use of quotation marks around key phrases cast doubt on the phenomenon it otherwise asserted to be "real." The headline, "White Slave Traffic Shown to Be Real," signaled a reluctance to embrace the concept of white slavery, and the consistent placement of quotation marks around the label *white slavery* and the word *bought* when describing the investigators' purchase of the girls similarly suggest a lingering doubt. Yet such statements as "There is a real traffic in 'white slaves' in this city" and "[The college women] have brought unmistakable evidence that the trade has existed for years" acted as counterpoint to this skepticism, suggesting that the writer's perspective had undergone a transformation from incredulity to a state of tentative belief.[24] The girls' story was said to have "stirred even men grown callous in the atmosphere of the Criminal Court Building."[25] Was the writer, as witness to the proceedings, including himself in this assortment of case-hardened men? Had the rhetorically potent mix of "hard" evidence provided by the DA harnessed to the sentimentalized representation of compromised femininity likewise awakened a sleeping compassion within this journalist? In a short month, this resurgence of simpering emotionalism would be put to rest.

This front-page article would soon propel the *New York Times* into something of a journalistic crisis. The paper's relationship to vice and crime reporting was already strained due to a journalistic turf war that had raged among New York dailies since at least the 1890s. As the investigation moved from the streets into the courtroom, the story was revealed as an elaborate ruse, a charade with stock characters played by second-rate actors unable to sustain their performances when placed on the stage of justice. The paper that built its reputation by eschewing sensationalism was thus put in the position of accounting for and defending its earlier articles. The public relations solution to this predicament was to portray the *Times* as a detached observer and recorder of a story that was in the midst of unraveling, while projecting a retrospective delight that "reason" had prevailed over anecdotal sensationalism. In fact, the *Times'* foray into sensationalism would ultimately serve a didactic purpose, lending credence to new developments in the journalistic profession that installed formal and institutional buffers between reporters and the streets.

FROM SENTIMENTALITY TO SKEPTICISM: WHITE SLAVERY ON TRIAL

If muckraking articles and the DA turned the public spotlight on white slavery in New York City, the *Times* kept it there by printing two or three weekly updates on the investigation's status. Since few new events related to the investigation had transpired, several articles were devoted to filling in missing details of the investigation itself. Readers' mental picture of white slavery's workings became clearer as more "insider knowledge" about the trade was offered via the college investigators, whose names were consistently omitted in order to "shield the two women in the dangerous paths into which their work took them."[26] Readers learned that the white slaves had price tags of $20 each for the two foreign girls and $60 each for the native-born ones. They also discovered that one of the four girls, said to be eleven years old, was promised by the traffickers but never produced. In the midst of bartering for her, news came that she had broken her leg and disappeared. The story indicated that "if they can find her now, and they are searching everywhere, the investigators hope to prefer charges of kidnapping," which carried a heavier sentence.[27] Several statements testifying to the effects of the investigation on Tenderloin activities were printed: "One large dealer declared to the agents that though two years ago he could have sold them all the girls they wanted for $5 to $10 apiece, he would not risk selling one now for $1000."[28] Such quotations lent much credence to the DA's work to combat white slavery. As news of the investigation spread throughout the city via the *Times* and other city papers, thousands of New Yorkers sent in letters and checks in support of the DA's activities. With the exception of the quotation marks around "white slavery" in these *Times* articles, any previous suspicion and doubt had been cast off in favor of thoroughgoing support for the investigation, its effects, and its compelling story line. *Times* readers were encouraged to indulge in each shocking revelation. Had they received the story from New York's more sensationalistic papers, the special combination of horror and fascination that white slavery induced in the public would have been a guilty pleasure at best. In the hands of the *Times*, however, the titillation became rationalized through the initial appeal to reality.

The New York trafficking narrative began to crack when the institutional location of the investigation moved out of the Tenderloin and into the Criminal Courts Building, nearly a month after the *Times* declared white slavery "real." Readers of a May 20, 1910, article were invited to share the shock expressed by the *Times* as the truth about each woman in the case was systematically revealed on the witness stand. The headline reads, "Belle Moore Guilty of Selling Girls," but the subheading delivers the jolt: "Some Surprises in Case—Girls Sold Not Children, as Supposed, but Women Beyond their Majority, Acting Voluntarily."[29] Despite the guilty verdict, the story indicated that "the day's testimony, even from the lips of the witnesses for the prosecution, did much to destroy the impression, so emphatically given when the women were arrested, that the District Attorney had captured a 'leading white slave dealer of the west side.'"[30] New revelations arose as each woman was brought to the stand. The appearance in court of the Radcliffe graduate caused "a great stir" in the audience. Mrs. Francis M. Foster was not the plucky New Woman as earlier surmised, but a woman in her forties described as having a surprisingly deep voice. Foster gave the single-occupancy New Amsterdam Hotel as her permanent address, and admitted to being abandoned by her husband the previous year. During cross-examination by the defense, Foster was asked whether it was "the proper thing for a college woman to go about among negro sporting joints."[31] To this query she replied that champagne was the only form of liquor she imbibed in these bars. In a revealing interjection, the *Times* offered a modicum of pity for the otherwise maligned Foster: "[Hers] was no pleasant task, to sit on the witness stand and tell a listening roomful of the weeks she spent in the Tenderloin, sometimes staying for weeks at a stretch in restaurants with colored men and women drinking at her elbow."[32] In addition to revealing a deep-seated fear of participation in social spheres outside one's own class and race, this passage offered a rather surreal image of time slipping by in Tenderloin bars without terminus, the white undercover investigator occupying a slightly higher social strata than the "colored" rabble down below.

After the rescued white slaves took the stand, the edifice upon which the New York white slavery investigation was built lay in ruins. While both girls were referred to in subheadings as "victims," one was described as "more than a child," while the other "had been married." The *Times* elaborated as follows: "It was these two girls [who were] described as children not more than 16 years old and around whom gathered the anecdotes of the wept-for Teddy Bear and the cherished 'dolly.' Alice Milton, not unlike the barn-storming Little Eva, confessed to 23, and looked the part despite a cluster of brown curls which she carefully arranged on either shoulder as she entered the room. She was pleasantly obscured by a mammoth scarlet hat, and throughout her testimony swung a patent leather toe in the neighborhood of the stenographer's left ear."[33] The other girl confessed on the stand that when Belle Moore approached her at the Magdalen home with the offer of work in a Seattle brothel, she consented with one word: "Sure."[34]

Each shocking performance was surpassed by the next in this courtroom drama. The women involved manifested neither their purported youth nor their previously implied social standing. In describing the scenario, the author repeatedly turned to themes of physical boundary and propriety that implied hierarchies of race and class. Neither naive, innocent, nor childlike, the erstwhile white slaves' coarse mannerisms impinged on the stenographer, while our errant college graduate was depicted hovering above the black restaurant patrons and their prominent elbows. In the courtroom, however, the female investigator's own innocent status and her reliability as an informant were stripped away by virtue of her physical location in that crowded club. By describing her in such unsavory environments as the club and the hotel, the defense was able to challenge Mrs. Foster's description of events. Early in the investigation coverage, the following quotation appeared in the *Times*: "The [white slaves] could not remain innocent twenty-four hours in the atmosphere into which they are forced."[35] Yet there is a sense in which this "twenty-four hour rule" was applied not only to the girls, but also to those journalists who voluntarily entered different social contexts and arenas in the pursuit of understanding.

As the New York white slavery story unfolded, the courtroom became the location where truth was revealed, and the street was shown to be the unreliable site of unbridled gossip. The title, "Belle Moore Guilty of Selling Girls," suggests a story of a procurer being convicted; however, its real shock value lay in the fact that a story told to prove the truth of white slavery—initially told by Turner, and repeated by activists, politicians, and the DA—was proven to be an empty hoax. The fake was exposed through a juridical process that could reliably distinguish fact from fiction, the real from the imaginary, and the objective from the merely subjective. The *New York Times* dutifully recorded these court proceedings, thus presenting to the public a media trial, one in which the guilty verdict of falsity was laid squarely on muckraking, which came to stand in for Turner, the DA, and especially unreliable, street-based knowledge. This may seem a minor point, as it may appear to be mere competition for audiences between competing media. However, the struggle was not so much over audiences per se as it was over definitions of which forms of knowledge and journalism would reign as dominant in the twentieth century, and which forms of truth-gathering and evidence would come to be seen as authoritative. Journalism, newly emerging as a profession in the early twentieth century, would adopt an analogous model of apparently disinterested impartiality as its central credo. This detached orientation toward reporting remains with us today as the ideal news-reporting style.

Claims linking sensationalism to fabrication became more abundant during this period, signaling a shift in the understanding and deployment of the term *sensationalism*. As the white slave trial reached its end, the *Times* printed a story claiming that a white slavery photograph featuring a suggestive heterosocial display with an employment agency as backdrop was a hoax. The agency's owner described in detail how his business became the stage and the men and women the character actors upon which new meanings were created:

> One day last Summer a traveling photographer came to me and said he would take a picture of my agency. I told him I did not want a picture. He begged me to let him take one, and said if it turned out to be a good one, he would sell it to me for 25 cents. He said I should give a poor man a chance. I then consented. He had another man with him who helped him to make the preparations for the photographs. They got a few girls who had been out in front of the store and brought them in and seated them in my office. Then they got my two young men clerks and seated them among the girls, telling the girls to look closely into the men's faces. When they had them posed in this way they took a flashlight picture and went away. I haven't seen them since, but I recognized the picture of my office as soon as the white slave article was shown to me.[36]

The agent's own testimony might have been suspect, but this discussion of photography exemplified a discourse linking falsification and sensationalism that was emerging at the time. Compared to the Reverend Ernest A. Bell, the Chicago anti-trafficking activist who lauded the media in 1910 for its potential to rouse public sentiment and galvanize social action, this employment agent offers a different narrative of white slavery media, accusing the commissioned photographer of turning the employment agency into a backdrop for a manipulated (and manipulative) drama. Bell's account portrayed the era's nationally distributed media as righteous and heroic conveyors of truth, but this 1910 representation highlights the potential of the media to act in an irresponsible manner, constructing fictitious, self-interested representations of cities and their institutions.

HIDDEN IN PLAIN SIGHT: THE (IN)VISIBILITY OF RACE

Just as newspapers like the *New York Times* spent little time reflecting on their portrayal of women, their codes for representing race were even less reflexive. As David Domke demonstrates, the mainstream northern press increasingly ignored race as a political issue after Reconstruction: "The . . . concern for Blacks' civil rights among many Northern Whites was replaced by a focus on taxes, free trade, women's suffrage, and other matters, particularly following the economic crisis that began in 1873."[37] From its first article in the series, the *Times* framed white slavery as an issue of truth or falsity. This frame put the reality of white slavery and the integrity of the DA's investigation on trial, turning Moore, the real defendant in the case, into little more than a bit character in the unfolding drama. Harry Levinson, the other accused trafficker, largely disappeared from the *Times'* reports on white slavery after the initial article based on the DA's press conference. However, an editorial after Belle Moore's trial noted that Levinson pleaded guilty to all white slavery charges against him.[38] In the wake of the Belle Moore trial debacle, Judge O'Sullivan retracted Levinson's guilty pleas.

In negotiating to purchase white slaves, Foster specifically requested a girl of European descent: "I told [Moore] that I was to open a house in Seattle—an expensive house. I told her that I would pay her well for an innocent girl and that at any rate I must have those who showed no trace of negro blood."[39] While much attention was focused on the supposed racial purity of white slavery's victims, few remember how many African American women and men were accused of trafficking during the white slavery scare and became pawns of the criminal justice system. Like Jack Johnson and Chuck Berry later in the century, the accused traffickers and those convicted under the Mann Act were disproportionately black. As Kevin Mumford points out, the irony of this was not lost on the Progressive Era black press.[40] In this particular case, the United States' legacy of racism and blacks' historical lack of protection and rights in the courtroom rendered Moore a conveniently expendable aspect of the investigation.

After a judge handed down Moore's sentence of up to five years' imprisonment, the *Times* summed up Moore's significance in the white slavery panic: "Her trial was notable for having brought out the seasonable age and sophistication of the 'girls' and the fact that the agents almost vied with Belle Moore in persuading them to be 'sold.'"[41] Once the allegations of white slavery were proven empty, a *Times* editorial downgraded her status from a wicked person to that of a mere criminal.[42] White slavery's popularity as an explanation for women's entry into prostitution served the double ideological function of rendering the black prostitute invisible while accounting for the racial mixing that occurred in vice districts with a theory that preserved white women's innocence by denying their agency. As a "mulatto," Moore represented the very racial mixing that white slavery so fervently attempted to deny.

THE INSTITUTIONS AND THE STREETS

The revelations in court prompted a number of letters to the editor, including an editorial from the *New York Times* itself. These letters read like postmortems for Progressivism. The day following Moore's conviction for white slavery, the *Times* printed its first editorial on the topic, entitled "Ill-Chosen Agents of Reform."[43] This editorial heaps scorn upon the "particularly obnoxious" investigation and its unskilled agents. Ironically presaging later sociological theory on deviance, the paper contends that the investigators were really "'provoking agents' laboriously creating the criminality they had been sent out to find."[44] The convicted trafficker, Moore, is called a victim, though the *Times* stops short of proclaiming her innocence in the matter: "While undoubtedly a person of evil life and reprehensible activities, she seems to be an exponent of no abnormal unfamiliar, or monstrous wickedness."[45] Defining itself as against "sensationalism," the *Times* attempted to counteract the tendency to focus on the abnormal, unfamiliar, and monstrous by recasting the "sensational" as the mundane and the deviant as the boringly average. This editorial advocated a careful modulation of emotion as a corrective to the fast tempo and hysterical pitch of modern urban life; it offered a yawning challenge to yellow newspapers and muckraking magazines to tell it something it could not find blasé.

In the penny presses of the 1830s, editorial pages had been overtly partisan, giving support to various politicians and candidly attempting to sway party platforms. As Michael Schudson notes, the typical reader of the nineteenth-century press was frequently also a news contributor. The rigid divisions between news and correspondence, newspaper reporter and reader, had not yet developed. However, "the metropolitan press, as it became [a] more insistent, self-conscious, and lucrative big business, increased its distance from readers. More and more, the voice of the professional newspaper was separated out from the voice of the readers; where once the two were undifferentiated, they became sharply divided."[46] Increasingly, newspapers ceased to assume a direct political affiliation with their readers. At the same time, the space devoted to editorials shrank considerably.

Letters to the editor continued to fulfill an ideological function, albeit a transformed one. In the *New York Times* of the 1900s, the editorial page became a site for the separation of "views" and "opinions" from information. Editors wrote on a variety of public issues and introduced controversial topics for a small percentage of their readers to debate. As the most powerful medium of its day, the press continued to view itself as a central forum for political discourse and allowed selected readers to "talk back" to both the newspaper and its readership in letters to the editor. This formal division between information and opinion served the developing framework of objective news reporting and bolstered the idea that conversation and dialogue, even through a mass medium, were subjective modes, whereas one-way communication—the monologue—was rationally objective.

What passes for dialogue in any given paper is subject to processes of filtering and censorship for reasons that can be as practical as space constraints or as political as partisan alignment. Nonetheless, letters to the editor can give us a sense of how a segment of the *Times'* readership actually engaged the paper's white slavery coverage. One letter lauds the *Times* for exposing the white slavery story as a ruse: "The thanks of a quite ordinary person for your well-balanced, topical comment on 'Ill-Chosen Agents of Reform,' are yours."[47] This engaged newspaper reader claimed that the farcical outcome of the New York investigation was "probably more surprising to those that 'walked in the light' than to the rest of us that viewed the 'drama' from the shadows of our crude understanding."[48] In mocking the prevalent reform imagery of darkness and light, sunlight and shadow, this anonymous contributor suggested that events can only be understood if viewed from afar, as if watching a play. To "walk in the light" (as the most zealous activists imagined themselves as doing) was to lose all perspective and social distance. It was tantamount to entering a fictional world, discarding critical distance to play a role in an overwrought drama. At the same time, conceiving of oneself as a viewer and reader as opposed to a participant was equated with rationality. The "shadows" from which the white slavery drama was viewed were in this letter-writer's own mind, a location that implied a degree of isolation and distance from the object at hand.

Transformations in styles of news reporting presuppose changes in the behavior and views of news consumers. This letter, signed "Commonplace," expressed the thinking of what certain strands of contemporary political and social theory took as the ideal rational democratic citizen. In the United States and western Europe, political theory and mass-media practice converged on a common theme during this period, that of the rational public versus the feminized and irrational crowd. This dichotomy was instrumental in reform discourse as well, insofar as reformers pointed to an orderly and rational future achieved through the shaping of public opinion.[49] However, this formulation was also implicated in the undoing of the reform impulse. According to Stuart Ewen, "If *the crowd* was perceived as dangerous, driven by irrational appetites, *the public*—as an audience of readers—seemed more receptive to ideas, to rationalization, to the allure of factual proof. Conceived of as spectators, it was also seen as infinitely safer and more controllable."[50] Like the *Times'* own editorial, the letter to the editor posits a prosaic, "commonplace" skepticism against "sensationalism." Everyday ennui is presented as a norm that renders deviant a passionate engagement with public life. The new reader and audience member avoided titillation at all cost, because that signaled an interactive and prepossessed orientation toward the object under consideration. This "commonplace" reader displayed arousal and passion only over his or her ability to confront the world from a skeptical distance and to sniff out Progressive Era hoaxes. Skeptical arousal was an internal state of mind, a pleasure contained within one's own rational faculties.

From the first article, "White Slave Traffic Shown to Be Real," to the editorials condemning the white slavery investigation as a hoax, the *Times* took its readers on a wild, paradigm-shifting ride. On the way, emotional and moral verities dissolved into cheap illusions. Figures that initially appeared to be national treasures came into focus as low-grade roadside attractions. The teddy bear and dolly—those unimpeachable symbols of little-girl innocence, lack of sexual knowledge, and freedom from desire—were revealed as dusty old props hastily plucked from some backstage storage bin. As the series concluded, sentimentalism was replaced by rational skepticism. These dueling frameworks were represented in print in varying ways. The image offered by the *Times* reporter of callous men being physically and emotionally moved upon hearing the girls' stories is characteristic of reform discourse, in which "shock was to be followed immediately by a recognition of one's duty and a move to take action."[51] As a newspaper representation, its power derived from its own description of the men being lured by the melodramatic plot. Like an unsuspecting attendee at a religious revival, the journalist found his own body beginning to stir during the DA's sermon-like press conference. Truth emanated from the collective body in the initial white slavery article. Yet only a month later, editorials condemned corporeal understanding in favor of a sharp critical faculty located in the mind and seemingly disconnected from the body. Importantly, this philosophical transition occurs as the investigation moves from the gossip-laden streets of the Tenderloin District to the conversationally controlled atmosphere of the Criminal Courts Building.

This trajectory paralleled developments in news reporting itself. At the time, the institutional location of journalism was moving from city streets to the university. Departments of journalism would soon sit alongside colleges of law. The reporter began to see it as his duty to separate emotions from facts, to be an arbiter of the real. Identifying with activities on the streets was a hindrance to such detachment. That *Times* coverage of white slavery followed this same pattern—from the sentimental but also overtly sexual streets to the "callous" courtroom—signals that to some degree white slavery was appropriated as a cultural metaphor for the mass media itself.

TRANSCENDING THE STREETS

As Michael Schudson explains, since the 1890s, the *New York Times* had built a reputation for focusing on "information" rather than sensationalistic storytelling, and actively defined itself against the more titillating and visually striking New York dailies. Clever marketing of this focus quickly earned the *Times* a national status and an elite urban readership. Because the daily devoted as much attention to national and international news as it did to news of the city itself, it helped to establish New York as a trend-setting, world-class city by suggesting that events occurring there were of international import. The paper also helped to consolidate New York City's image as a major financial center.[52]

In an attempt to interpellate and maintain an upper-class readership, the *Times* marketed itself in opposition to the "new journalism," as though its methods and conventions were fully established, emphasizing its utility as a source of information as opposed to titillation. The competition among city presses was overtly inscribed within the pages of the dailies themselves, and articles were frequently peppered with blatant self-endorsement. Crime was one arena in which the *Times* distinguished itself: in general, the *Times* considered local crime news less important than political news, while the *New York Journal* and the *New York World* specialized in reporting on street-based transgressions. These two dailies had stronger connections to law enforcement and often actively participated in the search for criminals by organizing public "manhunts" and offering rewards for tips on a suspect's whereabouts. The *Times*, in conscious contrast, considered crime and vice news too low and debased for its sophisticated audience. A *Times* article appearing on February 17, 1897, provocatively entitled "The New Journalism and Vice," took the occasion to lambaste its competitors for indulging in vice coverage, while aligning itself with an apparently global historical struggle for truth: "The press of this country is engaged in a fearful struggle, one class against another. On one side stand the reputable papers which represent decency and truth, and on the other, is what calls itself the new journalism, but which is in reality as old as sin itself."[53]

During the period in which the *Chicago Daily Tribune* and other city papers acknowledged white slavery as a real threat, the *New York Times* remained surprisingly silent on the topic. Its first report on this incendiary public issue appeared two full years after *McClure's* ran Turner's initial article in 1907. But by 1909, Turner's allegations had clearly provoked a consolidated effort by national and local forces to stem white slavery. Local campaigns against white slavery were taking root in cities across the country, while federal legislation to curb the traffic in women was being steamrolled through Congress. Local manifestations of white slavery were viewed as points in a vast network connecting each locale with national and even international flows of women. The perceived scale of the problem placed the *Times* in the awkward position of having to report on activities in the Tenderloin as though they had a national, political dimension. Much like the mass-distribution print media itself, white slavery connected not only the urban to the rural, but also cities to each other by linking the minutiae of vice districts—the carnal spectacles and daily sexual exchanges—to interstate commerce and larger exchanges between regions.

In its early reports on white slavery, the *Times* treated the New York investigation as a reasoned response to a possible threat, while representing Turner's *McClure's* articles as shot through with sloppy methods, suspect motives, and faulty conclusions. The paper conceded that Turner "touched off" the New York investigation but dismissed the muckraker's account as "entirely hearsay."[54] The *Times* then went on to establish terms on which it could appropriately cover such a story. Its strategy was to define the media event that called the public's attention to white slavery—Turner's article in *McClure's*—as different in nature from the multiple and unquestionably real institutional responses it triggered. In dividing the white slavery phenomenon into the "sensational" and the real, the *Times* managed to devalorize the Progressive Era dialectic between investigative reporting and public response, while simultaneously validating institutional responses to the public panic in the form of palpable attempts to restore public order.

The *Times'* attacks on the reporting of white slavery played into a larger assault on the investigative, street-based reporting conducted by the era's muckraker journalists. The Progressive Era idiom of anti-monopolism, so central to many popular movements of the day, was attacked through the white slavery narrative. Indeed, Turner's suggestion that white slavery rings were essentially vice *trusts* prompted Mayor Gaynor to organize a grand jury on white slavery and to appoint John D. Rockefeller Jr. as its head. This grand jury's primary mission was to investigate the claim that white slavers were organized in the form of traditional monopolies. In January 1910, the *Times* ran an article lauding Rockefeller for organizing the grand jury, predicting that the proceedings would put to rest the contentious debate over white slavery's existence in New York and elsewhere.[55]

Ultimately, the *Times* deferred not to knowledge but to institutions, which came to stand in for objectivity. This could not have made its elite readership happier. The voices of elites and their proxies would increasingly come to be defined as truthful and associated with truth through new journalistic methods that linked reputability and information. However, the *Times* and other objective papers still relied on the rhetorical deployment of truth to establish the reality of a phenomenon. In this early instance, muckraking as a whole was "convicted" in the *Times* through a form of symbolic slippage and metonymy. White slavery, the object of one of many popular Progressive campaigns, became metonymic for Progressivism generally and for the perils of investigative reporting specifically. In the minds of Progressivism's conservative critics, the white slavery phenomenon crystallized a range of fears about Progressive culture: the public's seeming lack of consensus, yellow journalism's ability to ignite controversy and organize social movements, and the potentially damaging effects of media exposés on big business.

These critics were often readers of the *Times*, members of an educated upper class that had little tolerance for street-based knowledge. As the newspaper that catered to this class, the *Times* quoted at length institutional sources that supported its campaign against sensationalism. When former Police Commissioner Bingham was called upon to testify before the Rockefeller grand jury, the *Times* devoted several paragraphs to his statement. On the issue of the *McClure's* article, Bingham stated,

> As far as we have been able to discover, the original charges in the George Kibbe Turner article have been sustained in so far as he pointed

> to the existence of a large traffic, and not sustained in so far as he said the traffic was organized. There is no organization to the point of pooling profits, with an executive head here and branches in other cities. There is, however, just so much organization as comes from a perfect understanding between the traders in different cities, an understanding that has grown in intimacy with the necessity of secret trading.[56]

As this statement illustrates, the question of how to represent the level and nature of association among those in alleged white slave rings dominated the proceedings of the Rockefeller grand jury hearings. The answer seemed to turn on a distinction between the notion of formal institutional organization, on the one hand, and necessary patterns of social communication, on the other. The traffickers were described in the *Times* as possessing "such organization as comes from a perfect understanding between those who ply it in different centres all over the country," and the DA as racing against an "underground channel" through which word spreads among those in the trade.[57] One article warns of "sensitive currents [that] seem to connect the Criminal Courts Building with the criminal reaches of the city."[58]

It was only when mass-mediated communication achieved a dominant role in public culture that face-to-face communication, with its promises and pitfalls, became an object of intense social scrutiny.[59] For a brief period before World War I, the concept of free speech became politically charged, temporarily uniting radicals and liberals, workers and elites, the vanguard and the avant-garde under the same political umbrella.[60] Indeed, these references in the *Times* series to communication among traffickers seem to suggest that information spread through talking and other point-to-point means compromised the ability of such "legitimate" institutions as the justice system, and perhaps even the *Times* itself, to function effectively. The traffickers present a threat not only because of their sexual violation of white women, but because they possess secrets to which neither the *Times* nor the investigators are privy. While reporters had to receive thirdhand information about white slavery through the police wards and courts, white slave traders potentially got firsthand, "perfect" information that did not have to be censored, screened, or fact-checked in the interests of a liberal democracy. Traffickers could bypass the mass media and even utilize the information they spread by this means to create an underground association that was not only invisible but inaudible. A fantasy of cultural consensus reached through the containment of information was implicit in these representations of traffickers, a vision in which the stream of illicit and potentially transgressive knowledge flowing through city streets was stemmed, while legitimate information traveled only through formal channels.

But traffickers were not the only ones who relied on hearsay, everyday conversation, and the proverbial "word on the street." Detectives, social workers, and, importantly, some investigative journalists did the same. Images of traffickers transmitting illicit messages across the vast US landscape reflected larger concerns about street-based talk and the journalism of exposure more generally—which was often disregarded by elites as mere "gossip," with all of that term's feminized connotations. The form of rationality preferred by the *Times* and its late Progressive Era readers was very much an indoor pursuit. As an institution through which the social world was represented, the *Times* was instrumental in constructing a mental enclave in which elites could represent supposed reality without undo reference to the streets. The streets were, among other things, sites of fervent democratic protest in the first decades of the twentieth century. But for the *Times*, they were conduits of unfiltered and potentially dangerous information, sirens deflecting men from their rational pursuits. Casting about in the "muck" of society was conceptualized as an outlet for baser instincts, such as lust and vanity, and also as a detour from truth and toward distortion and sensationalism. Like the hapless white slave, the investigative journalist was equally in danger of falling prey to the lures of the street.

THE CONSTRUCTION OF JOURNALISTIC KNOWLEDGE CIRCA 1910

It is difficult to characterize and place the first decade of the twentieth century in the evolution of journalism and news. Sandwiched between two significant social, political, and cultural events—the "rise of mass culture" in the 1890s and the massive social and cultural transformations wrought by World War I—this period is usually viewed as a further entrenchment and elaboration of commercialism and mass culture before the first shot was fired that changed everything. Many of today's big city newspapers were by the 1910s fully functioning institutions. But if the urban daily paper had established itself as the cultural institution *par excellence*, the role and identity of the individual reporter was still under construction. This decade marked the beginning of a half-century of the transformation of journalism from the part-time activity of writers with literary aspirations to the occupation of professionally trained men and women. Debates swirled in print-media circles over whether journalism should be a profession with its own philosophy, professional associations, training, and accreditation process. While some newspaper owners and editors welcomed the emergence of college programs devoted to journalism, others felt such training would detract from the lively and engaged journalistic style developed and practiced by the new journalism. Even Joseph Pulitzer, who in 1911 bequeathed two million dollars to Columbia University for a new school of journalism, did so with some reservation, not entirely convinced that reporters would benefit from such training.

As university programs in journalism proliferated, they brought with them changes in journalistic practice aimed at conferring a new legitimacy on reporters, one grounded in scientific and rational principles. These professional schools and associations introduced new perspectives on and methods for choosing topics, gathering and assembling information, and writing stories. By the 1930s, the notion of news objectivity would become journalism's crowning achievement and central doctrine.[61] As the news coverage of white slavery indicates, however, these larger concerns about professional autonomy, sourcing, and the institutional location of truth were stitched into the white slavery controversy as early as the 1910s; the white slavery coverage in the *Times* and elsewhere helped to shape and, to some degree, determine the outcome of debates over these institutions and practices, and thus to transform news media.

A struggle over institutional methods and strategies for producing journalistic knowledge was embedded in the news coverage of white slavery. White slavery came to symbolize an irrational historical order in the eyes of a cadre of conservative intellectuals, journalists, newspaper editors, and national elites—a constituency grown weary of a perceived causal link between muckraking investigative journalism and a politicized, incendiary public. In reality, the era's reform movements were heterogeneous, with frequently diverging political, social, and moral agendas. Within the skeptical reaction, however, white slavery became a metonym for the entirety of Progressivism and was used to discredit the entire range of media forms and much content as well that addressed the public as an audience for social and political reform. White slavery became the terrain upon which a struggle was waged over the journalist's proper social and political role. At stake was the vantage point from which reporters should view the world and how they should turn their worldly insights into a story. Should their knowledge base derive from what Progressive journalist William Dean Howells called "the university of the streets and the police stations, with its faculty of patrolmen and saloon keepers" or from the literal university classroom and other institutions of power?[62]

Claims linking objectivity to information and truth, and sensationalism to reform and falsity ignore the fact that there is no necessary connection between either objectivity or sensationalism and accuracy. At best, both are equally capable of pursuing and representing truth. This is certainly true of Progressive Era investigative reporting. While there are plenty of examples of poorly documented and overly simplistic exposés within the muckraking canon, there are also numerous examples of carefully researched work whose accuracy is still highly regarded (Ida Tarbell comes to mind). Turner's work exemplified neither the era's investigative reporting nor the general attitude toward accuracy at *McClure's*. However, over the course of the white slavery controversy, it came to stand in for the entire genre and contributed to the eventual demise of that journalistic mode.

CONCLUSION

In the 1910s, newspaper reports and other public commentary on white slavery suggest that both investigative journalism and reform movements became coded as feminine through their metonymic association with gossip. This new alignment of loquaciousness with gossip constituted a direct reversal of earlier Progressive Era notions of detachment and silence as effeminate, and being opinionated and contentious as manly. Between 1880 and 1910, such figures as Joseph Pulitzer and Samuel S. McClure, not to mention a host of famous muckraking reporters and fiction writers, embodied this model of manliness. By the 1910s, the discourse that such figures contributed to the public sphere was condemned as gossip and hearsay, printed "speech" lacking in journalistic integrity and rigor. By contrast, secrecy, expertise, and the calculated framing of public information became central features of an ascending model of masculine political behavior and journalistic modes to represent it authoritatively.

While Progressive Era newspapers and magazines played a pivotal role in popularizing and intensifying social movements, the symbiotic relationship that media and reformers seemingly shared was not a given. Alliances between social movements and the press shifted through time and across media institutions. In the 1910s, previously friendly relations between a number of city newspapers and anti-vice reformers soured once again during a period in which allegations of sensationalism reached a new peak. While some activists celebrated the press's ability to rouse the public, others sought a calmer public sphere, where social change was not spearheaded by an activist media but instead occurred among individuals and institutions specially trained to deal with social and political issues.

The next chapter examines the 1910 grand jury on white slavery that cast further doubt on Turner's claims. As John D. Rockefeller Jr. emerged as a major figure in the post-1910 white slavery movement, the movement increasingly adopted a business ethos that included mergers and was guided by a new managerial idiom. Chapter 6 traces Rockefeller's initiatives for circumventing public discourse and mass activism in the anti-vice arena, demonstrating that new managerial campaigns against prostitution had become a testing ground for new strategies of elite intervention and self-promotion, many of which took the form of "enlightened philanthropy."

CHAPTER SIX

From Sensation to Secrecy: The Rockefeller Grand Jury and Its Aftermath

In conclusion, it should be stated that the spirit which dominates the work of the Bureau is not sensational or sentimental or hysterical.
—John D. Rockefeller Jr., "The Origin, Work, and Plans of the Bureau of Social Hygiene" (1913)

The first step in any reasonable and effective reform is an entire change of attitude on the topic, and about the only good to be expected from the agitation about white slavery, with all its preposterous exaggerations and absurd sensationalism, is that it is perhaps making for a changed attitude, a new conception.
—Brand Whitlock, *Forty Years of It* (1914)

New York City's new mayor, William J. Gaynor, found himself the lone Tammany officeholder after the 1909 municipal election swept a slate of reform-minded Fusion Party candidates into the majority of lower posts. Gaynor was forced to preside over a city government that, just prior to the election, had seized upon George Kibbe Turner's claims in *McClure's Magazine* that an organized white slave trade operated out of New York City. As the Fusion candidate for district attorney, Charles Whitman had promised voters a grand jury inquiry into organized prostitution; despite Gaynor's condemnations of Turner during the campaign, it was incumbent on the incoming administration to deliver. On January 3, 1910, Judge Thomas O'Sullivan of the Court of General Sessions announced the formation of a grand jury investigation into Turner's allegations. O'Sullivan claimed that "some of these statements may have been published with an ulterior motive, and may have been mere sensationalism, but some are said to be based upon official investigation and charges made by persons who profess to have knowledge of the facts." The ultimate object of the grand jury, said O'Sullivan, was to "uncover not alone or isolated offenses, but [evidence of] an organization, if any such exists, for a traffic in the bodies of women."[1]

O'Sullivan appointed John D. Rockefeller Jr., heir to the Standard Oil fortune, as foreman of the twenty-three member white slave grand jury. Rockefeller initially expressed reluctance to serve, citing his "inexperience" and pressing business matters, but O'Sullivan insisted that the millionaire had a civic duty to fulfill. The next day Rockefeller promptly showed up for work at the Criminal Courts Building.[2] The jury was ordered to convene for three weeks. However, under Rockefeller's assiduous leadership and financial sponsorship, the jury inquired into sex trafficking allegations for a full six months. Grand jury members personally interviewed hundreds of people, hired a group of private detectives to find white slave rings in the city, and solicited sworn testimony from Turner, federal immigration officials, New York policemen, and members of the New York Independent Benevolent Association, as well as representatives from scores of religious and civic associations involved in moral reform. Rockefeller's experience investigating white slavery proved personally formative. Biographer Raymond Fosdick notes that after the grand jury, he resigned from all business posts and devoted all is time to funding social scientific endeavors.[3] Indeed, the son of America's richest man emerged from this experience as a key figure in conceptualizing and funding the "post–white slavery" agenda around prostitution.

The continued skepticism about white slavery allegations in New York City was connected to a mounting concern among elites over popular unrest and the perception that exposure-oriented magazines fueled this public discontent. This chapter chronicles the formation and effects of Rockefeller's intervention into white slavery charges. As a result of the grand jury, two significant developments occurred in the discourse surrounding white slavery during this period: (1) an increasingly explicit debate over sensationalism, hysteria, and the status of knowledge about prostitution and white slavery emerged and was elaborated in various print media forms, and (2) white slavery crusaders, while still championing the trafficking thesis, developed an ambivalent relationship toward the use of the white slavery captivity theme in mass entertainment and other artistic productions, precipitating a shift in political activism away from political representatives and their institutions and toward the mass media itself. This chapter situates these developments within broader shifts in cultural authority and strategies for producing and disseminating information to the public.

FROM STANDARD OIL TO THE WHITE SLAVE GRAND JURY

It may seem ironic that Rockefeller was appointed as foreman of a grand jury inquiry into allegations made in *McClure's*, the era's foremost muckraking publication. After all, exposés like Ida Tarbell's "History of the Standard Oil Company" in the same publication had solidified the elder Rockefeller's reputation as the most reviled man in America. Tarbell's series, along with Thomas Lawson's "Frenzied Finance," were only the most famous of dozens of exposés published after 1901 that pointed to John D. Rockefeller Sr.'s business and labor practices as the bane of American economic and political life. Before the Rockefellers hired Ivy Lee to handle Standard Oil public relations crises after the 1914 Ludlow Massacre, the elder Rockefeller had done nothing to dispel the public's perception of him as a ruthless monopolist who suppressed labor and bought off Republican leaders in industrial states. To make matters worse, his dour public demeanor (he was rarely photographed smiling) did him no favors in the eyes of the press. His son, by contrast, was deeply concerned about negative publicity, actively sought to change the family's image, and fought back against misleading press coverage. When a 1908 story in the *American Magazine* accused him of ordering a "peonage stockade" at the Corn Products Refining Company, the younger Rockefeller successfully sued for libel and was awarded $500 from the Hearst Publishing Company.[4]

In general the daily papers were kinder to the son than they were to his father; the younger Rockefeller had a reputation in New York City as a studious "good boy." Devout and conscientious, his weekly Men's Bible Class lectures for the Fifth Avenue Baptist Church on topics like the moral application of money and the importance of marriage were widely covered by city papers.[5] In the months before Rockefeller was selected as grand jury foreman, New York newspapers had praised his role in the campaign to eliminate hookworm from the south. Daily papers similarly reported favorably on Rockefeller's new identity as white slavery investigator. The *New York Evening Mail* wrote, "John D. Jr., White Slave Reformer—Reluctant to Head Grand Jury, He Quickly Becomes Most Ardent Prober."[6] The *Boston American* exulted, "J. D. Rockefeller, Jr., Backs Country-Wide Fight on 'White Slavers.'"[7] The *Troy Daily Press* claimed that Rockefeller's service was proof that America was a truly democratic country.[8] Rockefeller's appointment was not only noted in the Northeast. It became a national media event, with papers in Texas, Washington, California, Arizona, Nebraska, and numerous other states reporting on Rockefeller's involvement.[9] Much of this coverage suggested that Rockefeller would serve ably and ultimately determine the truth about white slavery. A week into the grand jury's work, the *San Francisco Call* even surmised that "the searching investigation undertaken by John D. Rockefeller, Jr.," had "already proceeded far enough to show not only that an organized white slave traffic really exists, but that there are close relations between traffickers in women in the principal cities of the country."[10]

While newspaper articles and editorials were generally positive about Rockefeller's role in the grand jury, not all white slavery activists immediately embraced the scion as one of their own. Activists had a tempered response, and some initially viewed the appointment with distrust. One letter-writer to the *New York Times* expressed fear that the young businessman had decided in advance to reach a different conclusion from the scores of commissions that had already "reported upon the wicked traffic in extensive and horrifying detail."[11] A reporter for the *Tacoma Times* interviewed two New York City rescue workers from the Florence Crittenton mission, who predicted that Rockefeller's "undertaking will come to nothing, because the victims seldom talk." Margaret Luther, a supervisor at a home for unwed and fallen women, told the paper that "in the years I have spent in this work I have questioned not less than 15,000 girls, and I do not know to this day why they refuse to give evidence. If they would talk, the conviction of the cadets and the smashing of the system would be easy."[12] Because the press generally presented Rockefeller as a hero bent on revealing the truth about white slavery syndicates, it is easy to see why invested anti-vice activists and rescue workers would express anxiety over the conclusions that a grand jury headed by someone unfamiliar with the broader movement might reach.[13]

THE GRAND JURY INVESTIGATION

Between January and May, the white slave grand jury subpoenaed twenty people who professed to have knowledge of or, in the case of the Independent Benevolent Association, were accused of white slavery, and interviewed numerous defense attorneys and rescue workers about cases of alleged forced prostitution. Reporters took photographs as grand jury members arrived at the Criminal Courts Building to receive sworn testimony. Because the press was denied access to the proceedings, for months papers had little to report aside from the comings and goings of jury members and minor leaked details about the testimony. Rockefeller routinely emphasized the need for secrecy to grand jurors, underscoring the need to withhold information from the press in the interest of establishing plans, gathering data, and cross-checking facts. When Rockefeller visited Mayor Gaynor's office on January 20 to secure further appropriations for the inquiry, extra policemen had to be ordered to stave off a growing crowd hoping to catch a glimpse of Rockefeller and gain information about the jury's findings. Rockefeller told the mass of reporters stationed outside the building: "It is not quite time for me to talk yet. When our work is completed, we will have much to say. We have certain matters before us which we wish to investigate. When we have done this we will talk readily enough."[14] This vow of silence became a constant refrain in the months leading up to the presentment.

The secrecy surrounding the investigation fueled media speculation about the discoveries taking place behind the Criminal Courts Building's doors and helped legitimize the investigation. In the story of the white slave grand jury, Rockefeller was the protagonist whose secrecy in the interest of accuracy was juxtaposed to muckrakers like Turner who engaged in unchecked and irresponsible talk. On January 6, Judge O'Sullivan elaborated on the reasons behind the appointment of a grand jury: "The finger of suspicion was pointed at decent men in New York City. . . . These articles, cleverly and cunningly, were brought in by irresponsible speakers on street corners and men were mentioned who never dreamed or heard of such a thing."[15] For O'Sullivan, magazine articles and talk on street corners were one and the same, helping to cement the association between muckraking magazines and street-based gossip.

Turner was the grand jury's second witness. During his first day of sworn testimony, questions from the jury centered primarily on the terms he used to describe the city's vice economy. Turner had to explain and justify the economic framework, which included terms like *organization*, *system*, *wholesale*, and *retail*, through which he understood prostitution. When pressed by jurors about sources, the muckraker conceded that many claims in "The Daughters of the Poor" were not based on firsthand knowledge of trafficking, but on secondhand information from informants whose names he could not recollect. Although Turner was not able to provide names, he assured jurors that his informants' identities were clearly documented in his notes. It is difficult to tell from the testimony whether the journalist was protecting his sources or genuinely could not remember names; on the second day of testimony, Turner did provide the name and address of a Chicago detective who had provided information for his "City of Chicago" piece.

Although the sworn testimony lasted two days, jurors quickly grew impatient with the circular nature of Turner's answers, which tended to point back to his written work and to conditions in Chicago, not New York City, as evidence. On the question of whether there was an organized system of commercial sex, the journalist deferred to his article and then finally suggested that there was a new system of male dominance in the sex trade that did not previously exist:

Q: What do you mean by "the system"? "And they have established, directly or indirectly, recruiting systems in every large city of the United States." Now that is a pretty broad statement. A recruiting system in New York City for prostitutes; that is what we are trying to find?

A: You see you are asking a question which I took the entire article to explain. The whole point of this matter is to demonstrate what I meant by that matter of system. What I mean is this . . .

Q: That is what we are trying to find out.

A: To put it another way, I went in Newark, starting here, in Philadelphia, in Pittsburgh, in Chicago, and by the government investigations at Washington I ran across the fact that this business had started out of New York, and the distinction was this: that formerly women were in charge of the general business of prostitution; that supplies came more or less readily out of the slums, but that since that time—here of course before, and to some of course before, and to some extent before in other cities—there had come up what I called here a system, by which men have taken charge of the business of prostitution.[16]

Several minutes later in the testimony, jurors again raised the question of whether the sex trade could be described as a system:

A: My statement—that is why I started with that definition of *pimp*, that there has grown up a new system of getting women and putting them in the houses and managing them when they get in the houses and taking charge of them when they are there; this man, as I started to say, gave a perfectly well-defined way that we should operate that place. In the first place he stated that he would go out—we did not have to get girls, he would go out and get them himself at the dances. In the second place he named the schedule prices which would have to be paid collectors in that district. This amounts, in my opinion, to a system.

Q: You are talking in that particular instance of Chicago?

A: Yes, but I think it exists everywhere.
Q: You have no knowledge it exists in New York that way, no practical knowledge?
A: I have no immediate knowledge; in fact, I don't think it does exist that way at the present time.
Q: You base your remarks on theories rather than facts?
A: No, I do not. (64–65)

Turner eventually conceded that there was no organized system for the purpose of trafficking in women in the New York City, "excepting possibly the Independent Benevolent Association" (67–68). When pressed on his knowledge of this Jewish organization, he stood by his claim that some members were involved in prostitution, but confessed that he knew of no instance where the association had "protected or been deployed to protect any traffic in women" or "resorted to political influence to protect its so-called pimp, or cadet, or prostitute" (110).

Asked on the second day of testimony what evidence he had to back up his claim that New York supplied prostitutes to cities around the country, Turner said that in small and large cities around the country, you could find women from New York. A juror asked if Turner was talking about "immigration or prostitution," and Turner was unable to provide an answer that did not sound like immigration (126). Turner stood by his claim, however, that a political organization had grown up around prostitution, making the trade more than a simple relationship between pimp and prostitute, but a business that was largely organized enough to fix prices and facilitate the movement of women across the country and abroad (136). On the question of politics, Turner flatly denied that *McClure's* had produced the article and published it before the election at the behest of any individual or political party (132).

SECRECY AND ANTICIPATION

As the release of the grand jury presentment grew near, the issue of secrecy and public access to knowledge took an unexpected turn. Rockefeller and O'Sullivan found themselves at odds over the rapidity with which the grand jury's findings should be released and whether anyone should be allowed to preview the document before it was circulated publicly. Rockefeller appeared at the Criminal Courts building on June 9 with presentment in hand, but he withheld it when O'Sullivan demanded the right to preview the document before it went public. The debate fueled suspicions that O'Sullivan, who had ties to Tammany Hall, had lost control of the grand jury. Indeed, jury members had deliberated far beyond the allotted three weeks, and the judge feared they had investigated aspects of the vice trade that fell outside the question of whether or not an organized white slave trade existed in the city. O'Sullivan's chief concern was that the document might incriminate political allies in Tammany Hall.

O'Sullivan's behavior in turn stoked Rockefeller's concern that the presentment might be subject to partisan censoring. Amidst much fanfare and publicity, members of the grand jury passed a resolution forbidding O'Sullivan and Whitman from accessing the presentment prior to its public release. A sealed copy of the presentment remained in Rockefeller's pocket for two weeks. This much-publicized conflict between Rockefeller and the judge over public access to information contributed to the presentment's mystique. On June 23, when Rockefeller attempted a second time to submit the document, the *New York Times* wrote, "Much curiosity is felt throughout the Criminal Court Building as to whether the Grand Jury will have its way to-day."[17] The grand jury resolution was a symbolic gesture of defiance. Under law, the presentment could not be released until O'Sullivan formally filed it with the court. O'Sullivan himself fueled suspicions when he fled New York with document in hand, delaying the release several days while he compared the grand jury's conclusions to the testimony it had received.

In the intervening days, newspapers speculated wildly about the document's content, and Rockefeller scored another public relations victory. News reports portrayed him as a champion of the disclosure of information. The millionaire's overt defiance of O'Sullivan was depicted in heroic terms; his visible disappointment over the inefficiency of the process met the approval of newspapers like the *Times*, which announced "[White Slave Report] Not Yet Filed—But Assurance Is Given That It Will All Become Public Somehow," and cited a source assuring that "before long, through one channel or another, each and every word of the presentment as handed up by Mr. Rockefeller would become known to the public."[18]

Rockefeller, who had been tight-lipped for months, was depicted as the radical proponent of free and open information who threatened to bypass the courts if necessary. O'Sullivan, the enemy of full public disclosure, appeared self-interested and fearful of the information contained in the document. Their conflict, and all the rampant speculation about what important words the hidden presentment might contain, helped to establish the legitimacy and gravity of the grand jury's findings. Newspaper descriptions of Rockefeller publicly snubbing partisan appointees created the impression that the grand jury was an objective body, driven only by a desire to establish and reveal the truth. The presentment controversy symbolically distanced elites like Rockefeller from the partisan realm of politics, positing them as more reliable, neutral, and efficient than civil servants. Polarizing the debate in this fashion also bolstered the notion that economic and political self-interest could only be expressed through transparent or at most thinly veiled acts of party and ethnic affiliation. The potentially greater interests that private-sector elites may have had in discrediting the literature of exposure went largely unexamined.

THE GRAND JURY PRESENTMENT

On June 29, the presentment was finally released. Much of that day's news coverage correctly noted that the grand jury dismissed claims of an organized traffic in women. The presentment did, however, indicate that "a trafficking in the bodies of women does exist and is carried on by individuals acting for their own individual benefit, and that those persons are known to each other and are more or less informally associated."[19] In emphasizing the initiative of individuals in sexual commerce, the grand jury sought to change the terms in which the traffic was discussed, reversing the polemical association of white slavery with big business and monopoly by reverting to the more standard idiom of the vice commissions. Instead of "incorporated syndicates" and "organized bands," the jury found casually related "associations" or "clubs." Traffickers did not operate from "international headquarters" or "clearing houses," but out of "cafés and other so-called hangouts." "Operators" or "retailers" were actually pimps, and "wholesalers" were brothel owners (5). The presentment upheld Turner's claim that individual members of the New York Independent Benevolent Association ran "disorderly houses" and that the president of the organization had provided bail in more than one instance, but the grand jury emphasized that the organization was not formed specifically for this purpose. However, because the association had members in other cities, it was the closest thing to a systematic traffic the jury could find (6).

Again echoing Turner's testimony (though not his exposé), the jury found that the newest and most egregious development in vice economies was the rise of the pimp, a figure who "in cold blood exploits a woman's body for his own maintenance and personal gain" and was "vile and despicable beyond expression" (14). The presentment offered seven recommendations for dealing with the traffic that ranged from imposing the strictest possible penalties on pimps in order to "exterminate them as a class" to increasing parental and guardian supervision at motion picture shows, imposing vigilant inspections of hotels suspected of tolerating prostitution, requiring public health licenses for massage and manicure parlors, devising curricula to educate children about sex, and conducting comparative studies on prostitution in US and European cities (15–16).

In *The Prodigal Daughter*, white slave activist, author, and prosecutor Clifford G. Roe described the day of the presentment's release ominously: "On the morning of the twenty-ninth of June in the summer of 1910 newspapers throughout the world printed glowing headlines that shocked the reading public and chilled the blood in the veins of those fighting the traffic in girls."[20] Echoing Roe, historian Ruth Rosen contends that the effects of this media event on public opinion constituted a major step backward for the anti-trafficking cause: "The public never received the actual details or conclusions of the Rockefeller grand jury. A delayed statement released to the press implied that the jury had found no evidence of an organized traffic in women. The next day . . . newspapers across the United States carried misleading stories indicating that no evidence of *white slavery* had been discovered."[21]

In fact, presentment coverage varied across newspapers. The *New York Times*, for example, did not commit the error that Rosen identifies. It announced the conclusions with the headline "White Slave Trade Is Not Organized. So Says the Rockefeller Grand Jury's Presentment, at Last Filed with the Court," followed by "no evidence of an organized traffic, but a traffic carried on by individuals." The paper then excerpted several pages of the actual presentment.[22] Some major dailies did grossly misrepresent the jury's conclusions and characterized white slavery as a myth. The *Chicago Daily Tribune*, for instance, claimed, "White Slavery? Not in New York.—Rockefeller Grand Jury Reports Allegations Are Largely Mythical—No Organized Traffic—Judge Says City's Fair Name Has Been Slandered by Muckraking Writers." This strange report cast New York City as a courtroom defendant seeking to establish its innocence in the face of "the most serious charge ever brought against it." It summed up the positive implications for Chicago of New York's "acquittal": "The acquittal of New York means basically similar exoneration for all other large cities in the United States, for it had been charged that, through New York as headquarters, traffic in women was carried on throughout the country."[23] A brief report in the *San Francisco Chronicle*, "No Evidence of the White Slave Traffic," summarized the grand jury's warnings about illicit activities in movie theaters and massage parlors, concluding that "in relation to the consorts of dissolute women, it recommends that legislation be effected looking toward their elimination."[24] Such articles prompted a number of letters to the editor decrying press handling of grand jury conclusions, including one printed in a Chicago paper stating, "The grand jury found plenty of traffic in unfortunate women carried on by unscrupulous individuals acting for their own benefit and with a certain amount of loose, joint cooperation. There is no evidence that the 'muck rakers' have exaggerated the volume or the seriousness of the social evil in the metropolis of this country."[25]

The grand jury kept abreast of its reception in the press and elsewhere. Assistant District Attorney James B. Reynolds—who had been instrumental in the Belle Moore case and was presiding over the District Attorney's Office while Whitman was in Europe—coordinated the post-presentment media blitz. Working closely with Rockefeller, he sent out two thousand copies of the presentment to the National Vigilance Committee and four hundred copies to newspapers, including fifty papers whose editorials "showed an ignorance of the exact findings of the Grand Jury." Attached to these fifty presentments was "a tactful and courteous note, calling their special attention to the presentment in view of their editorials." The presentment was also sent to "1,500 individuals who were on our list as being interested in the suppression of the white slave traffic." The document was also sent to the International Bureau of Vigilance Associations in Europe, the mayor of Tokyo, and government officials in France and England, who had specifically requested copies of the report.[26]

Despite Roe's depiction of June 29 as an Armageddon for white slavery crusaders, many activists, including Roe, came to view Rockefeller as an anti-vice hero. Activist response to the presentment itself was far different than response to the headlines it spawned. Many reformers took the occasion to praise the document, including the superintendent of the Society for the Prevention of Cruelty to Children, who wrote, "The presentment shows calm and careful consideration of the important subject which the Jury had in hand and with which it dealt in a manner which cannot have but good effect—That part of the presentment on pages 11 and 12 of the printed report dealing with moving picture shows is particularly pleasing to me personally. I shall take the liberty to use it in further action which the Society in considering against these nefarious places."[27]

Indeed, the presentment became the yardstick against which the "truth" about white slavery was measured in many subsequent discussions of the topic. But the presentment became a highly adaptable yardstick, one that could be used to measure truth wherever truth was seen. As such, it came to be wielded rhetorically to legitimize the validity of a range of claims about sex trafficking. White slavery crusaders, including Turner himself, were eager to demonstrate that the document captured their own beliefs about the traffic in women. Turner released a statement defending his work in light of the jury's findings. The journalist denied that his white slavery exposé asserted the existence of an organized traffic in women, arguing that the understanding of white slavery put forth in "The Daughters of the Poor" was nothing more than "the procuring and exploitation of women by men," and therefore identical to the presentment's own definition. He asserted that the facts in his article had been confirmed by four investigations, including the grand jury's, "and the attempt to belittle the danger from this evil, on the ground that either myself or others have misrepresented its exact form of organization, would be a contemptible evasion of the main issue, even if that excuse were true, which it is not."[28]

After 1910, a number of book-length, anti–white slavery polemics were published, and many of them took up the issue of the Rockefeller grand jury, frequently using its findings to bolster arguments about the reality of a white slave trade. The presentment, though not press coverage of it, was conceived as an appeal to reason and was perhaps a more flexible document than its creators had intended. Although white slave crusaders and anti-vice activists often used the rhetoric of monopolism to describe trafficking and prostitution (a rhetorical move that, as Mara Keire has shown, situated white slavery squarely within other Progressive Era campaigns), activists during this period were not fixated on whether white slave rings were actually vice trusts.[29] Belief in white slavery existed independently of questions about the level of association, cooperation, and communication that existed among traffickers (the issues that were central to the controversy among muckrakers, city officials, and elites). These activists were more concerned about perceived and actual moral threats and changes in the sex/gender system. Nonetheless, reformers after 1910 strove to defend themselves against charges of sensationalism and to bring the presentment into the evidence-of-white-slavery fold.

THE BUREAU OF SOCIAL HYGIENE

Mayor Gaynor responded to the presentment by calling for a commission to study conditions in the city. In a letter to Rockefeller, Assistant District Attorney James B. Reynolds noted that "at least [Gaynor] read, considered, replied and is open to suggestions,—none of which processes of mind on his part I had counted upon with certainty."[30] During the grand jury, Rockefeller had established trusting relationships with two of the jury's witnesses, Professor Jeremiah Jenks and Marcus Braun, both of whom conducted work for the Immigration Commission. During the inquiry, these investigators emphasized that their knowledge on the subject was not derived from reform movements. In a correspondence between Jenks and Rockefeller about Gaynor's proposed commission, the professor strongly urged Rockefeller to serve as head: "You have been the one who brings matters to a conclusion and gets things done, and you now have the experience and information on that question which would enable you to direct the work without waste of time or money." Jenks also warned against appointing affiliated reformers because one gets an "unprejudiced and wiser view of the question from a man who is not committed to a movement."[31] On the heels of this exchange, Rockefeller proposed the idea of establishing a privately funded permanent committee that would conduct its own research and shape public policy on prostitution-related issues.

Through his grand jury work, Rockefeller discovered a new role for the private philanthropist: to inform social policy and shape public opinion on important social issues. His experience convinced him of the necessity of a scientific approach to prostitution whose agenda was not driven by reform movements, muckraking magazines, or partisan elected officials and that would have lasting effects. To that end, he devised the Bureau of Social Hygiene (BSH) in 1911, an organization with four founding members and unlimited Rockefeller funds at its disposal. The bureau's aim was to devise concrete plans for "dealing with the social evil" that were based on scientific studies into the phenomenon. In order to arrive at a "deeply scientific as well as humane" understanding of commercial sex, the BSH sponsored research, including George Kneeland's *Commercialized Prostitution in New York City* and Abraham Flexner's *Prostitution in Europe*.[32] Rockefeller promoted these works as "dispassionate, objective accounts" of commercialized vice.[33] Flexner was handpicked by Rockefeller to conduct the comparative study of prostitution in Europe because he was an outsider to reform movements, was "without prejudice or preconception, . . . and had no previous opinion to sustain."[34] The BSH also established the Laboratory of Social Hygiene at Bedford Hills Reformatory. Under the guidance of Katherine Bement Davis, female prostitutes at the reformatory would become subjects of "physical, mental, social, and moral" studies with an eye toward understanding the causes of vice and answering the question of whether these women were capable of reform.[35]

The Laboratory of Social Hygiene was an unprecedented foray into joint private/public control over a state-funded institution. It turned a seemingly scientific gaze on individual prostitutes, invoking a pre–white slavery conception of the fallen woman and employing a medical discourse that offered biological explanations for women's "descent" into prostitution.

The knowledge produced by the laboratory marked prostitutes as social deviants. Guided by the increasingly popular science of eugenics, the BSH promoted the theory that there were two basic types of prostitutes: those capable of rehabilitation and those congenitally defective and therefore impervious to reform.[36] This division provided a mission and rationale for the creation of institutional facilities created with life imprisonment in mind. In the words of Maude Minor, a member of the newly formed American Social Hygiene Association, the objective of eugenics-based anti-prostitution programs was to segregate "mentally deficient persons and insur[e] a better inheritance."[37]

Rockefeller's efforts with the BSH were instrumental in transforming knowledge about prostitution and vice and transferring the locus of knowledge to experts. Motivated by the white slavery controversy, he created a new model of privately funded institutional inquiry into marginal groups. While citizens had used private capital to support vice committees in the past, they had never done so with the kind of resources wielded by Rockefeller. Rockefeller initially pledged up to twenty-five thousand dollars a year to the BSH. That amount increased steadily, and by 1920 he was contributing more than two hundred thousand a year.[38] Over his lifetime, he contributed more than five million dollars to the BSH. With this money, he helped dismantle the evangelical and woman-based social purity activist networks that had worked to abolish prostitution under the mantle of white slavery, essentially drowning out their voices and replacing them with a model based on medical experts and rooted in institutions of social hygiene.

Rockefeller also proposed and actively lobbied for a merger between the two main strains of the anti-vice movement, social purity and social hygiene. The result was the formal incorporation in 1913 of the American Vigilance Association and the American Federation for Sex Hygiene into the American Social Hygiene Association (ASHA). Through this incorporation, the professional, scientific wing of the movement subsumed the moral one. Rockefeller not only developed the blueprint for the ASHA, but also provided funding to the group in its early phases—between five thousand and ten thousand dollars per year to the ASHA between 1913 and 1918; he also engaged in fund-raising activities that led to a total budget of more than sixty thousand dollars a year. In overseeing this merger, he created a reform monopoly in which the physician-led social hygiene movement prevailed. The formation of the ASHA had paradoxical effects. While the restructuring was rationalized as an effort to increase the efficiency and strength of the anti-prostitution lobby, as its leadership shrank to a few prominent individuals, the movement in fact lost its strong public presence. In particular, the central role of nonprofessional women in leading earlier anti-prostitution activities was increasingly ceded to penologists, physicians, and social scientists.[39]

Assistant District Attorney Reynolds predicted a new era for anti-prostitution efforts. While reformers in the century's first decade had produced "searching investigations" that demonstrated the "calculating commercialism of aggressive vice," these works only paved the way for "serious investigations" in the second decade that would "more accurately determine the physical, mental, and social status of the classes involved in prostitution, the details of the traffic, and the general or particular effects of the evil."[40] Discourses of commercial sex were indeed radically transformed between 1910 and 1915, as beliefs in efficiency and in an expert-aided rational ascent from ignorance to social enlightenment took hold. By the time the United States entered World War I, concerns over prostitution were largely articulated through public health and eugenic discourses. However, this path was not an Enlightenment path to progress through equality and education but one based on eugenics and a transmogrified reactionary ideology, this time grounded not in religious or journalistic epistemologies, but in scientific ones.

Not everyone celebrated Rockefeller's foray into the problem of commercial sex. Walter Reedy, founder of the magazine the *Mirror*, charged that "as young Rockefeller is putting up money for the White Slave hunt, . . . White Slaves have to be produced" and referred to anti-prostitution campaigns as "anti-vice crusades financed by Standard Oil."[41] In addition to Reedy, radicals like Emma Goldman critiqued Rockefeller and suggested that even he could not rescue middle-class anti-prostitution movements from the grip of sensationalism. In response to such critiques, social purity activists like William Burgess defended Rockefeller and asserted a new public image for anti-prostitution movements. Because the financier had contributed "his business talent" and the "necessary funds" toward the continuation of the movement, the public "ought to be ready to accord him a full measure of gratitude for a service which is national and world-wide in its value." Turning to the charges of sensationalism, Burgess conceded that the social evil "inflames the minds of sensitive people and also attracts the headliners and seekers after the sensational" but asserted that, under new leadership, these tendencies would "doubtless subside." Burgess championed a vertical model of reform organizations that distinguished rational leaders from "passionate" followers: "But these [passionate reformers] are not the people into whose hands this movement is placed. They are sane, conservative people, statesmen, medical authorities and scientists, business men with a conscience, and eminent educators who are seeking uplift of society—not by sex hysteria, but by legislation and law enforcement, supported by an enlightened and awakened public conscience. To give support to these leaders in organized efforts throughout the country is the mission and work of the American Vigilance Association."[42] Burgess's statements here suggested an emerging corporate mentality within social reform movements and the possibility of increased affiliation with official institutions (a relationship that was not to be realized).

Rockefeller's model of enlightened philanthropy actually revealed a deep suspicion of public and political reform efforts.[43] While Rockefeller's interest in prostitution and social science was genuine, enlightened philanthropy also constituted a way to gain the public trust at the expense of the poor. The positive reaction his activities around vice and eugenics garnered in the nation's newspapers deflected attention from labor injustices committed by his family, particularly the bloody Colorado miners' strike of 1914.[44] Charity and endowments became the public face of the monopolists, and prostitution became one of the premiere domains in which early experiments in philanthropic social control and public relations were practiced. Or rather, conservative social hygiene and eugenics activities were successfully marketed as "charity," when they were actually medically justified and eugenically motivated attacks on the bodies of prostitutes.

THE CULTURAL AFTERMATH OF ROCKEFELLER: WHITE SLAVERY AND THE "NEW HYSTERIA"

After the grand jury presentment and especially after the barrage of news media, newspapers consciously distanced themselves from white slavery, possibly because of its association with sensationalism and because many of the stories that had been told about it had been debunked. Consequently, white slavery narratives lost their newsworthiness, and the media began looking toward institutional sources for guidance on issues of prostitution. Some newspapers came to duplicate the efforts of the Rockefeller grand jury in their privileging of secrecy, authoritative sources, expert testimony, and formal methods. The result was a decline in news about white slavery, except for an occasional flare-up, such as the "poisoned needle" controversy, which I discuss later in this chapter. These developments within journalism did not mean that the public's interest in white slavery similarly disappeared. Nor did it mean that white slavery disappeared from popular culture. Indeed, the intensity of public interest in white slavery if anything increased in the years following the Rockefeller presentment.

After the 1910 white slave grand jury, white slavery themes and plots increasingly appeared in other forms of cultural production, including novels, plays, and popular films, where they took on a life of their own. The introduction of white slavery narratives into the realm of entertainment and art precipitated a public outcry over the narrative and visual content of these productions rather than concern over the truth or falsity of claims made about the trade. Reformers who worked so passionately to abolish sex trafficking suddenly suspected the white slavery narrative was being used to arouse rather than inform. *House of Bondage*, a novel by Reginald Wright Kauffman that depicted innocent girls drugged and forced into prostitution, went through eleven printings within a year of its publication, and similar novels were equally popular.[45] Plays like *A Girl without a Chance, The Innocence of Youth, The Dangers of Innocence, The White Slavers of a Great City, Lured from Home, Escaped from the Harem,* and *Dealers in White Women* emphasized the dangers of city life to the unmarried girl.[46] White slavery films like *The Traffic in Souls*, released in 1913, and the film version of Kauffman's novel, released in 1914, were huge cinematic successes. *The Traffic in Souls* drew more than thirty thousand viewers in its opening week. As mainstream media coverage of trafficking waned, artistic cultural productions featuring the lurid white slavery plot were on the rise. In magazines and newspapers such narratives had come under attack for their lack of veracity. In popular culture they were titillating and were a legally and culturally appropriate means to discuss sex, in that they were presumably morally justified and, at least temporarily, flew under the radar of embarrassment and censorship.

Audiences eagerly devoured these cultural productions that represented rural and immigrant girls being drugged and forced into sexual servitude in prisonlike brothels. At the same time, moral controversies over white slavery as a supposedly material, social phenomenon were supplanted by debates over the ubiquity of sexualized media representations. Some of the same crusaders who had worked to prove the existence of white slavery became vocal opponents of obscene, sexualized portrayals, wanting to abolish them not only from popular culture, but from the pages of their own reform media. The new focus of cultural debate was media images and their effects. The ubiquity of "sex talk" in the nation's media led one writer to ask, "Does this overemphasis on sex indicate a permanent change in our temper? Has it struck sex o'clock permanently, or will time soon point to another hour?"[47]

Mrs. Barclay Hazard, a rescue worker at the New York branch of the Florence Crittenton mission, became an outspoken opponent of the use of white slavery themes in fiction, plays, and films. She became a prominent spokeswoman for the censorship of such forms of entertainment, popularizing a psychological theory of strong media effects that was subsequently reproduced in the *New York Times* and magazines like *Outlook* and *Current Opinion*.[48] According to Hazard, women who were "borderline cases" and "neurasthenics" were particularly prone to the suggestive power of trafficking plots. Borderline cases were women and girls "with very little active mentality," while neurasthenics were hysterical and "suffered from a disease requiring as much patience and skill in controlling as it would were the malady an active mania." Hazard particularly objected to the truncated endings of white slavery films, which breezily condensed the tragic fates of white slaves: "It is not a sudden nor a dramatic end which comes to the great majority. The films cannot show the slow disintegration of the nervous tissue; it cannot show the insidious advance of anemic disease; these things constitute the real and unavoidable tragedy."[49]

Some rescue workers attached themselves to an emerging rationalism and expert agenda while maintaining a strong belief in street-based reform. Hazard, once again, succinctly articulated the view that publicity and popular culture had corrupted the serious business of prostitution reform: "These subjects should be discussed sanely and quietly by experts. The result of the attention that has been called to the white slave traffic and subjects akin to it is that people are in a state of hysteria." Hazard accused women in particular of "talking about something of which they know absolutely nothing and [doing] a great deal of harm. They are sentimental about it; they give the wrong point of view." She not only derides the effects of middle-class women's talk, but also complains that claims of white slavery had become so ridiculous that even prostitutes were making jokes about what should be a grave topic. While attending a trafficking-themed play, Hazard allegedly overheard one "girl of the street" laughingly saying to another, "Did you know you were a little coozy, woozzy, pinky, winky, white slavey."[50]

A class of white slavery skeptics emerged during this period that often utilized allegations of sensationalism to describe reformers. The view of *Current Opinion* typified these claims: "The vice crusade . . . is being overdone. There is too much sensationalism in its campaigns. There is too much censorship of songs and dances. It is all as spasmodic and Saint Vitus dance-like as some of the condemned performances themselves. There's an epidemical frenzy in it, and the public isn't so much shocked. It rather enjoys the coprolalia of it all."[51]

New controversies over mass-mediated representations of white slaves frequently took place in letters to the editor. The publication of Carrie Weaver Smith's poem "The Cry to Christ of the Daughters of Shame" in *Survey* provoked heated controversy. Readers decried verses that compared the suffering of white slaves to that of Christ:

> But we—we are crucified daily,
> With never an Easter morn;
> But only the hell of human lust,
> And worse, of human scorn.
> For the sins of passionless women,
> For the sins of passionate men,
> Daily we make atonement:
> Golgotha again and again.[52]

One reader protested the romanticized portrayal of prostitutes implicit in such dramatic representations: "The quality of taste that can represent prostitutes as addressing the crucified Christ in terms of envy of his easy fate is offensive to some of your readers. . . . All harlots are not martyrs nor can we assert that a majority of them are victims of anything but their own frailty."[53]

Survey again came under attack (but also garnered publicity) when it used as its May 3, 1913, cover a photograph of a statuette by Abastenia St. Leger Eberle depicting a naked and cowering "white slave" being sold at the auction block. This photograph started a lengthy letter-writing campaign over the suggestive nature of the figurine. Letters of public outrage as well as support for the artist, her social vision, and the journal's decision to reproduce Eberle's "The White Slave" poured in to the editor between May 17 and July 24, when *Survey* decided to end the debate by halting publication of additional responses because they were repetitive.

The issue of *Survey* in which the photograph appeared contained a feature article on Eberle and her other works. The figurines themselves strike one less as shocking than as cheap. Nonetheless, the article sets her work apart from modern art more generally, which demonstrates "a frank disregard of what impression the mystified public carries away." Eberle's work, by contrast, reflected "the spirit of awakened social consciousness so apparent today." According to the article, Eberle's work had undergone a transformation from being objective in its depiction of day-to-day life to interpretive in its representation of social ills: "Just as The Windy Doorstep, with its fine feeling for the dignity of everyday homely tasks, outranks the Roller Skater, which she says, was done in a purely objective spirit, so the White

Slave records a forward step which is a difference in kind even more than degree. Here she has turned from her more objective work to the graphic interpretation of a social menace; and it is here, perhaps, that she finds herself with surest touch."[54]

Many readers disagreed with this assessment. Some were horrified that the photograph was carried through the mail and delivered into homes in plain view of their sons and daughters: "Grown people who urge full instruction and warning do not take into account the sensitive nervous systems of unformed youth."[55] Once again, echoing the response to Stead, we see an implicit media-effects model here in which the people vulnerable are not really women but young men who are feared to engage in self-pollution. Some wondered how Eberle could create such a portrayal: "The artist must have allowed her imagination to go deep into the haunts of vice before she made this statue."[56] Some canceled their subscriptions to the journal. However, reaction against the initial letters of protest soon overtook the shocked response. Far from restricting the distribution of the "The White Slave," the controversy actually encouraged a number of people to request reprints to use in lectures on the subject or to share with friends. In statements that promoted the efficacy of shock, others claimed that the statue provoked a conversion experience: "That picture was like a blow from a clenched fist at the end of a strong arm. I sat looking at it for quite half an hour, and never before did the horror of the traffic it represents so sink into my soul."[57]

The journal responded to the letters by printing a statement in defense of the cover photograph. This letter argued that it was the journal's social duty to promote rather than repress knowledge and appealed to the legitimacy of experts and professionals in this endeavor: "The *Survey* must draw its councils rather from those who bring [a] larger measure of social experience to the question—from superintendents of orphanages, . . . from neurologists, . . . from reformatory heads, . . . from physicians. . . . It is the duty of the *Survey* of all journals, standing as it does between the doctor, the social investigator, the criminologist, and the general public, to bring out the truth and to bring it out in ways that will strike fire."[58]

Here sensationalism was rationalized by its association with a growing class of experts. Reform rhetoric was transformed into a cultural narrative that represented reality through fiction and artistic productions rather than blunt assertions. Just as the media scandal in England over "The Maiden Tribute of Modern Babylon" quickly moved from moral questions of prostitution and trafficking toward debates over what it is proper to discuss and portray in publicly distributed media, so did the scandal incited by "The Daughters of the Poor" quickly become a debate about pornography in mass media. In this case the recursive backlash of the surplus scandal over sex was not aimed at *McClure's* or at the grand jury's investigation, but at the ensuing discussions, debates, exposés, stories, films, plays, and books that soon followed in a variety of informational, entertainment, and reformist media.

A POISONED POSTSCRIPT

In the 1910s, daily newspapers and reform movements began to distance themselves from one another, conceiving of their respective social goals and functions as increasingly distinct and perhaps even incompatible. The logic governing this developing polarization was a projection of the acts of sensationalism and exaggeration onto the other party and a concomitant disavowal of one's own stake in the practice. In 1915, Eric Hopwood of the *Cleveland Plain Dealer* addressed this increasingly strained relationship between the press and social movements: "I find repeated indications of a lack of confidence in the newspaper [by reform movements]. There are charges of sensationalism, of inaccuracy, of unfairness and lack of understanding. . . . In fact, most social betterment movements, of one sort or another, rank the average newspaper as a low grade moron. On the other hand there is too great a tendency among newspaper men to class reform advocates as nothing less than pests and madmen."[59] The press during this period began to posit a more objective and less grandiose social function. In turn, many reformers who had come to celebrate the ability of commercial newspapers and magazines to incite social change suddenly blamed those very media for making a mockery of reform movements.[60]

In 1913, theories surfaced in New York City and Newark that young women were being kidnapped in movie theaters by a new means, the poisoned needle, and that white slavers were pretending to be relatives and dragging the unconscious girls out of the theaters.[61] The *Washington Times* headlined one story "Many Young Girls Victims of Poisoned Needles" and went on to say that "hundreds of respectable girls and young women have been the victims of white slave traffickers operating with poisoned needles in the dimness of moving picture and other theaters."[62] The alleged crime scenes were the very cinemas where people were learning about these horrors. The "poisoned needle" stories were repeated in newspapers across the country, provoking a paranoid public response. After two months of panic over this new tool in the trafficker's arsenal, newspapers began distancing themselves from the stories. The *New York World*, which had contributed to their popularity, asked, "Are we losing our senses over white slavery?

This present phase of popular credulity on the subject would deserve to be regarded as merely silly if it were not for the tendency of an exaggeration of the fancied dangers of the evil to confuse the public mind about its real dangers."[63]

Calling this development the "new white slavery hysteria," one journal accused daily newspapers of first popularizing and subsequently distancing themselves from the pinprick tales: "'White slavery' as a popular catchword to cover a multitude of crimes, real and imaginary, has for the past year been greatly developed and strengthened by sensational 'stories' printed by the daily newspapers. It has remained for the newspapers themselves to calm the frenzied hysteria for which they themselves are partially responsible."[64]

Aside from the *World*, the dailies that now rejected white slavery claims were the *Chicago Tribune* and *Chicago Record-Herald*, the *San Francisco Chronicle* and *San Francisco Bulletin*, the *New York Times, Evening Post, Sun*, and *World*, the *Baltimore American* and *Baltimore Evening-Sun*, the *Pittsburgh Dispatch*, and the *Albany Herald*.[65] Some newspapers did continue to affirm the existence of white slavery during this period, most notably the *Cleveland Plain Dealer*, whose illustrations of white slaves and their corpulent captors were often reprinted in such social purity journals as *Vigilance* and the *Light* throughout the 1910s. Secondhand trafficking narratives from the *Joliet Republican* also turned up in a number of anti–white slavery publications in the prewar period. In 1914 the *New York Times* summed up the history of the white slavery controversy in an editorial on the Mann Act by suggesting that "[The act] was passed at a time when sensational magazines had created a belief in the existence of a great interstate 'white slave' trust. No such trust exists, nor is there any organized white slave industry anywhere."[66] In 1916 an article reported that the "myth of an international and interstate 'syndicate' trafficking in women" was "a figment of imaginative fly-gobblers."[67]

CONCLUSION

This chapter has traced a number of significant cultural developments emerging from the white slavery scandal, including the privileging of institutional and professional secrecy over disclosure as a way to arrive at truth; shifting relationships between the press and reform movements in the midst of an increasingly explicit public debate over sensationalism; and an increase in public debate over artistic representations of sexual slavery coupled with a decrease in the level of public activism concerned with the act of trafficking.

Explanations for the decline of investigative journalism after 1917 tend to focus on a gradual cultural waning of interest in exposés, the public's increased investment in capitalism due to rising corporate welfare after World War I, and the active appropriation of muckraking publications by corporate and governmental interests eager to eviscerate this threatening form of journalism.[68] Chapters 5 and 6 have demonstrated that controversies surrounding George Kibbe Turner's work in *McClure's* also played a role in delegitimizing Progressive Era muckraking. Played out in daily papers, in criminal courtrooms, and in grand juries, the surplus scandal generated by Turner's claims was not just rhetorical and symbolic. The backlash occurred simultaneously on many different levels and involved a number of actors and institutions threatened by allegations of widespread trafficking in women and the destabilizing power of muckraking productions. The momentous intervention of Rockefeller in the white slavery grand jury is important in this regard. Not only did Rockefeller engage in a public service in the interest of combating a social evil; he also succeeded in discrediting muckraking journalists more generally, and thus weakened a collective threat to big business in general (and Standard Oil in particular). At the same time, the debates that ensued in the media over the appropriateness of sensational articles addressing sexual slavery led to a toning down of news media coverage of white slavery. This did not immediately vanish, but petered out gradually with occasional punctuations of paranoia, generated by coverage of stories like the poisoned needle scare, that universally resulted in a backlash against sensational media and its methods and served as a reminder of the necessity for more objective and authoritative news sourcing.

Turner's "The Daughters of the Poor" presented itself as a high-profile straw man that was quickly and efficiently taken down, and with it the enterprise of exposure journalism, including its unruly methods and unacceptable conclusions, particularly in the eyes of elites. The institutions of economic power also fought back on the financial battleground, where they had an obvious advantage and were able simply to purchase magazines, as did the J. P. Morgan Trust. They fought back on the legal front, through court cases showing that although prostitution and sometimes trafficking occurred, they were not organized in the manner purported. And they fought back on the battlefield of mass culture, as when the *New York Times* authoritatively pronounced white slavery, and muckraking along with it, dead.

This transformation involved discursive battles, contests over meaning, the deployment and redeployment of narratives, and handed-down folk myths and other bits of cultural baggage that were utilized in a number of rhetorical ways. However, the meanings and shapes that these fragments took transformed news media at a particular moment in history in the context of existing institutional arrangements of power—a transformation that involved actors competing for legitimacy and power simultaneously within cultural, political, and economic fields. The object that was ultimately negated by the *Times*, by the criminal investigation, and by the grand jury was exposure journalism. However, dismissals of white slavery and muckraking did little to undo the setting into motion of institutional changes, surveillance, and policing practices.

As the news media retreated from white slavery claims, white slavery crusaders lost their stance as representing the vanguard in fighting the social evil of sexual vice and were increasingly supplanted by the rising, institutionally based social hygiene movement promoted by Rockefeller and others. Some of the loss of momentum in white slavery crusades had to do their mounting success in shutting down red-light districts in the 1910s, but it also was the product of interventions into organized social movements by people like Rockefeller. During this period, the news media and reform activists distanced themselves from each other; with the decline in muckraking, the news media did not necessarily wish to be associated with activism and street-based knowledge but began to desire the legitimacy of authoritative sources. Increasingly, following the *New York Times*' model, papers sought to attain an image of objectivity. Social activists began to distrust the news media, having come to view them as overly sensationalistic and opportunistic in the aftermath of the Turner article and the grand jury investigation. However, far from disappearing from popular culture, white slavery continued to be a major cultural preoccupation; indeed, there was a huge audience and market for entertainment-based media surrounding this topic. The controversies surrounding white slavery after the theme's expulsion from news media thus shifted from those concerning sensationalism and truth-production in the news to those concerning pornographic representations and the degree to which prostitution and sexuality should be represented in the media, even if purportedly done in the name of social reform.

CONCLUSION

In the 1910s business elites like the Rockefellers began asserting themselves, clamping down on street-based knowledge and using their own funds to initiate a new order in which expert knowledge took precedence over moral and political activist crusades. This new regime of knowledge production and governance emphasized authority and the one-way flow of information. More than any other commentator at the time, Walter Lippmann provided the theoretical rationale for these changes. At the moment Stead was going down on the *Titanic*, Lippmann was formulating a prescriptive model of the press that reversed many of the tenets of Stead's "Government by Journalism."[1] In 1886, Stead had posited the journalist as the true democratic ruler who spoke directly to and on behalf of a "vast congregation" from his pulpit of mass distribution. He called for elected officials to recognize editor-reporters' newfound power by granting them unrestricted access to interviews as well as right of entry to all social institutions. Lippmann, by contrast, sought to neutralize the potential power of journalism by reducing reporters to the status of passive intermediaries facilitating communication between experts, government officials, other elites, and their audiences. Stead's journalist-as-ruler became Lippmann's journalist-as-stenographer. Where Stead believed journalism should conduct major studies and investigations, managing entire apparatuses of knowledge production, after World War I Lippmann believed the role of journalism was to signalize an event, not to analyze it.[2] Reporters should be granted access to powerful figures, but only within highly structured environments and rarely on the journalist's own terms.

In 1913, Lippmann diagnosed modern life as a "monstrous confusion" due to the "tumultuous medley" of public demands for reform and social change.[3] Lively public participation in political life had led only to shortsighted reforms and was unlikely to produce social stability over the long term. Lippmann believed that underlying moral and political crusades were real social needs, but that these social movements should not be addressed in raw form. They had to be translated into rational terms by people in possession of a clearer understanding of the issues and possible solutions than the agitators themselves.

Progressive Era crusades around white slavery and vice provided the catalyst for some of Lippmann's early anti-rationalist assumptions, suggesting that the sex trafficking scandals of this period were sites of political conflict, not only over the ostensible events and issues at hand, but over the future and direction of mass media and politics. In *A Preface to Politics* Lippmann analyzed the 1911 report of the Vice Commission of Chicago as the product of an inflammatory press, a reactive public, and a hyper-responsive politician.[4] In doing so, he provided an early theoretical rationale for new developments in public opinion management that became central to both news practice and the professionalization of journalism after World War I. The solution to the endless crusade, Lippmann believed, lay in the implementation of additional stages of mediation between the public and elected officials. But while Lippmann saw practical problems with the multidirectional flow of information that characterized Progressive Era politics, he was blind to the potential pitfalls of expert knowledge and the rise of public relations.

Sex trafficking inspired large changes in the mass media and journalistic conventions particularly because they were the focal point for scandals that were uncontained. Sex trafficking also served as a politically expedient weapon for waging ideological battles on a variety of fronts: economic (monopolists), social (aristocrats and immigrants), and sexual. Since the white slavery scandals of the early twentieth century, the specter of sex trafficking had become a ready-made controversy that was always potentially there, lying dormant but becoming politically potent at moments of political transformation as well as social, demographic, and economic change.[5]

Media attention to white slavery had largely disappeared in the United States by the onset of World War I. International activism waned by the 1930s, although the League of Nations had an active sex trafficking agenda well into the 1930s, and the United Nations declared trafficking a human rights violation in 1949. Beginning in the 1990s, however, newspaper stories, television documentaries, magazine articles, as well as fictional and documentary films, again began to detail the emergence of global sex trafficking networks in the United States and abroad. Stories depicting the horrors of "modern-day sexual slavery" now appear with some regularity in the *New York Times*, the very paper that debunked early twentieth-century claims of white slavery in the United States. Sex trafficking narratives appear at specific moments in time corresponding with the rise of conflicts involving specific social and political movements and also in response to political and economic changes, such as regime instability and increased immigration.

However, current abolitionist campaigns against prostitution and media coverage of sex trafficking are not carbon copies of those from the earlier white slavery crusades. Current sex trafficking activism and media coverage is marked by historical continuities and discontinuities. Debates over prostitution more generally have shifted due to the emergence in the last twenty-five years of new activist groups with diverging understandings of sex trafficking, the rise of human rights as a central site for addressing claims, and the ascendancy of neoliberal political agendas. New trafficking discourses frequently reference such issues as globalization, the collapse of Communism, and the rise of global sex tourism. They also resurfaced in the midst of an ongoing AIDS epidemic that has altered the way our society thinks about sexuality, challenged journalistic conventions, and given rise to new political subjects and activist strategies.[6] Such developments as the formation of national and transnational movements supporting gay and lesbian rights as well as prostitutes' rights, the emergence of queer theory and activism, and the theorization of a sex-radical feminism have altered the political terrain upon which trafficking claims are made, but so has the rise of new evangelical movements that consider abolishing sexual slavery a top priority.[7]

Popular debates over trafficking now occur within a range of media (broadcast, film, and digital media), in additional to more traditional print media. Adversaries in the current "trafficking debates" offer competing definitions of commercial sex and differ sharply over issues concerning the legitimacy and legality of prostitution. New relations of reciprocity have emerged between mass media representational strategies and social movements seeking to gain access to mass audiences by positioning themselves as experts and commentators on issues concerning prostitution.

From an early twenty-first century vantage point, it is clear that issues of immigration, urbanization, heterosociability, and racial mixing were stitched into white slavery narratives. The social changes woven into current trafficking narratives are not as readily apparent, precisely because we are living and experiencing them in the moment. In a profession whose primary function is to report on the "new," journalists do not always reflect on the history of the stories they tell. Ideally, research on the intertwined histories of sex scandals and journalism will encourage media practitioners and consumers to reflect on linkages between journalistic methods and specific representations of sexuality, including portrayals of gendered and racialized sexual violence. Continued research in this area may also encourage a better understanding of how historically specific economic and political conditions determine relationships between dominant media forms at work in the production of truth, social/political movements, and the rise and fall of salient topics such as sex trafficking that are not only deemed newsworthy, but at particular historical moments may generate debates of such magnitude that they transform the media themselves.

NOTES

PREFACE

1. "Crime Beat," *New York Sun,* 29 September 1835, 2.

2. Letter, *Chicago Tribune,* 15 March 1862, 4.

3. "Rally to Crush White Slave Sin," *Chicago Tribune,* 21 November 1907, 3.

4. Michel Foucault, "Truth and Power," in *Power/Knowledge: Selected Interviews and Other Writings, 1972–1977,* ed. Colin Gordon (New York: Pantheon Books, 1980); Stephen Reese, "The News Paradigm and the Ideology of Objectivity: A Socialist at the Wall Street Journal," *Critical Studies in Mass Communication* 7, no. 4 (1990): 390–409; Paula Treichler, *How to Have Theory in an Epidemic: Cultural Chronicles of AIDS* (Durham, NC: Duke University Press, 1999).

5. On the treatment of the Helen Jewett murder in the penny press, see Patricia Cline Cohen, *The Murder of Helen Jewett: The Life and Death of a Prostitute in Nineteenth-Century New York* (New York: Alfred A. Knopf, 1998); Carol A. Stabile, *White Victims, Black Villains: Gender, Race, and Crime News in US Culture* (New York: Routledge, 2006), chap. 2; Andie Tucher, *Froth and Scum: Truth, Beauty, Goodness, and the Ax Murder in America's First Mass Medium* (Chapel Hill: University of North Carolina Press, 1994).

6. See, for example, Patricia Cline Cohen, Timothy J. Gilfoyle, and Helen Lefkowitz Horowitz, *The Flash Press: Sporting Male Weeklies in 1840s New York* (Chicago: University of Chicago Press, 2008); Lisa Duggan, *Sapphic Slashers: Sex, Violence, and American Modernity* (Durham, NC: Duke University Press, 2000); Joshua Gamson, "Jessica Hahn, Media Whore: Sex Scandals and Female Publicity," *Critical Studies in Media Communication* 18, no. 4 (2001): 157–73; Robert Hanczor, "Articulation Theory and Public Controversy: Taking Sides Over *NYPD Blue,*" *Critical Studies in Mass Communication* 14, no. 1 (1997): 1–30; Jean Marie Lutes, *Front-Page Girls: Women Journalists in American Culture and Fiction, 1880–1930* (Ithaca, NY: Cornell University Press, 2007); Kevin Mumford, *Interzones: Black/White Sex Districts in Chicago and New York in the Early Twentieth Century* (New York: Columbia University Press, 1997); Stabile 2006; Treichler 1999; Christopher Wilson, *Cop Knowledge: Police Power and Cultural Narrative in Twentieth-Century America* (Chicago: University of Chicago Press, 2000).

7. See, for example, Susan Jeffords and Lauren Rabinovitz, eds., *Seeing Through the Media: The Persian Gulf War* (New Brunswick, NJ: Rutgers University Press, 1994); Edward S. Herman and Noam Chomsky, *Manufacturing Consent: The Political Economy of the Mass Media* (New York: Pantheon Books, 1998); Michael Schudson, *The Power of News* (Cambridge, MA: Harvard University Press, 1995); Barbie Zelizer, "Achieving Journalistic Authority Through Narrative," *Critical Studies in Mass Communication* 7, no. 4 (1990): 366–76.

CHAPTER ONE

1. Patricia Cline Cohen, *The Murder of Helen Jewett: The Life and Death of a Prostitute in Nineteenth-Century New York* (New York: Alfred A. Knopf, 1998).

2. David R. Roediger, *The Wages of Whiteness: Race and the Making of the American Working Class* (New York: Verso, 2007), 65.

3. "White Slaves," *Chicago Tribune*, 18 August 1862, 2.

4. "White Slavery in Turkey," *Independent*, 17 January 1895, 11; David Langum, *Crossing Over the Line: Legislating Morality and the Mann Act* (Chicago: University of Chicago Press, 1994), 26.

5. "A System of White Slavery," *Chicago Daily Tribune*, 4 January 1888, 8.

6. John J. O'Shea, "The White Slave Trade," *Catholic World*, June 1894, 424.

7. "Four Thousand White Slaves," *San Francisco Call*, 13 March 1906, 11.

8. Stuart Hall, Charles Chritcher, Tony Jefferson, John Clarke, and Brian Robert, *Policing the Crisis: Mugging, the State, and Law and Order* (New York: Holmes and Meier, 1978), 21.

9. Mark Connelly, *The Response to Prostitution in the Progressive Era* (Chapel Hill: University of North Carolina Press, 1980); Langum 1994.

10. Kathleen Barry, *Female Sexual Slavery* (New York: New York University Press, 1979); Ruth Rosen, *The Lost Sisterhood: Prostitution in America, 1900–1918* (Baltimore, MD: Johns Hopkins University Press, 1982).

11. Connelly 1980; Stuart Ewen, *PR! A Social History of Spin* (New York: Basic Books, 1996); Joan McDermott and Sarah J. Blackstone, "White Slavery Plays of the 1910s: Fear of Victimization and the Social Control of Sexuality," *Theatre History Studies* 16 (June 1996): 141–55.

12. Connelly 1980; Sharon R. Ullman, *Sex Seen: The Emergence of Modern Sexuality in America* (Berkeley and Los Angeles: University of California Press, 1997).

13. Janet Beer and Katherine Joslin, "Diseases of the Body Politic: White Slavery in Jane Addams' *A New Conscience and an Ancient Evil* and Selected Short Stories by Charlotte Perkins Gilman," *Journal of American Studies* 33, no. 1 (1999): 1–18; Connelly 1980; Christopher Diffee, "Sex and the City: The White Slavery Scare and Social Governance in the Progressive Era," *American Quarterly* 57, no. 2 (2005): 411–37; Brian Donovan, *White Slave Crusades: Race, Gender, and Anti-vice Activism, 1887–1917* (Urbana: University of Illinois Press, 2006); Frederick K. Grittner, *White Slavery: Myth, Ideology, and American Law* (New York: Garland, 1990); Mara L. Keire, "The Vice Trust: A Reinterpretation of the White Slavery Scare in the United States, 1907–1917," *Journal of Social History* 35, no. 1 (2001): 5–41; Kevin Mumford, *Interzones: Black/White Sex*

Districts in Chicago and New York in the Early Twentieth Century (New York: Columbia University Press, 1997).

14. Cynthia M. Blair, *I've Got to Make my Livin': Black Women's Sex Work in Turn-of-the-Century Chicago* (Chicago: University of Chicago Press, 2010); Alain Corbin, "Commercial Sexuality in Nineteenth-Century France: A System of Images and Regulations," in *The Making of the Modern Body*, ed. Catherine Gallagher and Thomas Laqueur (Berkeley and Los Angeles: University of California Press, 1987), 209–19; Timothy Gilfoyle, *City of Eros* (New York: W. W. Norton, 1992); Stephanie A. Limoncelli, *The Politics of Trafficking: The First International Movement to Combat the Sexual Exploitation of Women* (Stanford, CA: Stanford University Press, 2010); Benson Tong, *Unsubmissive Women: Chinese Prostitutes in Nineteenth-Century San Francisco* (Norman: University of Oklahoma Press, 1994); Judith R. Walkowitz, *Prostitution and Victorian Society: Women, Class, and the State* (Cambridge: Cambridge University Press, 1980), and *City of Dreadful Delight: Narratives of Sexual Danger in Late-Victorian London* (Chicago: University of Chicago Press, 1992).

15. Jeannette Delamoir, "'It Pulsates with Dramatic Power': White Slavery, Popular Culture and Modernity in Australia in 1913," *Journal of Australian Studies* 82 (June 2004): 25–36; Shelley Stamp Lindsey, "Is Any Girl Safe? Female Spectators and the White Slave Films, *Screen* 37, no. 1 (1996): 1–15, and "'Oil Upon the Flames of Vice': The Battle over White Slave Films in New York City," *Film History* 9, no. 4 (1997): 351–64.

16. "The Dangers of a Large City, Or The System of the Underworld: Exposing the White Slave Traffic" (Chicago: n.p., n.d.).

17. Clifford G. Roe, *Panders and Their White Slaves* (New York: Fleming H. Revell, 1910), n.p. The image was also featured on the cover of Ernest A. Bell, ed., *Fighting the Traffic in Young Girls, or War on the White Slave Trade* (Chicago: G. S. Ball, 1910).

18. Jean Turner Zimmermann, *Chicago's Black Traffic in White Girls* (Chicago: Chicago Rescue Mission, 1912); Bell 1910, n.p. (opening page of book).

19. Blair 2010, 3; See also Donovan 2006.

20. Mumford 1997, 16.

21. Tong 1994, 11.

22. "Startling Facts," *Sacramento Record-Union*, 22 July 1885, 1.

23. See Lucie Cheng Hirata, "Free, Indentured, Enslaved: Chinese Prostitutes in Nineteenth-Century America," *Signs* 5, no. 1 (1979): 3–29; Jean Pfaelzer, *Driven Out: The Forgotten War Against Chinese Americans* (New York: Random House, 2007); Tong 1994.

24. See, for example, "The Yellow Slave Trade," in Bell 1910, 213–22.

25. Jean Turner Zimmermann, *White or Yellow? A Story of America's Great White Slave Trade with Asia* (Chicago: n.p., 1916).

26. John B. Thompson, "Scandal and Social Theory," in *Media Scandals: Morality and Desire in Popular Culture*, ed. James Lull and Stephen Hinerman (New York: Columbia University Press, 1997), 50.

27. James Lull and Stephen Hinerman, "The Search for Scandal," in *Media Scandals: Morality and Desire in Popular Culture*, ed. James Lull and Stephen Hinerman (New York: Columbia University Press, 1997), 3.

28. Paul Apostolidis and Juliet A. Williams, "Sex Scandals and Discourses of Power," in *Public Affairs: Politics in the Age of Sex Scandal*, ed. Paul Apostolidis and

Juliet A. Williams (Durham, NC: Duke University Press, 2004), 1–37; Joshua Gamson, "Jessica Hahn, Media Whore: Sex Scandals and Female Publicity," *Critical Studies in Media Communication* 18, no. 2 (2001): 157–73.

29. For a more recent example of this dynamic, see Gretchen Soderlund, "Journalist or Panderer? Framing Underage Webcam Sites," *Sexuality Research and Social Policy* 5, no. 4 (2008): 62–72.

30. Emma Goldman, *The Traffic in Women and Other Essays on Feminism* (Ojai, CA: Times Change Press, 1970), 20. (Orig. pub. 1917.)

31. Walter Lippmann, *A Preface to Politics* (New York: MacMillan, 1913), 145.

32. See Allan M. Brandt, *No Magic Bullet: A Social History of Venereal Disease in the United States Since 1880* (Oxford: Oxford University Press, 1985).

33. Michel Foucault, "Truth and Power," in *Power/Knowledge: Selected Interviews and Other Writings, 1972–1977*, ed. Colin Gordon (New York: Pantheon Books, 1980), 131.

34. Foucault 1980, 132.

35. Michel Foucault, *The Order of Things: An Archaeology of Knowledge* (New York: Routledge, 2002).

36. Foucault 1980, 114.

37. Thomas Kuhn, *The Structure of Scientific Revolutions* (Chicago: University of Chicago Press, 1996).

38. Michael Schudson, *Discovering the News: A Social History of American Newspapers* (New York: Basic Books, 1978), 3–11.

39. Kevin G. Barnhurst and John Nerone, *The Form of News: A History* (New York: Guilford Press, 2001).

40. In the chapters that follow I use quotation marks around "sensationalism" to signal that it is an attributed construct. When there are no quotation marks, *sensationalism* is meant as a descriptive and analytical term whose meaning can be contested. However, I rarely place quotation marks around the term *white slavery* because it always was and still is a term whose meaning and even existence was contested. The term *white slavery* comes preloaded with dynamic chains of signification, some of which are quite evident today.

41. Michael Ayers Trotti, *The Body in the Reservoir: Murder and Sensationalism in the South* (Chapel Hill: University of North Carolina Press, 2008), 5.

42. See, for example, David R. Spencer, *The Yellow Journalism: The Press and America's Emergence as a World Power* (Evanston, IL: Northwestern University Press, 2007).

43. Michael Emery, Edwin Emery, and Nancy L. Roberts, *The Press and America: An Interpretive History*, 9th ed. (Boston: Allyn and Bacon, 2000), 97.

44. I am obviously indebted to Michel Foucault's discussion of repression in *The History of Sexuality*, vol. 1 (Harmondsworth, UK: Penguin, 1979) for my understanding of sensationalism as an overwhelmingly positive strategy.

45. Lisa Duggan, *Sapphic Slashers: Sex, Violence, and American Modernity* (Durham, NC: Duke University Press, 2000), 35. For another nuanced, though less analytical, approach to sensationalism that considers its use in the generation of audiences, this time in Gilded Age illustrated weeklies, see Joshua Brown, *Beyond the Lines: Pictorial Reporting, Everyday Life, and the Crisis of Gilded Age America* (Berkeley and Los Angeles: University of California Press, 2002).

46. Hazel Dicken-Garcia, *Journalistic Standards in Nineteenth-Century America* (Madison: University of Wisconsin Press, 1989), 123–28.

47. Warren Francke, "Sensationalism and the Development of 19th-Century Reporting: The Broom Sweeps Sensory Details," *Journalism History* 12, nos. 3–4 (1985): 82.

48. Schudson 1978, 95.

49. In this regard, we see a resurgence of the trope of the journalistic hoax after the turn of the century, but couched in terms of sensationalism. For a discussion of earlier controversies over the hoax (or the "humbug") in the penny presses, see Brown 2002, chap. 1; Andie Tucher, *Froth and Scum: Truth, Beauty, Goodness, and the Ax Murder in America's First Mass Medium* (Chapel Hill: University of North Carolina Press, 1994).

50. "A.B.C.'s," 1, cited in Rosen 1982, 114.

51. Edwin W. Sims, "The Menace of the White Slave Trade," in Bell 1910, 63. See also Edwin W. Sims, *The White Slave Trade of Today* (Chicago: n.p., 1911), 73.

52. "White Slave Story False, Says Guide," *New York Times*, 28 October 1909, 3.

53. See James W. Carey, *Communication as Culture: Essays on Media and Society* (New York: Routledge, 1988); Michael Schudson, *The Power of News* (Cambridge, MA: Harvard University Press, 1995); Barbie Zelizer, "Achieving Journalistic Authority Through Narrative," *Critical Studies in Mass Communication* 7, no. 4 (1990): 366–76.

54. See Frank D. Durham, "News Frames as Social Narratives: TWA Flight 800," *Journal of Communication* 48, no. 4 (1998): 100–117; Robert Hackett, "Decline of a Paradigm? Bias and Objectivity in News Media Studies," *Critical Studies in Mass Communication* 1, no. 3 (1984): 229–59; Edward Herman and Noam Chomsky, *Manufacturing Consent: The Political Economy of the Mass Media* (New York: Pantheon Books, 1998); Ekaterina Ognianova and James Endersby, "Objectivity Revisited: a Spatial Model of Political Ideology and Mass Communication," *Journalism and Mass Communication Monographs* 159 (October 1996): 660–79; Stephen Reese, "The News Paradigm and the Ideology of Objectivity: A Socialist at the Wall Street Journal," *Critical Studies in Mass Communication* 7, no. 4 (1990): 390–409; Gayle Tuchman, "Objectivity as Strategic Ritual: An Examination of Newsmen's Notions of Objectivity," *American Journal of Sociology* 77, no. 4 (1972): 660–79.

55. Michael Schudson, "The Objectivity Norm in American Journalism," *Journalism: Theory, Practice and Criticism* 2, no. 2 (2001): 149–70.

56. S. Elizabeth Bird, "Storytelling on the Far Side: Journalism and the Weekly Tabloid," *Critical Studies in Mass Communication* 7, no. 4 (1990): 378.

57. Stuart Ewen, *PR! A Social History of Spin* (New York: Basic Books, 1996); Harlan Stensaas, "Development of the Objectivity Ethic in U.S. Daily Newspapers," *Journal of Mass Media Ethics* 2, no. 1 (1986–87): 50–60; Michael Schudson 1978.

58. Kevin Stoker, "Existential Objectivity: Freeing Journalists to be Ethical." *Journal of Mass Media Ethics* 10, no. 1 (1995): 6.

59. Daniel Schiller, *Objectivity and the News: The Public and the Rise of Commercial Journalism* (Philadelphia: University of Pennsylvania Press, 1981).

60. Michael Emery, Edwin Emery, and Nancy Roberts, *The Press and America: An Interpretive History of the Mass Media* (Boston: Allyn and Bacon, 1978), 145.

61. David T. Z. Mindich, *Just the Facts: How "Objectivity" Came to Define American Journalism* (New York: New York University Press, 2000). For another example

of work that takes issue with the clear delineation of phases in the history of American journalism, see John Nerone, "The Mythology of the Penny Press," *Critical Studies in Mass Communication* 4, no. 4 (1987): 376–404.

62. Francke 1985, 82.

63. William T. Stead, "Government by Journalism," *Contemporary Review* 49 (May 1886): 670.

64. Stead 1886, 671.

CHAPTER TWO

1. *Pall Mall Gazette*, 23 February 1884, 1.

2. See Edward Bristow, *Vice and Vigilance: Purity Movements in Britain since 1700* (Totowa, NJ: Rowman and Littlefield, 1977); Raymond L. Schultz, *Crusader in Babylon: W. T. Stead and the Pall Mall Gazette* (Lincoln: University of Nebraska Press, 1972).

3. See Bristow 1977; Josephine Butler, *Personal Reminiscences of a Great Crusade* (Cheshire, UK: Portrayer, 1896); Judith R. Walkowitz, *Prostitution and Victorian Society: Women, Class, and the State* (Cambridge: Cambridge University Press, 1980).

4. Stead, quoted in Bristow 1977, 77.

5. See Bristow 1977, 103–6.

6. Bristow 1977, 107.

7. W. T. Stead, *The Maiden Tribute of Modern Babylon: The Report of the Secret Commission*, ed. Antony E. Simpson (Lambertville, NJ: True Bill Press, 2007), 143. Originally published in 1885 in the *Pall Mall Gazette*. All quotations from "The Maiden Tribute" come from this edition, which is hereafter cited parenthetically by page number in the text.

8. Though the "investigative team" is mentioned at the beginning of the text, details of the role this collective played in the collection and production of knowledge were largely omitted from the published version. The actual investigation and its published narrative likely bore little resemblance to one another. In the exposé, Stead described a snowball effect: one source directed him to the next. The number of sources grew exponentially until he became satisfied that he had consulted a representative sample of informants and had encountered a sufficient variety of situations to construct his social object. The investigation's story began with Stead's conversation about prostitution, age, and agency with an anonymous member of Parliament. The M.P., though professing skepticism about the existence of unwilling virgin prostitutes, nonetheless introduced Stead to an old "friend to whom the brothels of Europe were as familiar as Notre Dame and St. Paul's." This "evergreen old gentleman" referred Stead to several brothels. However, it was difficult to gain access to them because the vice world was on high alert after Mrs. Jeffries' arrest. Nonetheless, Stead managed to gain some "trustworthy and experienced friends" who used their influence and credibility in the vice world to overcome obstacles to access. Ultimately, Stead interviewed several brothel keepers on London's east and west sides, as well as a team of procuresses, at least two midwives (who apparently did side work certifying virginity, repairing hymens, and performing abortions), and several teenage girls involved in the sex trade in various ways. See Stead 2007, 66.

9. On the history of this reportorial strategy, see Warren Francke, "Sensationalism and the Development of 19th-Century Reporting: The Broom Sweeps Sensory Details," *Journalism History* 12, nos. 3–4 (1985): 80–85.

10. Stuart Hall, "The Narrative Construction of Reality: An Interview with Stuart Hall," *Southern Review* 17 (March 1984): 7.

11. Sally Mitchell, "Sentiment and Suffering: Women's Recreational Reading in the 1860s," *Victorian Studies* 21, no. 1 (1977): 34.

12. See Raymond Williams, *The Country and the City* (Oxford: Oxford University Press, 1975); Mary Poovey, *Making a Social Body: British Cultural Formation, 1830–1864* (Chicago: University of Chicago Press, 1995).

13. See Rita Felski, *The Gender of Modernity* (Cambridge, MA: Harvard University Press, 1995); Judith Walkowitz, *City of Dreadful Delight: Narratives of Sexual Danger in Late-Victorian London* (Chicago: University of Chicago Press, 1992).

14. Deborah Gorham, "The 'Maiden Tribute of Modern Babylon' Re-Examined: Child Prostitution and the Idea of Childhood in Late-Victorian England," *Victorian Studies* 21 (Spring 1978): 355.

15. Walkowitz 1992, 85.

16. See Walkowitz 1992.

17. Ibid., 97.

18. Walkowitz points out that Stead continued to conduct interviews with prostitutes well after the publication of "The Maiden Tribute" and wrote of his investigative exploits in his diary, which Walkowitz likens to his "field notes." From her reading of this diary, she concludes that Stead's paid informants told stories of abduction and seduction, while his unpaid informants "spoke the unsensational language of sexual bartering" (ibid., 114).

19. William T. Stead, "Government by Journalism," *Contemporary Review* 49 (May 1886): 653–74.

20. In the Monday, July 6, installment of the exposé, Stead posited two types of prostitution, "willing and unwilling." He suggested "the vast majority" of prostitutes in London did not "come there by the road of organized rape." Of these, he argued "most fall either by the seduction of individuals or by the temptation which well-dressed vice can offer to the poor." However, "a minority" of "victims" were forced into the trade. Within this subset some were "snared, trapped, and outraged" after being placed "under the influence of drugs or after a prolonged struggle in a locked room." Others were "bought at so much per head," or "enticed under various promises into the fatal chamber from which they [were] never allowed to emerge." Despite Stead's acknowledgment that willing prostitution existed in the city, there was considerable slippage between his two typologies. Both willing and unwilling prostitutes were seduced or lured using various methods. Violence and torture, however, set unwilling apart from willing prostitution. Poverty, on the other hand, was the only characteristic of willing prostitution that was not simultaneously offered as an explanation for unwilling prostitution. While Stead refers to teenage prostitutes as the "daughters of the poor," he denied the possibility that they, and not just their parents, might be actively motivated by poverty (ibid., 64–65).

21. Male purveyors of prostitutes preferred the contractual model, which ignored the role of larger structural forces and saw only the simplest dyadic form of buyer and seller.

They feigned disbelief when approached with the possibility of abusive practices on the streets and in brothels. This view was embodied by the "evergreen old gentleman," who "entirely denied that there was such a thing as the procuring of virgins, willing or unwilling, either here or on the continent." However, when pressed, the man admitted that in some cases "little girls were bought and sold for vicious purposes" and that, for this reason alone, Stead's investigation was probably justified (Stead 2007, 66).

22. Stead 2007, 68. However, other girls and two entrepreneurial procuresses, Mesdames X. and Z., specialized in part-time opportunistic prostitution. They argued, both to Stead and to the girls they recruited, that the loss of virginity was more-or-less inevitable, and therefore the best approach is to lose it for money. As they put it, "If a girl is to be seduced it is better she should be seduced by a gentleman, and get something for it than let herself be seduced by a boy or young fellow who gives her nothing for it." The Mesdames thus offered an opportunistic model of prostitution in which girls made active choices from among a limited set of options. As with Stead's one-pound versus two-pound formulation, this perspective is not given calculative legitimacy in his exposé (Stead 2007, 99).

23. Francke 1985, 82.

24. Stead, quoted in Schultz 1972, 86.

25. Nils Gunnar Nilsson, "The Origin of the Interview," *Journalism Quarterly* 48 (Winter 1971): 707–13.

26. George Rider, quoted in Hazel Dicken-Garcia, *Journalistic Standards in Nineteenth Century America* (Madison: University of Wisconsin Press, 1989), 201.

27. See Dicken-Garcia 1989; Frank Luther Mott, *American Journalism, A History: 1890–1960* (New York: MacMillan, 1962).

28. Stead 1886, 669.

29. On the relationship between early sociology and urban reportage, see Rolf Lindner, *The Reportage of Urban Culture: Robert Park and the Chicago School* (Cambridge: Cambridge University Press, 1996).

30. On the history of eyewitnessing in journalism, see Barbie Zelizer, "On 'Having Been There': 'Eyewitnessing' as a Journalistic Keyword," *Critical Studies in Media Communication* 24, no. 5 (2007): 408–28.

31. Walkowitz (1992) originally pointed out this irony.

32. Bristow 1977.

33. Ibid.

34. George Cavendish Bentinck, quoted in Schultz 1972, 137.

35. Schultz 1972, 146.

36. H. A. D. Philips, "Offenses Against Marriage and the Relations of the Sexes," *Law Quarterly Journal* 47 (October 18[illegible]) 47[illegible]

37. Ibid., 483.

38. Schultz 1972, 141.

39. Ibid., 146.

40. Ibid., 147.

41. Alison Plowden, *The Case of Eliza Armstrong: A Child of 13 Bought for £5* (London: British Broadcasting Corporation, 1974); J. W. Robertson Scott, *The Life and Death of a Newspaper: An Account of the Temperaments, Perturbations, and Achievements of*

John Morley, W. T. Stead, E. T. Cook, Harry Cust, J. L. Garvin, and Three Other Editors of the Pall Mall Gazette (London: Methuen, 1952), 136; Schultz 1972; Walkowitz 1992.

42. Henry Poland, quoted in Plowden 1974, 16.

43. This quotation comes from a public announcement made by Stead at St. James Hall; quoted in Plowden 1974, 10.

44. Ibid., 34.

45. Ibid., 23.

46. Ibid., 34

47. Ibid., 35

48. The trial itself said much about social class and the power of language, spoken and written. Stead's implicit argument was that it was incumbent upon the middle class to protect young girls because the other classes were in collusion and equally morally bereft. His worldview placed the middle class at the center of a new moral authority. Literacy was a tool of this ascension.

49. Plowden 1974, 97

50. Ibid., 109–10.

51. Ibid., 111.

52. Scott 1952.

53. Ibid., 135.

54. Ibid., 146–47.

55. Ibid., 147.

56. Plowden 1974, 137.

57. Stead 1886, 653.

58. Ibid., 661.

59. Ibid., 659. Stead excoriates other journalists for failing to recognize this power and imagining a limited role for the media. These journalists believe that "leadership, guidance, governance, are alien to the calling of the journalist. These conceptions of what is a journalist's duty, if indeed they recognize that imperious word as having any bearing upon their profession, is hid in mystery. If it may be inferred from their practice, their ideal is to grind out a column of more or less well-balanced sentences, capable of grammatical construction, conflicting with no social conventionality or party prejudice. . . . How can they help to make up other people's minds when they have never made up their own?" (Stead 1886, 667). This description of the nineteenth-century journalist bears a striking resemblance to the image of the unbiased, objective journalist capable of sifting through information and alerting audiences to pertinent debates, but avoiding telling people what to think.

60. Ibid., 664.

61. Ibid., 656.

62. Ibid., 657.

63. Ibid., 667.

64. Ibid., 660.

65. Ibid., 671. Stead saw newspapers standing silent as abuses were committed and wanted to render his profession more responsive to social evils. The prostitute was always the limit case in hypothetical press scenarios. In one hypothetical case, Stead declared that if prostitutes were used as subjects for vivisection, only a couple of papers

would protest. The rest would "avoid the subject as much as possible, in the interests of public morality and public decency," while "the *Saturday Review* would empty vials of its sourest ink over the indecent Maenads and shrieking sisters who publicly denounced such an outrage on humanity and womanhood" (670).

66. Stead thus anticipated a major, late twentieth-century Marxist critique of the commodity audience among political economists of the media. See Eileen R. Meehan, "Why We Don't Count: The Commodity Audience," *Logics of Television: Essays in Cultural Criticism*, ed. Patricia Mellencamp (Bloomington: Indiana University Press, 1990), 117–37.

67. Stead 1886, 673–74.

68. William T. Stead, "The Future of Journalism," *Contemporary Review* 50 (November 1887): 664.

69. Ibid., 666.

70. Ibid., 672.

71. Ibid., 674.

72. Ibid., 678.

CHAPTER THREE

1. See John D'Emilio and Estelle Freedman, *Intimate Matters: A History of Sexuality in America* (Chicago: University of Chicago Press, 1997), 50–52, 130–38; Ruth Rosen, *The Lost Sisterhood: Prostitution in America, 1900–1918* (Baltimore, MD: Johns Hopkins University Press, 1982), chap. 1.

2. See Barbara Meil Hobson, *Uneasy Virtue: The Politics of Prostitution and the American Reform Tradition* (New York: Basic Books, 1987), 147–49.

3. In spite of abolitionists' victorious campaigns against regulation, regulationists attained some of their goals tacitly through zoning ordinances that segregated brothels into red-light districts, rendering them easier to manage and oversee. See David J. Pivar, *Purity Crusade: Sexual Morality and Social Control, 1868–1900* (Westport, CT: Greenwood Press, 1973); Rosen 1982.

4. Josephine Butler, "Mrs. Butler's Appeal to the Women of America," *Philanthropist*, October 1888, 16.

5. Frances E. Willard, *Address Before the Second Biennial Convention of the World's Woman's Christian Temperance Union, and the Twentieth Annual Convention of the National WCTU*, Chicago, 29 October–1 November (Chicago: Women's Temperance Publishing Association, 1893), 37.

6. "The Social Purity Movement in Europe," *Philanthropist*, August 1886, 4.

7. There were some earlier examples of moral reform politics sponsored by women, including New York City's Female Benevolent Society and Female Moral Reform Society, which both formed in the 1830s. See Larry Whiteakre, *Seduction, Prostitution, and Moral Reform in New York, 1830–1860* (New York: Garland, 1997).

8. Barbara L. Epstein, *The Politics of Domesticity: Women, Evangelism, and Temperance in Nineteenth-Century America* (Middletown, CT: Wesleyan University Press, 1981); Susanne M. Marilley, "Frances Willard and the Feminism of Fear," *Feminist*

Studies 19, no. 1 (1993): 123–46; Alison M. Parker, *Purifying America: Women, Cultural Reform, and Pro-Censorship Activism, 1873–1933* (Urbana: University of Illinois Press, 1997).

9. Willard 1893, 2.

10. Frances E. Willard, *A White Life for Two* (Chicago: Women's Temperance Publication Association, 1890), 1.

11. Ibid., 7.

12. By 1890 the WCTU had 150,000 dues-paying members, while the NAWSA had only 13,000. See Ruth Bordin, *Woman and Temperance: The Quest for Power and Liberty, 1873–1900* (Philadelphia, PA: Temple University Press, 1981), 3–4.

13. Carrie Chapman Catt, "Religion and Women's Rights," in *Up From the Pedestal: Selected Writings in the History of American Feminism*, ed. Aileen Kraditor (Chicago: Quadrangle Books, 1968), 261–62; orig. pub. 1894.

14. See D'Emilio and Freedman 1997.

15. See Ian Tyrrell, *Woman's World/Woman's Empire: The Woman's Christian Temperance Union in International Perspective, 1880–1930* (Chapel Hill: University of North Carolina Press, 1991).

16. Epstein 1981, 5.

17. See Mary Poovey, *Uneven Developments: The Ideological Work of Gender in Mid-Victorian England* (Chicago: University of Chicago Press, 1988); Judith R. Walkowitz, *Prostitution and Victorian Society: Women, Class, and the State* (Cambridge: Cambridge University Press, 1980), and *City of Dreadful Delight: Narratives of Sexual Danger in Late-Victorian London* (Chicago: University of Chicago Press, 1992).

18. See Caroll Smith-Rosenberg, *Disorderly Conduct: Visions of Gender in Victorian America* (New York: Alfred A. Knopf, 1985); Christine Stansell, *City of Women: Sex and Class in New York, 1789–1860* (Urbana: University of Illinois Press, 1987).

19. See Paula Baker, "The Domestication of Politics: Women and American Political Society, 1780–1920," *American Historical Review* 89, no. 3 (1984): 620–47.

20. See Carl F. Kaestle, "The History of Readers," in *Literacy in the United States: Readers and Reading since 1880*, ed. Carl F. Kaestle, Helen Damon Moore, Lawrence C. Stedman, Katherine Tinsley, and William Vance Trollinger Jr. (New Haven, CT: Yale University Press, 1991), 33–72; David Paul Nord, *Communities of Journalism: A History of American Newspapers and Their Readers* (Urbana: University of Illinois Press, 2001).

21. See Michael Emery, Edwin Emery, and Nancy L. Roberts, *The Press and America: An Interpretive History of the Mass Media* (Boston: Allyn and Bacon, 2000), esp. chap. 8.

22. S. N. D. North, "History and Present Conditions of the Newspaper and Periodical Press of the United States with a Catalogue of the publications of the Census Year," in *Tenth Census* (Washington, DC: U.S. Department of the Interior, Bureau of the Census, 1884), 8:51.

23. The terms *associational press* and *informational press* come from Nord 2001.

24. See Michael Schudson, *Discovering the News: A Social History of American Newspapers* (New York: Basic Books, 1978).

25. For an analysis of the scope of religious publishing in the nineteenth century and an account of its decline, see Paul C. Gutjahr, "Diversification in American Religious

Publishing," in *A History of the Book in America*, vol. 3, *The Industrial Book, 1840–1880*, ed. Scott E. Casper, Jeffrey D. Groves, Stephen Nissenbaum, and Michael Winship (Chapel Hill: University of North Carolina Press, 2007), 194–202.

26. Anna Garlin Spencer, *Literature and Vice* (Chicago: Women's Temperance Publication Association, 1887), 1.

27. Ibid.

28. M. Y. Beach. "The Accuracy of Reporters," *Writer* 10, no. 6 (1891): 112–13.

29. James Parton, "Journalism as a Profession for Young Men," *Writer* 7, no. 5 (1988): 105.

30. See Alison M. Parker, *Purifying America: Women, Cultural Reform, and Pro-Censorship Activism, 1873–1933* (Urbana: University of Illinois Press, 1997).

31. "Women's Press Associations," *Union Signal*, 20 January 1887, 2.

32. "To Our Censors," *Pall Mall Gazette*, 13 July 1885, 1.

33. For a discussion of the wire service, see Daniel J. Czitrom, *Media and the American Mind: From Morse to McLuhan* (Chapel Hill: University of North Carolina Press, 1982), chap. 1.

34. "The Immorality of London," *New York Herald*, 7 July 1885, 4.

35. "Obscene London," *New York Herald*, 9 July 1885, 4.

36. "The Morals of Mayfair," *New York Herald*, 10 July 1885, 5.

37. "Prurience and Politics," *New York Herald*, 13 July 1885, 4.

38. "The London Scandal," *New York Sun*, 10 July 1885, 2.

39. "A Terrible Picture of Vice," *New York Sun*, 12 July 1885, 2.

40. W. T. Stead, "To Our Censors," *Pall Mall Gazette*, 13 July 1885, 1; "The Iniquity of London," *New York Sun*, 13 July 1885, 1.

41. "The Newspaper's Proper Work," *New York Daily Graphic*, 9 July 1885, 1.

42. "Public Abuses and the Press," *New York Daily Graphic*, 9 July 1885, 1.

43. "Scandals in Washington," *New York Daily Graphic*, 13 July 1885, 1.

44. "Dirty Reform," *Nation* July 1885, 40.

45. See Rosen 1982.

46. Frances E. Willard, *Glimpses of Fifty Years: The Autobiography of an American Woman* (Chicago: Woman's Temperance Publication Association, 1889), 419–20.

47. "Age of Consent," *Union Signal*, 3 December 1885, 4.

48. "Stockholders' Meeting," *Union Signal*, 12 November 1885, 3.

49. Frances E. Willard, *Address Before the Twenty-Second Annual Convention of the Woman's Christian Temperance Union*, Baltimore, MD, 18–23 October (Chicago: Women's Temperance Publishing Association, 1895), 24.

50. Josephine Butler, "Address by Mrs. Josephine Butler," *Philanthropist*, January 1886, 3.

51. Aaron Powell, "Mr. Stead and His 'Party,'" *Philanthropist*, January 1886, 8.

52. See Pivar 1973, 132–35.

53. Nord 2001, 111.

54. Willard 1893, 5.

55. Ibid., 42.

56. Ibid., 44.

57. "On the Watchtower," *Union Signal*, 4 January 1883, 12.

58. "Press Department," *Union Signal*, 19 November 1885, 6.

59. Ruth Bordin, *Woman and Temperance: The Quest for Power and Liberty, 1873–1900* (Philadelphia, PA: Temple University Press, 1981), 93.

60. "Press Department," 6.

61. Annual Address of Frances E. Willard, President of Nat'l Woman's Christian Temperance Union, 1889, Philadelphia, PA.

62. Both quotations in this paragraph are from "Women and Press Reform," *Woman's Journal*, 13 January 1894, 1.

63. "To Advertisers: Prosperity Attends the Judicious Advertiser," *Union Signal*, 26 April 1883, 14.

64. "Since Our Last Issue," *Union Signal*, 19 November 1885, 1.

65. "The Traffic in Girls," *Philanthropist*, February 1887, 1.

66. For an insightful discussion of the World's Women's Christian Temperance Union's adoption of these methods to discover and represent prostitution in British-controlled India, Hong Kong, and the Philippines, see Tyrrell 1991.

67. "The Illinois Women's Press Association," *Union Signal*, 20 May 1886, 2.

68. "Notes and Comments," *Philanthropist*, February 1887, 1.

69. "The Traffic in Girls," 4–5.

70. Contrast this emphasis on movement in U.S. depictions of trafficking with Stead's understanding of white slavery, which was largely static.

71. "The Traffic in Girls," 4–5.

72. Frances E. Willard, "Social Purity Work for 1887," *Union Signal*, 13 January 1887, 12.

73. "The New Crusade," *Philanthropist*, January 1887, 6.

74. "Another Marinette Victim," *Chicago Inter-Ocean*, 18 January 1888, 7.

75. "A Week in the 'Upper Peninsula,'" *Union Signal*, 31 March 1887, 8. See also "Since Our Last Issue," *Union Signal*, 31 March 1887, 1.

76. Frances E. Willard, "Michigan's Battle," *Union Signal*, 21 April 1887, 7.

77. "Stockade Dens in Michigan," *Chicago Inter-Ocean*, 14 June 1888, 4; "Marinette's Dens of Infamy," *Chicago Inter-Ocean*, 30 October 1887, 1; "Dives Raided," *Chicago Inter-Ocean*, 4 November 1887, 1.

78. "Where Satan Rules," *Milwaukee Daily Journal*, 7 February 1888, 1.

79. Bessie V. Cushman, "Another Maiden Tribute," *Union Signal*, 17 February 1887, 9.

80. For a keen analysis of Bushnell's belief that masculine culture and interpretive practices had adulterated the true meaning of God's work, see Dana Hardwick, "Man's Prattle, Woman's Word: The Biblical Mission of Katharine Bushnell," in *Spirituality and Social Responsibility: Vocational Vision of Women in the United Methodist Tradition*, ed. Rosemary Skinner Keller (Nashville, TN: Abingdon Press, 1993). For discussions of the nativist and racist dimensions of the WCTU's convictions and practices, see Brian Donovan, *White Slave Crusades: Race, Gender, and Anti-vice Activism, 1887–1917* (Urbana: University of Illinois Press, 2006); and Tyrrell 1991.

81. "Slavery Up North," *Milwaukee Sentinel*, 8 January 1889, 3.

82. Ibid.

83. "Social Crimes," *Milwaukee Daily Journal*, 9 January 1889, 1.

84. "She Rides a Hobby," *Milwaukee Daily Journal*, 16 January 1889, 1.

85. "Resented By All," *Milwaukee Sentinel*, 16 January 1889, 1.

86. See Hardwick 1993, 169. Hardwick points out, however, that Bushnell was not alone in her crusade, but received the assistance and support of WCTU members, Wisconsin clergy, and prohibitionists.

87. Quoted in Frederick K. Grittner, *White Slavery: Myth, Ideology, and American Law* (New York: Garland, 1990), 89.

88. James C. Ambrose, "Press Brakes on Womanhood," *Union Signal*, 24 January 188, 3–4.

89. "Impure Stories," *New York Tribune*, 20 December 1887, 3.

90. "The Press and Vice," *Philanthropist*, September 1886, 6.

91. Louis N. Megargee, "A Newspaper Sensation." *Lippincott's Magazine* 52 (December 1893): 729.

CHAPTER FOUR

1. Ernest A. Bell, *Fighting the Traffic in Young Girls* (Chicago: G. S. Ball, 1910), 10. The article he referred to was "The White Slave Traffic of Today," by US District Attorney Edwin Sims.

2. Committee of Fifteen, *The Social Evil: With Special Reference to Conditions Existing in the City of New York* (New York: G. P. Putnam and Sons, 1902), 11.

3. U.S. Senate, *Importing Women for Immoral Purposes: A Partial Report from the Immigration Commission on the Importation and Harboring of Women for Immoral Purposes*, 61st Cong., 2nd sess., 1909, doc. 196; U.S. Senate, *Reports of the Immigration Commission*, vol. 19, *Importation and Harboring of Women for Immoral Purposes*, 61st Cong., 3rd sess., 1910.

4. George Kibbe Turner, "The City of Chicago: A Study of the Great Immoralities," *McClure's* 28 (April 1907): 575–92; George Kibbe Turner, "The Daughters of the Poor: A Plain Story of the Development of New York City as a Leading Center of the White Slave Trade of the World, Under Tammany Hall," *McClure's* 34 (November 1909): 45–61.

5. For detailed discussion of the multiplicity of vice commission reports that it seems each major city generated during this period, see Mark Connelly, *The Response to Prostitution in the Progressive Era* (Chapel Hill: University of North Carolina Press, 1980). On the historical, juridical, and social implications of the Mann Act, see David Langum, *Crossing Over the Line: Legislating Morality and the Mann Act* (Chicago: University of Chicago Press, 1994).

6. Paul Starr, *The Creation of the Media: Political Origins of Modern Communications* (New York: Basic Books, 2004), 254.

7. See Dustin Harp, *Desperately Seeking Women Readers: U.S. Newspapers and the Construction of a Female Readership* (Lanham, MD: Lexington Books, 2007); Phyllis Leslie Abramson, *Sob Sister Journalism* (New York: Greenwood Press, 1990).

8. See S. S. McClure, "Cheap Magazines," *McClure's* 5 (August 1895): 4–6, on the cost-lowering strategy of new magazines.

9. On the "new" topical focus in magazines, see Arthur Reed Kimball, "The Invasion of Journalism," *Atlantic Monthly* 86 (July 1900): 119–25; Julian Hawthorne, "Journalism the Destroyer of Literature," *Critic* 48 (February 1906): 166–71. For a discussion of the

structure of the late nineteenth- and early twentieth-century literary marketplace, see Christopher Wilson, *The Labor of Words: Literary Professionalism in the Progressive Era* (Athens: University of Georgia Press, 1985).

10. Ray Stannard Baker, *American Chronicle* (New York: Charles Scribner and Sons, 1945), 28–32.

11. For a detailed discussion of the relationship between muckrakers and socialists, see Sheila Reeves, "How Radical Were the Muckrakers?" *Journalism Quarterly* 61, no. 4 (1984): 763–70.

12. Theodore Roosevelt, "The Man with the Muck-Rake," in *The Essential Theodore Roosevelt*, ed. John Gabriel Hunt (New York: Gramercy Books, 1994), 194.

13. Roosevelt 1994, 187.

14. Baker 1945, 2.

15. Ibid., 93.

16. The rise of national brands reinforced this process, as did a 1979 act of Congress that reduced mailing rates for magazines and the 1886 invention of an effective linotype machine.

17. One could find scathing investigative reports in some daily papers in New York City, including Joseph Pulitzer's *World*, William Randolph Hearst's *New York Journal*, the *New York Sun*, New York's *Commercial Advertiser*, and in a handful of other papers like the *San Francisco Chronicle*, the *Baltimore Evening News*, and the *Emporia Gazette*. This suggests that by 1890 the advertising revenues of some urban dailies had reached a scale and level of mass distribution that could fund independent, costly investigative forays. However, the vast majority of urban papers still operated at a smaller level and could neither afford expensive, and therefore commercially risky, journalistic stunts nor adopt an overly critical stance toward corruption in their own cities. There were many book-length precursors to the muckrakers, including Charles F. Adams and Henry Adam, *A Chapter of Erie* (Boston: James R. Osgood, 1871); Henry Demarest Lloyd, *Wealth Against Commonwealth* (New York: Harper and Brother Publishers, 1899); William T. Stead's *If Christ Came to Chicago! A Plea for the Union of All Who Love in the Service of All Who Suffer* (London: Review of Reviews, 1894).

18. Richard Hofstader, *The Age of Reform: From Bryan to F. D. R.* (New York: Vintage Books, 1955), 187.

19. Will Irwin, *Propaganda and the News; or, What Makes You Think So?* (Westport, CT: Greenwood Press, 1970), 69–70 (orig. pub. 1936).

20. Cecilia Tichi, *Exposés and Excess: Muckraking in America, 1900/2000* (Philadelphia: University of Pennsylvania Press, 2004) 72. In his autobiography McClure noted that Tarbell's articles on Standard Oil cost him $4,000 an article, while Steffen's articles averaged $2,000 each. See S. S. McClure, *My Autobiography* (F. Ungar, 1963).

21. Wilson 1985, 65.

22. Mark David Chalmers, *The Social and Political Ideas of the Muckrakers* (New York: Citadel Press, 1964), 6.

23. Several simmering, behind-the-scenes conflicts contributed to this mass exodus, but the immediate disagreement was over a business scheme devised by McClure to form a corporation that would proximally include another magazine, a bank, an insurance company, and an educational publishing company and expand considerably from there.

McClure presented this idea to his staff as a foregone conclusion and refused to listen when they critiqued the plan as financially risky, akin to the kind of wild economic speculation the magazine had spent the last four years protesting. See John Semonche, "The American Magazine of 1906–15: Principle vs. Profit," *Journalism Quarterly* 40 (Winter 1963): 36–37.

24. Wilson 1985, 192.

25. George Kibbe Turner, "Galveston: A Business Corporation," *McClure's* 27 (October 1906): 611.

26. Peter Lyon, *Success Story: The Life and Times of S. S. McClure* (New York: Charles Scribner's Sons, 1963), 305; McClure 1963, 259.

27. George Kibbe Turner, "The Confession and Autobiography of Harry Orchard," *McClure's Magazine* 29 (May 1907): 294–365.

28. George Kibbe Turner, *The Confessions and Autobiography of Harry Orchard [pseud.]* (New York: S. S. McClure, 1907).

29. George Kibbe Turner, "Our Navy on Land," *McClure's Magazine* 32 (February 1909): 411–17.

30. Because he never published an autobiography, little is known about Turner's life. See Chalmers 1964; Lamar W. Bridges, "George Kibbe Turner of *McClure's Magazine*," *Journalism Quarterly* 61, no. 1 (1984): 178–82.

31. Lincoln Steffens, "Chicago: Half-Free and Fighting On," *McClure's Magazine* 21 (October 1903): 563–77.

32. McClure 1963, 257–58. "Chicago As Seen By Herself" was published in the May 1907 issue.

33. Chalmers 1964.

34. Compare, for example, Turner's "The Daughters of the Poor" to Ray Stannard Baker, "What Is a Lynching? A Study of Mob Justice, South and North," *McClure's Magazine* 24 (January 1905): 299–314.

35. Turner, "City of Chicago," 582.

36. Edward W. Bristow, *Prostitution and Prejudice: The Jewish Fight Against White Slavery, 1870–1939* (New York: Schocken, 1983); Eric Goldstein, "The Unstable Other: Locating the Jew in Progressive-Era American Racial Discourse," *American Jewish History* 89, no. 4 (2001).

37. Thomas Lee Philpott, *The Slum and the Ghetto: Neighborhood Deterioration and Middle-Class Reform, Chicago, 1880–1930* (New York: Oxford University Press, 1978); Richard Lindberg, *Chicago by Gaslight: A History of Chicago's Netherworld, 1880–1920* (Chicago: Academy Chicago, 1996).

38. Kevin Mumford, *Interzones: Black/White Sex Districts in Chicago and New York in the Early Twentieth Century* (New York: Columbia University Press, 1997).

39. Turner, "City of Chicago, 581.

40. Joanne Meyerowitz, *Women Adrift: Independent Wage Earners in Chicago, 1880–1930* (Chicago: University of Chicago Press, 1988).

41. Ibid., 39.

42. This economic analysis was at the center of Jane Addams' understanding of prostitution and white slavery. See Jane Addams, *A New Conscience and an Ancient Evil*

(New York: MacMillan, 1912); Brian Donovan, *White Slave Crusades: Race, Gender, and Anti-Vice Activism, 1887–1917* (Urbana: University of Illinois Press, 2006).

43. Lindberg 1996, 116.

44. Turner, "City of Chicago," 575. In the following discussion, this work will be cited parenthetically by page number in the text.

45. "Police Protection of Vice," *Chicago Daily Tribune*, 23 April 1907, 8.

46. "A 'Bad City,'" *Chicago Daily Tribune*, 29 April 1907, 8.

47. Clifford W. Barnes, "The Story of the Committee of Fifteen of Chicago," *Social Hygiene* 4 (January 1918): 145.

48. Clifford G. Roe, *Panders and Their White Slaves* (New York: Fleming H. Revel, 1910), 26.

49. Ibid., 32.

50. See Barnes 1918, 146–48; Donovan 2006, 71–87; Roe 1910, 155–59.

51. Roe 1910; Clifford G. Roe, *Horrors of the White Slave Trade* (London: Stationers Hall, 1911), and *The Girl Who Disappeared* (Naperville, IL: World's Purity Federation, 1914). Roe chose to focus on cases where the female victim was native-born and the trafficker an immigrant. For more on Roe's nativism, see Donovan 2006.

52. Addams 1912.

53. Bell 1910; Donovan 2006, 63.

54. Bell 1910.

55. Jean Turner Zimmermann, *Chicago's Black Traffic in White Girls* (Chicago: Chicago Rescue Mission, 1910).

56. Ibid., 10.

57. Jean Turner Zimmermann, *White or Yellow? A Story of America's Great White Slave Trade with Asia* (Chicago, n.p.: 1916).

58. Roe 1910, 156–59.

59. See Barnes 1918.

60. See Langum 1994. For more on Mann, see Herbert F. Margulies, *Reconciliation and Revival: James R. Mann and the House Republicans in the Wilson Era* (Westport, CT: Greenwood Press, 1996).

61. The early activities of the National Vigilance Committee under its president O. Edward Janney prefigured those of the Bureau of Investigation. The NVC sent out five investigators to cities from New York to Virginia and to San Francisco and Oakland in California to inquire into the crib system of sexual slavery involving "Japanese and Chinese slavegirls." They also broke up a number of employment agencies along the West Coast and a Nebraskan child-prostitution ring. See O. Edward Janney, "Purity Alliance and Vigilance Work," *Friend's Intelligencer* 65, no. 2 (1910): 25.

62. "Registration of Prostitutes," *Vigilance* 25, no. 1 (1912): 18.

63. Ibid.

64. For more on Johnson, see Mumford 1997.

65. George Kibbe Turner, "Tammany's Control of New York by Professional Criminals: A Study of a New Period of Decadence in the Popular Government of Great Cities," *McClure's* 33 (April 1909): 121.

66. Ibid., 132.

67. Quoted in Arthur Weinberg and Lila Weinberg, eds., *The Muckrakers* (Urbana: University of Illinois Press, 2001), 387–88 (orig. pub. 1961).

68. See M. R. Werner, *Tammany Hall* (New York: Greenwood Press, 1968); S. S. McClure, "The Tammanyizing of a Civilization," *McClure's* 34 (November 1909): 117–28.

69. Turner, "Daughters of the Poor," 46–47.

70. Raines-law hotels were saloons that exploited a loophole in 1896 New York law that prohibited the sale of alcohol on Sundays except by hotels. In order to serve on Sunday, saloons added small bedrooms to their establishments and applied for hotel licenses. See Committee of Fifteen 1902.

71. Turner, "Daughters of the Poor," 48. Cited parenthetically by page number in the text in the discussion in the next two paragraphs.

72. McClure 1909, 117.

73. Ibid.

74. Ibid.

75. Weinberg and Weinberg 2001, 388.

76. Werner 1968, 503.

CHAPTER FIVE

1. "Murphy and Gaynor Answer Vice Charge," *New York Times*, 25 October 1909, 2; "Mulry Says Turner Slandered the City," *New York Times*, 29 October 1909, 4.

2. Barbie Zelizer, "Achieving Journalistic Authority Through Narrative," *Critical Studies in Mass Communication* 7, no. 4 (1990): 367.

3. Kevin Stoker, "Existential Objectivity: Freeing Journalists to Be Ethical," *Journal of Mass Media Ethics* 10, no. 1 (1995): 7.

4. Harlan Stensaas, "Development of the Objectivity Ethic in U.S. Daily Newspapers," *Journal of Mass Media Ethics* 2, no. 1 (1986–87): 58.

5. George H. Douglas, *The Golden Age of the Newspaper* (Westport, CT: Greenwood Press, 1999); Michael Schudson, *Discovering the News: A Social History of American Newspapers* (New York: Basic Books, 1978).

6. Mark Connelly, *The Response to Prostitution in the Progressive Era* (Chapel Hill: University of North Carolina Press, 1980); David Langum, *Crossing Over the Line: Legislating Morality and the Mann Act* (Chicago: University of Chicago Press, 1994).

7. Stephen Reese, "The News Paradigm and the Ideology of Objectivity: A Socialist at the Wall Street Journal," *Critical Studies in Mass Communication* 7, no. 4 (1990): 394.

8. Ibid., 395.

9. "Murphy and Gaynor," 2.

10. Ibid.

11. "Gaynor's Reply to Turner," *New York Sun*, 25 October 1909, 2.

12. "Libel, Says Gaynor Again," *New York Sun*, 26 October 1909, 2.

13. "White Slave Story False, Says Guide," *New York Times*, 28 October 1909, 3.

14. "Murphy's Defense Untrue, They Say," *New York Times*, 26 October 1909, 3.

15. Edward Bristow, *Prostitution and Prejudice* (Oxford: Oxford University Press, 1982), esp. chaps. 7 and 8.

16. "Murphy's Defense Untrue," 3.

17. "Attack on Gaynor," *New York Times*, 28 October 1909, 3.

18. "White Slave Story False," 3

19. "Gaynor Wins; Tammany Loses All the Rest," *New York Times*, 3 November 1909, 1.

20. "Whitman on 'White Slaves,'" *New York Sun*, 26 October 1909, 2.

21. "White Slave Traffic Shown to Be Real," *New York Times*, 30 April 1910, 1.

22. Ibid.

23. Ibid.

24. Ibid.

25. Ibid.

26. "Four White Slaves Were Sold for $160," *New York Times*, 3 May 1910, 20.

27. Ibid.

28. "White Slave Traffic," 1.

29. "Belle Moore Guilty of Selling Girls," *New York Times*, 20 May 1910, 18.

30. Ibid.

31. Ibid.

32. Ibid.

33. Ibid.

34. Ibid.

35. "Four White Slaves," 20.

36. "Defends Employment Agents," *New York Times*, 1 May 1910, 20.

37. David Domke, "The Press, Race Relations, and Social Change," *Journal of Communication* 51, no. 2 (2001): 322.

38. "Belle Moore's Case," Letter, *New York Times*, 27 May 1910, 8.

39. "Belle Moore Guilty," 1910, 18.

40. See Kevin Mumford, *Interzones: Black/White Sex Districts in Chicago and New York in the Early Twentieth Century* (New York: Columbia University Press, 1997).

41. "Prison for Belle Moore," *New York Times*, 27 May 1910, 4.

42. "Ill-Chosen Agents," *New York Times*, 21 May 1910, 8.

43. Ibid.

44. Ibid.

45. Ibid.

46. Michael Schudson, *The Power of News* (Cambridge, MA: Harvard University Press, 1995), 51.

47. "To the Editor of the New York Times," *New York Times*, 24 May 1910, 8.

48. Ibid.

49. See, for example Edward Bellamy, *Looking Backward: 2000–1887* (New York: Houghton Mifflin, 1887).

50. Stuart Ewen, *PR! A Social History of Spin* (New York: Basic Books, 1996), 73.

51. Sonya Michel, "Dorothea Dix; or, the Voice of the Maniac," *Discourse* 17, no. 2 (1995): 54.

52. Schudson 1978.

53. Ibid., 114.

54. "White Slave Traffic," 1.

55. "Rockefeller, Jr.," *New York Times*, 5 January 1910, 7.

56. "Four White Slaves," 20.

57. "White Slave Traffic," 1.

58. "More White Slave Arrests," *New York Times*, 1 May 1910, 20.

59. See John Durham Peters, *Speaking Into the Air: A History of the Idea of Communication* (Chicago: University of Chicago Press, 1999).

60. See Christine Stansell, *American Moderns: Bohemian New York and the Creation of a New Century* (New York: Metropolitan Books, 2000).

61. Schudson 1978.

62. William Dean Howells, *Years of My Youth* (New York: Harper, 1916), 140.

CHAPTER SIX

1. Transcript, Court of General Sessions of Peace in and for the County of New York, "The Court's Charge to the Grand Jury in the Matter of the Investigation into the charges made as to the existence of an organized traffic in women for immoral purposes, or what has come to be known as the 'White Slave' traffic," 3 January 1910, folder 56, box 8, series O, BSH, RAC, Sleepy Hollow, New York.

2. "John D. Rockefeller, Jr. is Foreman of Grand Jury to Probe 'White Slave' Trade," *New York Evening Telegram*, 4 January 1910, 1.

3. Raymond B. Fosdick, *John D. Rockefeller, Jr.: A Portrait* (New York: Harper and Brothers, 1956), 137.

4. See ibid., 125–42.

5. "J. D. Rockefeller, Jr., Speaks," *New York Tribune*, 17 October 1900, 3; "Stand Shoulder to Shoulder with All Men," *New York World*, 14 March 1904, 8.

6. "John D., Jr., White Slave Reformer," *New York Evening Mail*, 4 January 1910, 1.

7. "J. D. Rockefeller, Jr., Backs Country-Wide Fight on 'Slavers,'" *Boston American*, 7 January 1910, 3.

8. *Troy Daily Press*, 7 January 1910, 5.

9. Exemplary stories include "White Slave Probe Will Begin in Earnest Next Week," *Paducah Evening Sun*, 6 January 1910, 7; "White Slave Traffic Is to Be Investigated by Special New York Grand Jury," *Palestine Daily Herald*, 3 January 1910, 1.

10. "Oil King's Son Wars on White Slavery," *San Francisco Call*, 11 January 1910, 3.

11. "Uncertain About a Certainty," *New York Times*, 6 January 1910, 8.

12. "Rescue Workers Say Power of Rockefeller Will Not Solve the Infamous White Slave Problem," *Tacoma Times*, 13 January 1910, 8.

13. While Raymond Fosdick claims that Rockefeller had no interest in vice issues until the grand jury, he did donate $2,500 to the Committee of Fifteen in 1901 and a lesser amount to the Committee of Fourteen. See "Pledge to the Committee of Fifteen," 1901, folder 39, box 6, series O, BSH, RAC.

14. "Rockefeller, Jr., Sees Mayor," *New York Times*, 21 January 1910, 4.

15. "Wants White Slave Inquiry," *New York Times*, 6 January 1910, 3.

16. Testimony of George Kibbe Turner, Grand Jury Transcript, Transcripts of the County of New York, Court of General Sessions, 1883–1927, Lloyd Sealy Library, John Jay College of Criminal Justice, New York City, case 3317, roll 420, page 63. Cited parenthetically by page number in the following discussion.

17. "White Slave Jury Defies O'Sullivan," *New York Times*, 23 June 1910, 12.

18. "O'Sullivan Gets White Slave Report," *New York Times*, 24 June 1910, 18.

19. White Slave Grand Jury, Grand Jury Presentment, July 1910, folder 58, box 8, series O, BSH, RAC, 4–5. Cited parenthetically by page number in the following discussion.

20. Clifford G. Roe, *The Prodigal Daughter: The White Slave Evil and the Remedy* (Chicago: L. W. Walter, 1911), 237.

21. Ruth Rosen, *The Lost Sisterhood: Prostitution in America, 1900–1918* (Baltimore, MD: Johns Hopkins University Press, 1982), 124.

22. "White Slave Trade Is Not Organized," *New York Times*, 29 June 1910, 16.

23. "White Slavery? Not in New York," *Chicago Daily Tribune*, 29 June 1910, 5.

24. "No Evidence of the White Slave Traffic," *San Francisco Chronicle*, 29 June 1910, 2.

25. Quoted in Roe 1911, 238.

26. James B. Reynolds to Rockefeller, 22 July 1910, folder 59, box 8, series O, BSH, RAC.

27. Quoted in James B. Reynolds to Rockefeller, 22 July 1910, folder 59, box 8, series O, BSH, RAC.

28. "Defends White Slave Story," *New York Times*, 2 July 1910, 2.

29. Mara Keire, *For Business and Pleasure: Red Light Districts and the Regulation of Vice in the United States, 1890–1933* (Baltimore, MD: Johns Hopkins University Press, 2010).

30. James B. Reynolds to Rockefeller, 8 July 1910, folder 59, box 8, series O, BSH, RAC.

31. Jeremiah W. Jenks to Rockefeller, 20 July 1910, folder 59, box 8, series O, BSH, RAC.

32. Abraham Flexner, *Prostitution in Europe* (New York: Century, 1914); George Kneeland, *Commercialized Prostitution in New York City* (New York: Century, 1913).

33. Rockefeller, quoted in Kneeland 1913, x.

34. Rockefeller, quoted in Flexner 1914, xiii–ix.

35. John D. Rockefeller Jr., press release, "The Origin, Work, and Plans of the Bureau of Social Hygiene," 18 January 1913, folder 67, box 9, series O, Bureau of Social Hygiene Records (BSH), Rockefeller Archive Center (RAC), Sleepy Hollow, NY. For more on the Bureau of Social Hygiene, see Allen M. Brandt, *No Magic Bullet: A Social History of Venereal Disease in the United States Since 1880* (Oxford: Oxford University Press, 1987); Judith Sealander, *Private Wealth and Public Life: Foundation Philanthropy and the Reshaping of American Social Policy from the Progressive Era to the New Deal* (Baltimore, MD: Johns Hopkins University Press, 1997).

36. See Hastings H. Hart, "A Working Program for the Extinction of the Defective Delinquent," *Survey*, 24 May 1913, 277–79; Maude E. Minor, "Report of the Commission of Social Hygiene," *Journal of Social Hygiene* 1, no. 2 (1914): 81–92; Nicole Hahn Rafter, *Creating Born Criminals* (Urbana: University of Illinois Press, 1997).

37. Minor 1914, 92.

38. "BSH Pledges and Payment, 1911–1925," box 9, folder 71, series O, BSH, RAC.

39. See Brandt 1987.

40. James B. Reynolds, "Commercialized Vice," *Survey*, 13 December 1913, 354.

41. William Reedy, cited in "Sex O'Clock in America [editorial]," *Current Opinion* 55 (August 1913): 113.

42. W. Burgess, "A Wave of Sex Hysteria?" *Vigilance* 27 (September 1913): 8–9.

43. Marvin E. Gettleman, "Philanthropy as Social Control in Late Nineteenth-Century America: Some Hypotheses and Data on the Rise of Social Work," *Societas* 5, no. 1 (1975): 49–59.

44. Eleanor L. Brilliant, *Private Charity and Public Inquiry: A History of the Filer and Peterson Commissions* (Bloomington: Indiana University Press, 2000); Stuart Ewen, *PR! A Social History of Spin* (New York: Basic Books, 1996); Rafter 1997.

45. Reginald Kauffman, *The House of Bondage* (New York: Moffat, Yard, 1910). For a discussion of the white slavery novels published during this period, see Frederick K. Grittner, *White Slavery: Myth, Ideology, and American Law* (New York: Garland, 1990).

46. Joan McDermott and Sarah J. Blackstone, "White Slavery Plays of the 1910s: Fear of Victimization and the Social Control of Sexuality," *Theatre History Studies* 16 (June 1996): 141.

47. "Sex O'Clock" 1913, 113.

48. "Lectures in Lent to Check Hysteria," *New York Times*, 2 January 1914, 5.

49. "The Moral Havoc Wrought by Moving Picture Shows," *Current Opinion* 56 (April 1914): 290.

50. "Lectures in Lent" 1914.

51. "Sex O'Clock" 1913, 113.

52. Carrie Weaver Smith, "The Cry to Christ of the Daughters of Shame," poem, *Survey*, 1 November 1913, 116.

53. H. H. Knox, "Daughters of Shame," letter, *Survey*, 29 November 1913, 229.

54. Christina Merriman, "New Bottles for New Wine: The Work of Abastenia St. Leger Eberle," *Survey*, 3 May 1913, 196–98.

55. A. W. Allen, letter, *Survey*, 12 July 1913, 510.

56. R. I. Newport, letter, *Survey*, 31 May 1913, 313.

57. R. F. Carter, letter, *Survey*, 12 July 1913: 507.

58. "Communications," editorial, *Survey*, 31 May 1913, 314.

59. Eric C. Hopwood, "The Opportunity of the Press as a Moral Educator," *Journal of Social Hygiene* 2 (January 1915): 21–22.

60. Burgess 1913; "Lectures in Lent" 1914.

61. "Poison Needles Used by Slavers to Kidnap Women from Streets," *New York World*, 6 December 1913, 1.

62. "Deadly Hyoscine Has Quick Effect," *Washington Times*, 7 December 1913, 1.

63. Cited in "Popular Gullibility as Exhibited in the New White Slave Hysteria," *Current Opinion* 56 (February 1914): 129.

64. Ibid.

65. Ibid.

66. "Does Not Fit the Crime," editorial, *New York Times*, 19 July 1914, 4.

67. "The Blackmail Act," *New York Times*, 20 September 1916, 8.

68. In 1911 members of the press watched and speculated as Thomas Lamont, a member of the J. P. Morgan financial group and major stakeholder of the Crowell Publish-

ing Company as well as Duffield & Company, bought a majority share of *Harper's*, *The Woman's Home Companion*, and eventually *The American Magazine*. Some muckrakers alleged a conspiracy in which the trusts were buying up the muckraking publications in order to silence them. By 1912, conflicts had already arisen. One incident in particular featured massive editing of an article written by Baker that was sympathetic to textile workers striking in Lawrence, Massachusetts. The account was so heavily altered that the published version upheld police accounts of unruly workers and championed capitalist principles with which Baker disagreed. See John E. Semonche, "The 'American Magazine' of 1906–1915: Principle vs. Profit," *Journalism Quarterly* 40, no. 1 (1963) 36–44; "The Rumored 'Magazine Trust,'" *Literary Digest* 25 February, 1911, 344. See also "A Word to the Muckrakers," *Independent* 6 February 1911, 319–20.

CONCLUSION

1. Stead was on the *Titanic* when it went down, and an interesting mythology surrounds the event of his death. Stead had predicted that he would meet a violent and catastrophic end, and he had even written an 1892 story, "From the Old World to the New," published in the *Review of Reviews*, in which an ocean liner collides with an iceberg and the passengers are rescued by another ship.

2. Walter Lippmann, *Public Opinion* (New York: The Free Press, 1977); orig. pub. 1922.

3. Walter Lippmann, *A Preface to Politics* (New York: MacMillan, 1913), 8.

4. The Chicago Vice Commission, appointed by Mayor Fred Busse after allegations of regional sex trafficking, documented widespread prostitution in the city and identified the varied social spaces in which vice occurred. It offered a staggering number of suggestions for attaining the proximal and long-term goals expressed in its motto, "The Constant and Persistent Repression of Prostitution the Immediate Method: Absolute Annihilation the Ultimate Ideal," including better lighting in parks at night, regular police raids on brothels, heightened police surveillance of youth, censorship of prurient advertising, stronger sentencing laws for prostitutes, stringent curfews, increased policing of public spaces, and the prohibition of lewd dancing. See Vice Commission of Chicago, *The Social Evil in Chicago: A Study of Existing Conditions* (Chicago: Gunthorp Warren Printing Co., 1911).

5. Elizabeth Bernstein, *Temporarily Yours: Intimacy, Authenticity, and the Commerce of Sex* (Chicago: University of Chicago Press, 2007); Jo Doezema, "Loose Women or Lost Women? The Reemergence of the Myth of White Slavery in Contemporary Discourses of Trafficking in Women," *Gender Issues* 18, no. 1 (2000): 23–50; Gretchen Soderlund, "Running from the Rescuers," *National Women's Studies Association Journal* 17, no. 3 (2005): 64–87.

6. Paula Treichler, *How to Have Theory in an Epidemic: Cultural Chronicles of AIDS* (Durham, NC: Duke University Press, 1999).

7. Elizabeth Bernstein, "The Sexual Politics of the 'New Abolitionism,'" *Differences* 18, no. 3 (2007): 128–57; Soderlund 2005.

INDEX